Terror.

2.99
1 Saue
d
44

Terrorism for Humanity
Inquiries in Political Philosophy

Ted Honderich

Pluto Press
LONDON • STERLING, VIRGINIA

First published as *Violence for Equality: Inquiries in Political Philosophy*, 1989 by Routledge

This revised edition published 2003 by
Pluto Press
345 Archway Road, London N6 5AA
and 22883 Quicksilver Drive, Sterling, VA 20166-2012, USA

www.plutobooks.com

British Library Cataloguing in Publication Data
A catalogue record for this book is available from the British Library

ISBN   0 7453 2134 8 hardback
ISBN   0 7453 2133 X paperback

Library of Congress Cataloging in Publication Data
Honderich, Ted.
   Terrorism for humanity : inquiries in political philosophy / Ted Honderich.— Rev. ed.
      p. cm.
Rev. ed. of: Violence for equality. Enl. and rev. ed. 1989. Includes bibliographical references and index.
   ISBN 0–7453–2134–8 — ISBN 0–7453–2133–X (pbk.)
   1. Political violence. 2. Terrorism. 3. Government, Resistance to.
4. Democracy. I. Honderich, Ted. Violence for equality. II. Title.
   JC328.6 .H66 2003
   172'.1—dc22
                                                            2003018185

10   9   8   7   6   5   4   3   2   1

Designed and produced for Pluto Press by
Chase Publishing Services, Fortescue, Sidmouth, EX10 9QG, England
Typeset from disk by Stanford DTP Services, Northampton, England
Printed and bound in the European Union by
Antony Rowe Ltd, Chippenham and Eastbourne, England

To Ruth and Bee

Contents

Introduction

The six essays of this book, now revised after having previously been published as *Violence for Equality: Inquiries in Political Philosophy*, are the result of trying to inquire with an open mind into terrorism and more particularly what some people think are justifications of it or would be justifications of it. If you actually think about it, what can be said for and against terrorism or political violence? When, if ever, is terrorism right?

What can be said for or against terrorism of the kind of which we know too well – the actual terrorism in Ireland, Colombia, flight 103 over Scotland, Palestine and elsewhere before September 11, and in the United States on that day, and since then? Can some of this terrorism have the name of being *terrorism for humanity*? What can be said for or against not this actual terrorism, but possible or conceivable terrorism instead, including terrorism for humanity?

To start with the actual terrorism we know and its possible grounds and their relative worth is indeed to be led on to think of different and perhaps better grounds – in fact to think of terrorism that does not happen, or has not happened yet. To think about this is to shed another light on our world as it is, with the injustice of ordinary and extraordinary wretchedness and distress in it. What we in our comfort do to others and what we could stop doing. To think about it is to shed light on our own moral standing, and what we are obliged to do about our world, whether or not with a prudential eye on the future. This is my subject too.

Actually to inquire, to try to get away from preconception and automatism and the like, this was my explicit intention, and indeed I have found my way to some propositions uncongenial to me. Still, I have done rather better at finding congenial ones. Perhaps this helps to show that to open one's mind is not necessarily to lose one's convictions.

All of the essays in this book are exercises in political philosophy, or anyway attempts at it. Political philosophy is none of political theory, political history, or the sceptical and rightly cynical examination of our past and present politics, economics and international relations. It is not political science, reflective journalism however good, religious morality however enlightened.[1] Nor, of course, does

1

political philosophy consist in Hymns to Democracy, or Reflections on the Danger to the Liberal Society – let alone works of ideological self-deception, assumptions of a kind of stupidity in a society and making for more of it, propaganda of traditional kinds, and governmental lying by official vocabulary and by obfuscation. After the second Iraq war, our newspapers and screens remain full of the latter stuff, and also the Hymns and the Reflections, mainly because our politicians are full of it, Bush and Blair to the fore, so suited to one another.

There are other respectable and indeed essential books on terrorism and/or the decency or indecency of our own lives, some of them being sorts of books just mentioned – political theory and history, and the rightly cynical examinations. They have strengths not aspired to by this book. Political philosophy is what results from a different kind of concern for clarity and for orderly reflection and full argument. It has in it that commitment to *logic* in a general sense that is the distinction of all philosophy worth the name. It abstracts from kinds of details. That remains true of political philosophy when it is, as it usually is, a part of moral philosophy, indeed what should be about half of moral philosophy.

Although the essays have been revised since September 11, they were written before then. About this fact, you can have the reassurance that books are not news, which is near to being their general recommendation. Burke's *Reflections on the Revolution in France*, if you will allow me the comparison, and whatever you think of it, is not much touched by having been written before the revolution ran its course. Nor is Marx's *Capital* not to be reprinted because a wall fell down in Germany, or Paine's *The Rights of Man* left unread because the nation he was welcoming into being does no honour to his radicalism. But no doubt, even if this lesser book is about more than the terrorism we know, and about ourselves in addition to terrorism, it might be thought to lack something more as a result of having been written before the act of September 11, sometimes said to have changed the world. What is it that it might be thought to lack?

Perhaps a horror that goes with having really *personally identified* for the first time with victims of terrorism? Maybe the people leaping from the twin towers. Well, that fact of personally identifying does prompt some new lines in this revised edition, but not any change in its conclusions. Does the book, having been written before September 11, need a fuller conception of Islamic terrorism and its relation to terrorism for humanity, and a fuller sense of what we who have been attacked can do and will do in counter-attack for whatever reason? One reply is that philosophy is more general than that, which fact is connected with its distinctive commitment to the clarity, consistency and completeness of our natural logic.

Should I, after September 11, amend the book's conclusions? To do more did not seem necessary or right. One large reason is that books such as this one are long arguments claiming serious attention, however hopefully. It is no bad idea to leave them standing. They may put a case worth hearing. There is always the possibility, for anyone having some of the self-scepticism of a proper philosopher, that first thoughts rather than second thoughts are best.

If what you are about to read might have been a little longer, for having been written after September 11, it might also have been a little worse. Perhaps no single event in our lifetimes, certainly no single day's event, has been so *used*. If September 11 has had its natural effects on our feelings and in other ways, it has also been used by most of our politicians and also others to fortify the conformity in which so many of us live our lives. That is the social stupidity that is not a matter of our natures but of an ignorance satisfactory to others and thus a weakness and absurdity in judgement. This book came before the reinforcement. It did not run the risk of being distorted by it.

Still, there would have been no risk of a comma in it being changed as a consequence of reading pieces after September 11 by one or two of my fellow philosophers. The American John Searle occurs to me, a bully boy who has done some service in the philosophy of mind. He wrote a piece during the course of the war against the Taliban in Afghanistan, in 2001, when the bombing and missiling were in progress. He provided us with what he said was needed, 'an intelligent response' to terrorism and in particular Islamic terrorism.[2]

There should be more such wars carried forward, he said, one by one. Removals one by one of governments that somehow support or tolerate terrorism. These wars are needed, he said, to avert what will otherwise happen, the anthrax pandemic of 2003 in America, the germ terrorism of 2004 killing a million Americans, and the smuggled nuclear bombs of 2008 killing five million Americans – these various weapons having been prepared, as he knew, in the laboratories of Iraq.

But the war-mongering and the awful predictions, the latter having some reason and sense in them despite their drama, were not what was most notable in this philosopher's thinking. What was most notable was another reasoned proposal to his country.

> We need to give up on the illusion that there is some policy change on our part that will change the attitude of the terrorists. Short of all of us converting to an extreme version of fundamentalist Islam and driving all the Israelis into the sea, there is no policy change that will alter their determination to kill us. The policy changes that are urged on us – stop the bombing, use the United Nations, etc. – might peel off some of their moderate supporters but will not weaken the resolve of the terrorists.

To say that no reasonable American policy change would have any effect on the terrorism in question is to contribute, out of ideological or other passion, to the stupidity of nations, America above all if not America alone, the stupidity of ignorance and weak and absurd judgement.

The revisions throughout this book are more stylistic than substantial. One revision brings the book into line with an indomitable linguistic fact, the universal use of the term 'terrorism' rather than 'political violence'. The revision is also in line with the fact that reasonable definitions make the two terms mean the same thing.[3] There is no great point in making a distinction. Another revision is owed to a change of mind about a great principle, the moral principle that informs the whole book. It will meet with less confusion and less protestation of confusion if it has the name of being the Principle of Humanity.

The use of the term 'terrorism' did indeed seem necessary. That is not to say that it is comfortable to me. The word has taken over partly the result of a choice and indeed a manipulation of language by governments, allied interests and sometimes parts of peoples for their own ends, sometimes ends that remain transparently vicious, as in the case of contemporary Zionism in Palestine.[4] Still, there is little gain in being a Canute against the tide of language. More important, there is reason to keep in view the human fact of the victims of political violence, to which the use of 'terrorism' with its connotations is also owed. It would be no service to truth or morality to shrink from the term, as it is no service to truth or morality to use it in the common politician's way that not merely implies but declares in passing that all of it is wrong.

The necessity of the term 'terrorism' remains a necessity despite another fact. It is that much terrorism is absolutely as rightly spoken of in other ways. It is also an ongoing reply to state-terrorism, self-defence, defence of a homeland, freedom-fighting, liberation struggle, personal self-sacrifice in the hope of gaining great goods for others, defence against ethnic cleansing, a struggle of a people for their survival, terrorism for humanity.

You will anticipate my saying that something else is also true. Terrorism is not the only horror. There is another horror, another evil, another inhumanity. It is also necessary to have and keep *it* in view, to resist the language of avoidance and concealment that serves ends as much as the name 'terrorism', including ends that remain transparently vicious. Moral intelligence now requires excess in language, what others take to be excess. Do you say philosophy is not the place for this? It is not clear to me why. Its logic is as much about wretchedness and distress as anything else.

The first essay of this book, if it aspires to that logic that is the distinction of all decent philosophy, is unlike others in not dealing with the question of what can be said for and against terrorism or political violence entirely by way of argument and reflection of a philosophical kind. That is, 'Wretchedness and Terrorism, and Differences We Make Between Them' *is* partly empirical.

The facts that are brought to political philosophy, and I trust to its improvement, concern average lifetimes of certain groups and classes. It is remarked that these facts must touch our reflections on terrorism. For the rest, the particular subject of the first essay is certain of our first responses to the facts of political violence and what can be called the facts of inequality, responses both in feeling and in doctrine.

Several pieces of reasoning by others are examined in the second essay, and perhaps handled too roughly. One has to do with the obligation to obey the law and to abstain from violence, and also with what is taken to be a conflicting and a higher demand, essentially a demand of conscience. It is the work of Robert Paul Wolff. The other argument examined in the essay is founded on the idea of a hypothetical social contract, and issues in particular propositions about the obligation to obey the law and to abstain from violence. It also issues in two large principles of justice. This theory of justice is the work of the liberal John Rawls.

The third essay, 'The Principle of Humanity', sets out what is argued to be the proper answer to the question of what distribution of well-being and distress there ought to be in societies and between societies. That is, the essay tries to deal rightly with the problem of justice, the first and main problem of moral and political philosophy, the first problem in thinking about terrorism and about wretchedness and other distress.

The solution offered to the problem, the Principle of Humanity, derives from a conception of categories of desire fundamental to all our lives. The principle considers general policies for achieving the end or goal of the principle, having to do with those great desires. The concern of the book is mainly with terrorism related to this principle, and our world as it is in relation to this principle.

The fourth essay, 'Our Omissions and Their Terrorism', begins from what is said by the violent, or some of them, against those of us who are law-abiding. It is that despite our moral confidence we contribute in an essential way, by our omissions, to denials of life, to wretchedness and other distress. The essay has to do with the reply that there is a great difference between acts and omissions, whatever else is to be said. It has to do, too, with another reply to terrorists and those who at least understand them. I mean the inevitable refrain about any *tu quoque*, that the guilty are trying to avoid the subject of their guilt. Those who kill and devastate are merely attempting an evasion.

'On Democratic Terrorism', the fifth essay, concerns democracy and violence. It sets out answers to the questions of how violence stands to the practice and to the rules of democracy, and, more importantly, an answer to the question of how it stands to the ends or values that are proposed in the fundamental arguments for democracy. There is, as a result, analysis of a particular kind of terrorism, named the democratic kind.

What can be saved of the tradition of an actual rather than hypothetical social contract is a first part of the subject of the last essay, 'Four Conclusions About Terrorism for Humanity'. Another part is the consequences of a certain moralism, an affirmation of moral necessities. Reflection on these two things leads to a further consideration of the empirical issues of wretchedness and other distress raised in the first essay and other great facts of distress. These in turn lead to the four principal questions about terrorism for humanity, and responses to them.

The essays were written as papers for philosophy conferences and the like. They have had some unity put on them, but they remain separate. Can they be thought to measure up to their awful, spreading and sometimes intractable subject? Sometimes they seem to me a bundle of materials for inquiry and argument, not an assembled thing. You, reader, can decide, and also wonder about the usefulness of imperfect things in a dark time of need, a time of attack on moral intelligence.[5]

The essays taken together will not fully satisfy a tidy kind of reader. They deal more with our omissions than our commissions. They bring together the subject of terrorism against our commissions, say Islamic terrorism against our commission in supporting Israel in Palestine, with the subject of our omissions elsewhere, omissions that might have given rise to other terrorism, say African terrorism, and may still do so. There are reasons for this over and above the truth that there is no law of subject-matters for books, and that one thing, as already remarked, leads to another. One reason is that moral questions ask themselves, and certainly cannot be ruled out by tidy or self-interested or cozened persons. There is some assertive truth in morality. Another reason is that propositions turn up. One is that our indubitably being in the wrong with respect to omissions, if that is the case, must raise a doubt about any *presumption* of our being in the right with respect to our commissions. Sometimes a guilt is unlikely to go with an innocence.

The answers given to the four questions about terrorism in the last essay, as I say after making them, give rise to an idea that also has a place in this introduction. It needs somehow to be brought into consistency with something said at the beginning of it, about inquiring with an open mind.

If political philosophy should be an attempt to inquire with an open mind, it is also something else. If it is not ideology, it is *advocacy*, in a way related to the work of a decent barrister. Political philosophers are more like barristers than judges, even if barristers more or less convinced of the rightness of their cases, and it is worth remembering.

22 May 2003

1
Wretchedness and Terrorism, and Differences We Make Between Them

So much of what passes for decent political philosophy is factless and presumptuous. It is of some use in trying to decide how our societies ought to be, and how to get or keep them that way. But that it is of use is only to be explained by the want of something better.

We can agree that all of philosophy, in order to come within sight of its end, must have far less to do with empirical fact than those disciplines, the sciences, that have the discovery of it and its explanation as their end. However, in the political philosophy that explicitly or implicitly recommends action to us, or more likely inaction, premises of empirical fact necessarily have a larger importance than elsewhere in philosophy. It is not to be overlooked that recommendations with specific consequences are made. We are in fact urged to take a political side. We are urged to take a side that will determine whether some children remain uneducated, or emaciated, or a side that may commit us to support a war, or terrorism by a state – the latter being, very roughly, small-scale and illegal violence by a state.

Political philosophy of this kind, to its lesser credit, is different even from moral philosophy of the traditional kind. There, we used to be urged towards such outlooks as the Utilitarian one, and more recently we have been urged to such commitments as *integrity*, and to obligations so undemanding that we do customarily act on them. Neither the Principle of Utility by itself, nor stuff about integrity or the easy obligations, is presumed to settle particular questions in private morality for one. It is understood that to settle answers to questions of conduct in marriage, say, one needs something in addition to general principles, which by themselves do not tell one what to do. The additional factual premises are not and could not easily be supplied, and so, very reasonably, recommendations of a specific nature are not made. One is rarely told what to do in marriage, or when to leave one.

In political philosophy of the recommending kind, one is told what to do in politics, in a way that matters. For such recommendations to rise to being *argued* recommendations, they clearly need to be preceded by premises about society, empirical premises of a quite particular kind about conditions of life. Typically they are not. Nor does one have much confidence that what is said for our guidance was in fact derived, in private reflection off the page, from factual premises worth the name. If political philosophy of the kind in question, just about all of it, is as little empirical as the rest of philosophy, and has such need to be more so that it may with justice be called factless, it is therefore presumptuous in its conclusions. However, there is also presumption in it for an entirely different reason.

The issue of terrorism, to come down to that, is typically handled in what purports to be a conclusive article or book, a thing that ends, or as likely begins, with a conclusion on the principal question. In our part of the world, we may be expected to assume that all terrorism is unspeakable, an atrocity. In other parts of the world, we may be given to understand that Islamic terrorism, or terrorism to free a people, or terrorism against inhuman or violating conditions of life, must at least be *understood*. It may be implied in both cases, as certainly it ought to be stated, that what has actually been set out in support of the chosen conclusion is no more than a sketch or impression of an argument for it, or, certainly better, only a part of an argument. Still, we are offered the intimation about this simulacrum that all of the real thing, the conclusive argument itself, exists somewhere else.

This political philosophy, then, begins without essential premises of fact, and proceeds by way of gesturing. It delivers conclusions to us none the less. Let us make a beginning at trying to put things right, by looking at one of several pertinent sets of facts.

LIFETIMES

In the United States, on average, blacks live for about six years less than whites.[1] About thirty million individuals now alive will have an average of about six years less of life than, on average, other members of their society. This average of deprivation is produced, of course, by more deaths of babies, of children, of young people, and of their parents. Fewer make it through each of these stages of life. Those who die are denied what almost all of us desire above all and to the end, the great good of a full length of life. If there are no very fundamental economic and social changes in America, it is likely that the next 'generation', the blacks who are alive 20 years from now, will still have a life-expectancy much shorter than that of their white contemporaries. The rate of improvement in the past gives one of several bases for this guess about the future.[2] An optimistic guess is that blacks alive 20 years from now, if fundamental economic and social changes do not come about, will have an average lifetime about five years shorter than their white contemporaries.

The population of England and Wales has been divided into five of what are officially called social classes. They might also be called occupational groups, since they are in fact defined by the occupations of their members. They are labelled professional, intermediate, skilled, partly skilled and unskilled. The average lifetime of males in the fifth social class is seven years shorter than the average lifetime of males in the first social class.[3] There are about 1.5 million individuals in question. One can guess that in 20 years' time, if fundamental social and economic changes are not made in Britain, the unskilled class may be in an improved position but still have a life-expectancy very considerably shorter than that of a professional class – more deaths at each stage of life.

Let us have before us, beside the truths and suppositions about individual lifetimes in contemporary America and Britain, two uncontentious generalisations about all of the western rich societies. We can proceed towards these by remembering that blacks in America and unskilled workers in Britain have greatly less material wealth and income than other groups in their societies. There are, of course, some blacks who are better off than some whites, and some unskilled workers who are better off than some members of some other occupational groups. On the whole, none the less, blacks in America and unskilled workers and their families in Britain each are large parts of a poorest group in each of the two societies. We have, then, a correlation between an economic fact and a fact about lifetimes. If qualification is needed in stating it, it is unsurprising. Indeed, the fact that the people in question come at the bottom of scales of wealth and income is the principal part of the complex cause of their shorter lives. This consideration, and many related truths about groups in the other western rich societies, give rise to the two generalisations I have in mind about all such societies.

The first one has to do with roughly the one tenth of each western society's population that has less wealth and income than any other tenth in that society. The generalisation is that the worst-off tenth now living in each one of the rich societies will have considerably shorter lives than the individuals in the best-off tenth. It is as good as certain that they will live less long, on average, by about six years or more.[4] We must wait for precision until the time, if ever it comes, when more statistical work is done. The second generalisation, as may be anticipated, is that if there are not fundamental social and economic changes in the societies in question, the situation will be better in 20 years but not greatly better.

As with of what was said of America and Britain, the numbers of people involved is of an obvious importance, making for a very large loss of living-time. There are now, in all of the bottom tenths of the poor societies, something like a hundred million individuals.

To turn to a related and yet heavier subject-matter, here are the life-expectancies at birth for a few poor societies, and then a few rich societies.[5]

Malawi 39 yrs
Mozambique 44 yrs
Zambia 40 yrs
Sierra Leone 38 yrs
United States 77 yrs
United Kingdom 77 yrs
France 78 yrs
Germany 77 yrs

So people born in Sierra Leone have an average lifetime of 38 years. People born in America and Britain, taking all classes together, have an average lifetime of 77 years. On average, people in Sierra Leone die before what is regarded as early middle age in Britain and America. It is not too much to say that what we have before us are different kinds of human existence.

The average figures for the two groups of societies, as the specimen figures indicate, hide still greater inequalities. There is the greater difference in lifetimes between the bottom tenth of population in the poor countries and the top tenth of population in the rich countries. There are no figures available, to my knowledge, for the latter tenth. Given evidence of various kinds, it is certain that the bottom tenth in poor societies have average lifetimes very much more than around 40 years shorter than the average lifetimes of the top tenth in rich societies. Their lives, on average, are in the neighbourhood of 50 years shorter. So the wealthiest in the wealthy countries have two lives for each single life of the poorest in the poor countries. That is not really a metaphor. It is not too much to say that if one knew only the average lifetimes of these two groups of beings, one would suppose they were different species.

Is it likely that such inequalities in life-expectancy between poor and rich societies, and groups within them, will be smaller in 20 years? What is certain is that unless there is a transformation in the relations between the wealthy and the poor parts of the world, there will remain an immense difference in lifetimes 20 years from now.

Do some of us say there is no possibility of real change, either in the inequalities of lifetime within rich societies or in the inequalities of lifetime between rich and poor societies? Are some of us inclined to suppose that whatever morality may say or not say, we do not have the relevant capability? And thus that there is misconception in talk of large changes in lifetimes that might follow on fundamental social and economic changes? It may be objected, in effect, that it is already inevitable that the next generation of the groups in question will have a life-expectancy much like that of the present generation of the same groups.

This is mistaken, certainly or probably. Given the wealth and efficiency of the rich societies, proved in many different ways, it is clear enough that we could change very radically the life-expectancy of the groups in question. One needs to reflect, in part, on the magnitude of just such changes in the past. To consider the inequalities within rich societies, the following figures give the change in life-expectancy of American whites, at birth, over a period of 40 years.[6]

1920	54.9 yrs
1940	64.2 yrs
1960	70.6 yrs

One fact of relevance, then, is that in each of two 20-year periods in the fairly recent past, the life-expectancy of American whites was improved to a considerably greater extent than would be required in the coming 20 years if American blacks were to come up to the level of American whites.

It is to be admitted, certainly, that the case is not *clear* with respect to the possibility of change in the lifetime-inequalities between rich and poor societies. None the less, it is beyond question that the inequalities could be dramatically reduced. The lifetime-inequalities are consequences of economic inequalities. It is plain that no amount of economic theory can put in doubt the truth that the present economic inequalities are open to change, change which would not be damaging to present economic totals and which would dramatically reduce lifetime-inequalities.

It is worth remarking in this connection, to those who are struck by how very little has been achieved, that not much more than nothing has been attempted. In 1964 a number of the rich countries pledged to 'contribute' a percentage of their future gross national products to the poor countries. This 'contribution' was to include loans and private investment. The figure agreed upon was 1 per cent. This has not come near to happening. Nothing of any significance whatever has been attempted by Blair, the sometimes feelingful and moralising leader of the New Labour Party in Britain. The pledged total of 1 per cent of the gross national products of the rich countries in question has not been met in any year. These nullities are not the kind of thing to be kept in mind in considering the question of capability. A better thing is the 'war efforts' of the past and no doubt the future.

All of the generalisations about lifetimes have all of their importance in the fact that they have to do with individual human experience. They do not have to do most importantly with *differences* in experience, comparisons between people, relative positions. They have to do *most* importantly with the badness of bad experience, distress. The comparisons serve the purpose of indicating actual states of distress, and they also illustrate that the cause of this distress has greatly to do with the fact of others having the means to radically different lives. So they are also about injustice, monstrous injustice.[7]

It is a banal truth that typically we escape these propositions, or give them the attention of a moment. It is necessary to come closer to the reality of experience. We may do so through one woman's recorded recollection of her daughter.

She was doing fine, real fine. I thought she was going to be fine, too. I did. There wasn't a thing wrong with her, and suddenly she was in real trouble, bad trouble, yes sir, she was. She started coughing, like her throat was hurting, and I thought she must be catching a cold or something. I thought I'd better go get her some water, but it wasn't easy, because there were the other kids, and it's far away to go. So I sent my husband when he came home, and I tried to hold her, and I sang and sang, and it helped. But she got real hot, and she was sleepy all right, but I knew it wasn't good, no sir. I'd rather hear her cry, that's what I kept saying. My boy, he knew it too. He said, 'Ma, she's real quiet, isn't she?' Then I started praying, and I thought maybe it'll go the way it came, real fast, and by morning there won't be anything but Rachel feeling a little tired, that's all. We got the water to her, and I tried to get her to take something, a little cereal, like she was doing all along. I didn't have any more milk maybe that's how it started. And I had a can of tomato juice, that we had in case of real trouble, and I opened it and tried to get it down her. But she'd throw it all back at me, and I gave up, to tell the truth. I figured it was best to let her rest, and then she could fight back with all the strength she had, and as I said, maybe by the morning she'd be the winner, and then I could go get a bottle of milk from my boss man and we could really care for her real good, until she'd be back to her self again. But it got worse, I guess, and by morning she was so bad there was nothing she'd take, and hot all over, she was hot all over. And then she went, all of a sudden. There was no more breathing, and it must have been around noon by the light.[8]

No breath of apology is owed to those who may say to themselves that they do not expect to find emotional matter within serious reflection. On the contrary, one must feel remiss for offering so small a reminder of human experience.

TERRORISM

The facts of terrorism or political violence are not so much in need of being brought forward. It is a part of what I shall discuss in this essay that we have an immediate and a sharp awareness of them. Nonetheless, should any remaining Trotskyite or the like still persist in regarding the effects of terrorism as no more than calculable expenses to be paid for the march of history, it will be as well to assert what should need no asserting. It is that here too we find facts of human experience. Bombs injure, disfigure, maim and kill. They end or devastate the lives of their first victims, and they bring agony or ruin to the lives of their second victims, those who suffer through others being disfigured, injured, maimed or killed. The effects of explosions are not only those effects which we find detailed in our newspapers. A man who is blinded or a girl who loses a hand lives on, and, for everyone who is killed, there are others who continue to be affected.

If these are the things of importance about terrorism, there is a need for a general definition. Terrorism or political violence, in all its elements, is

a use of physical force that injures, damages, violates or destroys people or things, with a political and social intention, and whether or not intended to cause fear to people in general, and raising a question of its moral justification – either illegal violence within a society or violence between states and societies not according to international law, and smaller-scale than war.

Some comments on this may be useful.[9] The definition, although like all definitions a matter of some decision-making as well as reporting, is in some accord with ordinary and current usage. It is about violence, illegality and scale. It covers terrorism aimed at the freedom of a people, which may be seen or merely tagged in terms of religion. It also covers terrorism by a state or government, *state-terrorism*, perhaps aimed at denying the freedom of a people, usually in order to enlarge or engorge the freedom of the people of the state in question. It covers terrorism for humanity, as it will be called, and it covers terrorism directly opposed to this.

The definition does not require of terrorism that it cause fear more or less throughout a society. In this connection, note that the murder of a leader, a political murder and very likely regarded as terrorism, may not cause general fear. Indeed there can be socially-reassuring violence that now would be called terrorism. The definition, if it registers a *prima facie* moral case against terrorism, does not automatically condemn all of it. It leaves open the question, for example, of whether the terrorism that contributed to the establishing of the state of Israel was right. Certainly the definition carries no implication whatever that *war*, by contrast, has a moral justification. There can be wrong and vicious war against right and principled terrorism.

One other remark. The definition does not specify that victims of terrorism by the state or by others are innocent people or non-combatants. This is not because of some difficulties in defining the innocent, which difficulties do exist, but mainly because many victims of war are also innocent people or non-combatants. Morever, by an arguable understanding of intention, the deaths of innocents in war, being foreseen, are within the intentions of the makers of war. Further, the deaths of innocents can be means to ends in both terrorism and war. It is not a good idea to forget, for example, the terror-bombing of World War II.

The definition covers more than the terrorism we have known, above all that of September 11, 2001. There can or could be terrorism directed to other ends than those of which we commonly think. My concern in this book, as already noted, will be with both actual and also possible and conceivable terrorism. Finally, it is to be allowed that there are other definitions of political violence, certainly, including definitions thought to be more enlightened or virtuous, and we shall return to the matter.[10]

FACTS AND REASONINGS

There are the facts of violence, then, and there are what can be called, if we persist in the use of an anodyne label, the facts of inequality. The latter, of which we have considered only one particular set, claim attention not strictly because they consist in inequalities: situations such that one group of people has *less* of something than another. What is mainly important, as already remarked, is that some people have so little, judged in an absolute rather than a comparative way – and, further, that this has to do with the distribution of things. They are in conditions of distress – conditions of being badly-off ranging from deprivation to wretchedness and indeed to agony. They lack or are denied lives of well-being. The circumstance is not an unreal one which can be imagined, where inequality does not matter much because the worst-off are nonetheless splendidly off and in no real sense deprived by the better-off. Our real circumstance is one in which the facts of inequality include, and might alternatively be described as, the many facts of distress. This, further, is principally explained by the larger shares of goods of the better-off, by injustice.

My intentions in this essay, which have to do with these facts and with the facts of violence, are two in number. One of them is 'unphilosophical' and has already been realised. It was to make a small contribution, the first of two in this book,[11] to a realisation of the facts of inequality. Any such realisation, of course, must touch one's view of actual, possible and conceivable political violence, whatever the final effect.

The particular set of facts noticed, those about lives cut short, have a natural priority. *Time alive* is not all that matters, but it matters very much indeed. Certain other facts of deprivation and worse may be separated into two families. There are those that have to do with economic and social life. The list begins with lacks in decent food, shelter and health – something more than is actually necessary to sustain life. The extent of such inequalities is only barely indicated by the known immense disparities in wealth and income. Another set of deprivations is political in kind, and has to do with certain freedoms and the lack of them. It is here that one finds demands for national self-determination, and demands of peoples to lands to which they have rights that are alive. The demands of the Palestinians against the further violation of their homeland by Israel comes here. There are also other great things we want.

It cannot be that rationality allows us to avoid informing ourselves of these things which are more or less directly relevant to political violence. No more is meant than said: that we are obliged in rationality *to inform ourselves*. As I have already implied, a part of this is a decent approach to human experience in its detail. What is needed first is knowledge, knowledge of particulars, which is to be distinguished from responses of feeling to general facts of distress of various kinds, and from judgements about them. No one should overlook, for example, that shorter lifetimes are in clear ways within the anticipation of very many of those who have them, and also within the experience of others. With respect to the latter point, there is the fact that if the daughter of whom you have heard had lived longer, her death would not have been within the experience of the mother.

If we were better informed of the facts of deprivation and worse, the denials of well-being, we could with propriety pass on to further things. What is customarily done, as I have remarked, is to press on improperly, to conclusions. What we shall do here, less improperly, is to move forward slowly. We shall not come quickly to a conclusion about the rightness, the permissibility, the wrongfulness, or the monstrousness of political violence. The matters we shall consider, like the facts of inequality and violence, have a natural place near the beginning of an orderly inquiry.

There is a certain welter of propositions, arguments, theories, and doctrines which comes in between the factual premises about terrorism and about wretchedness and the rest, on the one hand, and, on the other hand, any final conclusions about the morality of this terrorism. I mean, in saying that these things in the middle come in, that they must be considered. All of them are reasons or reasonings, or else they can be improved into reasons or reasonings. All of them, obviously, must be made decently clear and explicit before their value is judged. In the end, of course, since they point in different directions, some of them must be rejected, or regarded as of lesser weight.

Here are some examples, all of one kind. We may believe that some governments, perhaps democratic ones, have a rightful authority over the members of the societies in question, and hence that the members have an obligation of obedience. We may believe that all members of pretty well any society, simply by living in it, acquire an obligation to keep some or all of its laws. We may have some idealised conception of the society of justice, and suppose that our actual society is within sight of realising this conception. Very differently, we may have some ordered set of fundamental moral principles, or a belief as to the best or the only acceptable way of drawing moral conclusions, perhaps a way that is thought to guarantee fairness. Differently, we may be committed to a number af propositions, perhaps got by historical inquiry, about the probability that violence will secure or give rise to social change. Differently again, we may suppose that some political violence has important affinities with the practice of democracy.

Whatever their final value, such reasons and reasonings are certainly of relevance to any verdict on violence. I shall consider most of them, and some others, in the essays of this book. Still, these are examples of reasons and reasonings of a kind correctly described as being at a certain distance from the facts, the facts of distress and violence. There are things which are closer to the facts and which may be considerably more persuasive for many people, whether or not they should be such. Some of these latter things, indeed, may determine the weight given to the more distant reasons and reasonings. They often have the character of unreflective responses and assumptions, but, as I have said, they can be other than that.

My second intention in this essay is to look at four of them, perhaps the four which are most important. They have to do with immediate feelings about distress and violence, the existence of moral prohibitions on certain kinds of action, the supposed irrationality of violence, and the very possibility of having satisfactory principles of equality. The last subject will be no more than introduced, and will get full attention in the following essay. As you will guess, these reasons and reasonings, while the middle two are relevant to all terrorism, have most to do with terrorism in the pursuit of freedom and the like – what has been anticipated as terrorism for humanity.

CIRCUMSTANCES OF FEELING

If we were to assemble the facts of distress before ourselves as best we could, as we have not done, what would be our untutored feelings about them? Among the facts would be those at which we have looked, about more deaths at every age. (i) Within rich societies a bottom group of individuals, many million people, have lives six years shorter on average than other members of their societies. They want the six years, as much as you do. (ii) In a sample of poor societies, the populations can expect to live only to what we regard as middle age. (iii) The worst-off in these countries, compared with the best-off in other countries, have less than half-lives. They have death-in-life, death intruding into life as a matter of course, rather than death after life. Among the facts of distress before us, as well, would be those of socio-economic and political kinds. We have not even glanced at those. Also, for all these general facts, there would be particulars, particulars of human experience.

We who are contemplating these facts of distress, we may suppose, are people who are moved to some decent degree by the situations of others and have only an ordinary amount of prejudice. We are not possessed or taken over by ideology or doctrine. We may, as people do, incline to certain social and economic beliefs, but these are not so much a part of us that we have no independent attitude to the facts of distress, down to wretchedness.

What would be our feelings about them? The question could do with sharper expression, but let us take it as we have it. Our feelings in the imagined state of knowledge would be considerably different from our ordinary responses now, in our actual state of ignorance. They would be stronger. As I have already implied, we feel less than we might about the facts of inequality, much less, simply because we are ignorant of them. That, however, is not my principal point, which may be approached by noticing that our feelings would have a certain character. Many of us, faced with the facts of inequality, would be appalled, dismayed, saddened, affected, sympathetic, wearied, or resentful. The character of these feelings is one of passivity or quietness.

Suppose that on another occasion we have assembled before us some facts of terrorism. Suppose we have before us killing, wounding, kidnapping, such destruction of property as touches closely on the lives of individuals, and also the consequences of these several things. Suppose, more simply, that we remember the facts of September 11. We feel horror, shock, repugnance, disgust, rage, or vengefulness. The terms 'atrocity' and 'savagery' have a place in the expression of these emotions. To come to the principal point, these emotions do not have about them the passivity or quietness of the emotions called up by the facts of inequality. They have a different character.

This difference is a fact about the feelings which we would have, given a fuller knowledge of deprivation and other distress, but obviously there is a related fact about the feelings we actually do have, with the knowledge we actually do have. It has seemed to me right to come to the matter by way of supposing our being more responsible about informing ourselves, about assembling the dark facts. Certainly it is the difference in *informed* feelings, as they might be called, which is most important. In what follows, nonetheless, we shall almost inevitably have in mind our feelings as they are, and this will not be disastrous. It will certainly not be to the advantage of my argument, but rather the reverse.

Feelings about distress and terrorism are obviously of great effect on final moral views about violence. Furthermore, it is certainly possible to regard the responses as reasons, or to derive reasons from them. That is, it can be argued that we ought to be directed in our judgements by such differences in feeling, that such differences are right determinants of judgement.

The general ideas that we are guided by feeling in morality, and that we ought to be, are somehow true. That is, some understanding of these ideas makes them beyond denial. Obviously, both matters are complex ones.[12] Let us look a bit at the second one, to the effect that we ought to be guided by differences in feeling.

It is clear enough that we must pay attention to what can be called the *circumstance of feeling*. We must look to the question of how it is that we come to feel as we do. Few people will say, except in heat, or with personal excuse, that we should not inquire into this. Very nearly all recent moral philosophy, in one way or another, gives explicit adherence to a general proposition of this kind about judging feelings, despite the fact that this philosophy has not got down to hard cases and hard details. What I should like to consider is whether our circumstance is such that we can give an unquestioned importance to our feelings about distress and terrorism. There are quite a few plain propositions which are of relevance, things which go unnoticed but which are there for the eye to see.

One notable difference between our awarenesses of the two orders of fact is that the agents of violence are inevitably in the foreground, but the agents of wretchedness and lesser ways of being badly-off are not immediately to be seen. The young man or woman who blows up a crowd at a bus-stop is precisely within our focus. Not so with agents of inequality. We may of course set out to find them. We may attempt some distinction of the kind that has informed whole traditions of political reflection and action, and issued in condemnatory works of various kinds.

If we attempt to find the greyer agents, we may have some tolerable success.[13] We shall certainly find a class of people who may be said to accede to the system of inequalities, and who could contribute to change if they wanted. It does not stand in the way of this enterprise that their motivations and personalities are not greatly different from those of the victims of inequality. They do not contribute to change and, unlike almost all of the victims of inequality, they could do so. Their simplest contribution would be part of their wealth.

At least three relevant things are true of this class of agents of distress. One is that very nearly all of us, readers of books, are members of the class. A second is that the class is immense and hence, so to speak, anonymous. Its members are not some few identified individuals. The third is that the relation of these agents to the facts of inequality is quite unlike the relation of the agents of violence to the facts of that order. No one with his own hands sets a fuse which secures an immense loss of living-time for American blacks or a part of the English people, ordinary working men. Much of the latter difference, to which we will certainly be returning, remains if we narrow down our conception of the agents of inequality to individuals who actively obstruct change or, differently, individuals who by their own actions do make for the distress of identifiable victims of inequality.

Our feeling about terrorism, then, has very much to do with its agents, while our feeling about deprivation and worse has less or indeed little to do with its agents. The latter is true because these latter agents are pretty well out of sight or, if they are in sight, they are ourselves, they are many and impersonal, and they are distant from their work. The character of our feeling about terrorism, against the character of our feeling about inequality, is in significant part explained by the matter of agents.

However, to move towards the principal point, there is reason for saying that our feelings about distress and terrorism are principally relevant in so far as they are feelings about victims rather than agents. That, although we shall in a way come back to the question, will be agreed by almost all who consider distress and terrorism, no matter to what conclusion they are inclined. What matters is awfulness, and not, by itself, what may be regarded as an agent's callous deliberateness in intention. It is impossible to agree with the agent-obsessed Kant that a good will, or a bad will, matters far more than its effects on others, that a good will is the only unqualifiedly good thing and a bad will, presumably, the only unqualifiedly bad thing. If we could subtract all bad and terrible intentions or all suffering from the world, we would rightly not be in doubt for a moment about which to do.

We thus have a consideration which must lead us in some degree to discount the vehemence, indeed the violence, of our feeling about violence. If that vehemence were more the product of an awareness of victims, of both kinds, the circumstance would be importantly different.

There is a complication with which we shall be faced. There are those who will urge upon us what they regard as plain rationality. They will object that if it is agreed that our concern must principally be with victims, it must also be agreed as a consequence that we must concern ourselves with agents, conceived just as causers of distress, makers of victims. That is, we must look upon agents of violence as we look upon ordinary nonpolitical lawbreakers if we subscribe to the deterrence theory of punishment. Like an ordinary offender, a man who sets a bomb is a man who is likely to act in the same way again, and also a man who encourages others to do likewise.

It may thus be suggested, by way of a ramshackle argument, that we should in no way discount our feeling about violence on the ground that it is to some significant degree called up by agents. The argument, in essence, will be that any discounting of feeling leads to inhibition of it, that inhibition will have an effect on what is done to agents, and that if less is done there will be more victims. Of course, the same sort of premises may also be taken to lead in another direction, towards doubt about the validity of our passive or quiet response to the facts of inequality. That is, the premise about the necessary connection of agents and upshots may be thought also to contribute to the conclusion that we should try to have stronger feelings about the agents of distress, or compensate in our reflection for the weakness of our feelings.

I shall not examine either this retort or the supposed plain rationality about victims and agents. All I wish to notice is another fact about our actual responses to the agents of violence. In those responses we are not in fact persistently rational in the given sense, or anything like it. Our responses to the agents of violence, perhaps, are in part 'useful' responses to causes of suffering or, in the relevant sense, makers of victims. However, our responses are very much more than that. They are accusatory or vengeful. The machine that maims a worker and the man who maims another man are naturally regarded by us in quite different ways. In the latter case, there is the fact of our beliefs and attitudes having to do with responsibility and culpability of persons. Hence, even should we be inclined to give some attention to the rationalist argument about feeling, it would remain the case that our feeling about the facts of violence has much to do with agents regarded as other than past and perhaps future causes of distress. It is not what some would call rational feeling, in the end about victims.

In sum, the different character of our feelings about political violence and distress has in part to do with awareness of some agents and our want of awareness of others. To the extent that the resulting feelings are not related to the matter of prevention, they are not of the first importance. What is of the first importance is victims. We have, then, a reason for questioning a large reliance on the contrast in our feelings about violence and distress.

You may see, as once I did not, that there is a kind of corollary to this line of thought, a second proposition. On September 11, 2001, if we were aware of agents who were hideous and monstrous to us, we were yet more aware of their victims. Indeed, and for human reasons, victims have never been more in the minds and lives of a people and of other peoples. That this fact was owed not only to the event itself but also to television and the rest, new facts of communication and the immediate entering into the lives of others, does not diminish it.

To diminish it is far from my intent. What needs to be remarked on is only the truth that we have been so aware of these victims of terrorism to the exclusion of the victims of other things, those multitudes of people in wretched lives. Do you take this reminder to be somehow tasteless? Is it yet more tasteless to make another remark about the day of September 11, when 3000 were killed at the

Twin Towers and the Pentagon? On that day, if deaths by starvation for 2001 were spread evenly throughout the year, 23,000 people died of hunger. Each was as individual as the black mother's child who went when it must have been around noon by the light. Each was as individual as each of the 3000.

It is not my intention to presume or claim any simple connection between the two sets of victims. The point is that in considering our feelings about terrorism and about lives of distress, and in particular our feelings about both categories of victims, we need to remember that both categories do not exist for us in the same way. They do not exist *for us* in the same way. But they do both exist in the same real way. One cannot rightly be treated as unreal when the general subjects of terrorism and lives of distress are under consideration. We do treat one category as unreal, and we need to reflect on this circumstance of feeling.

Given all that, a third proposition about our different responses to inequality and violence may strike you as paradoxical. It is that we are familiar with inequality and unfamiliar with the violence. The real humanity of the victims of inequality, and the absolute as against the comparative condition of those who are badly-off, and even the magnitude of the inequalities, are not things of which we have much grasp. Still, if we were to assemble the facts of inequality, we would not then have a grasp of something new, something with which we had had no previous familiarity. In a general way, we know about the dying, and about other things. We've heard of them, most of us. As for violence being different in not being within the awareness of most of us, no doubt that is a generality pertaining only to most times and most places. As such, it stands high among useful generalisations in political philosophy.

It is to be remarked, then, that the quiet feelings evoked by inequality are in part to be explained by the relative familiarity of the subject-matter. The feelings evoked by violence are in part to be explained by the relative unfamiliarity of violence. There is support for this in the truism that there is a deadening or quieting of feeling in certain circumstances, usually in war, when violence becomes familiar.

The suggestion that must emerge here is that the moral relevance of feelings is the less if they owe something, perhaps a good deal, to the familiarity or unfamiliarity of their objects. It surely cannot be that the 'natural' death of a child or the murder of a man has a significantly different value in virtue of there being many or few such deaths, many or few murders. One may think of ways in which the proposition might be qualified, but the qualifications are slight ones, of secondary importance. Thus our circumstance in responding to wretchedness and the like as against violence is, for a third reason, one in which our first feelings are not to be accorded an unquestioned deference.

A fourth proposition to be considered has to do with the common perception of inequality as entrenched. Violence is rightly seen differently. Setting a bomb is a human action which like other human actions might not have been performed. The man could have done otherwise. That, however the belief is to be analysed, is our belief. The action is something, too, which quickly raises in the mind the possibility of prevention by others. The inequalities, by contrast, and for good reason, do not have the perceived character of things that easily might not have been, or things that we can briskly set about altering.

The point again is that if our feelings about human experience are in part given their character by a factor external to that experience, such a fact must be paid attention. If the quiet of our feelings about wretchedness and the like is in part owed to a perception of it as settled and resistant, this is a fact to be paid attention. The terribleness of human experience, the terribleness of having a child whose lifetime is five years, remains just that, whatever may be true about persistence and change. If the inequalities were not merely entrenched, but in fact necessary and inevitable, which is different, the situation would be otherwise. That they are in fact necessary and inevitable is a simple error corrected by some reflection on history. It was once thought to be necessary and inevitable that children worked in mines, and the example can be multiplied many times.

It is to be admitted, certainly, that it would be irrational to come to a verdict about political violence without paying careful attention to the probability of its actually achieving ends of social change. That is something of which I shall have a good deal more to say.[14] However, it is one thing to take the matter into account, in full consciousness and in the right place, and another thing not to notice its effect, or rather the effect of something less precise, on our feelings about the human experience of inequality.

Fifthly, it is at least arguable that our feelings about inequalities and about violence are influenced by the correct perception of the inequalities as constituting a state of *order*, and violence as constituting a circumstance of *disorder*. Inequality is a product of law, of diverse settled institutions, of custom, and indeed of assent. The vast majority of those who are worse-off do not resist, because they cannot. Violence is otherwise. A man shot by a political assassin is one of two figures in a circumstance of a wholly different character, a circumstance of anarchy. No restraint is put on one's feeling about his death by a recognition of it as ordained.

To repeat, if our concern is rightly our feelings about the experience of others, it is important to be sure that we take into account precisely these feelings. The present point, then, is that the distress of others should not come upon one, in the first instance, as items of order or of disorder. It may be that they should be so considered, at some later point in reflection. They should not be regarded in this way in the first instance if a primary matter is not to be confused. If, therefore, pain and distress do in fact have an effect upon us which is partly a consequence of something that is external to them, we must recognise this fact.

A sixth consideration has to do with the difference, not necessarily a reasonable difference, in our response to being attacked or wounded on the one hand, and, on the other, being made to suffer for much longer periods but not as a consequence of being attacked, wounded, or the like. Before one rests a conclusion quickly on our primitive impulse to choose, say, lasting hunger rather than an injury, it is useful to consider what one would choose for another person, perhaps a person about whom one cares. Would we have our children hungry for life? Not literally attacked but nonetheless crushed and brutalized by life? It is safe to observe that first impulses are not certain to be last judgements. A seventh consideration has to do with the indiscriminateness or the undirectedness of much political violence. One thing to be remarked here is that the particular victims of inequality are not carefully chosen either. However, I shall leave undiscussed these considerations, the sixth and the seventh, and finish here with something else.

There is not a great deal in common, you may say, between two large figures of the nineteenth century, Friedrich Engels and John Stuart Mill. Well, there is something. The collaborator of Marx characterises all morality as class-morality.[15] It is, in his view, an instrument of a ruling class or of an oppressed but rising class. In *On Liberty*, although the fact is often forgotten, the great liberal says much the same. 'Wherever there is an ascendant class, a large part of the morality of the country emanates from its class interests, and its feelings of class superiority.'[16] Should you spend some time with the writings of the father of conservatism Edmund Burke, you will find him in no doubt that a society's morality is and must be owed not to its hairdressers but mainly to its natural aristocracy.[17] To the testimony of these diverse worthies can be added not only that of a thousand lesser thinkers, as well as the evidence of your own reflections. One proposition, which does not presuppose a ruling class's *devising* of morality, is that moral feeling has much of its genesis in the general self-interest of ascendant classes.

The relative quietness of our feelings about the distress of inequality, and the violence of our feelings about violence, are related to our own places in the world. You who are reading this essay, in all likelihood, are a beneficiary of the system of inequality. Perhaps more important, you have no human connection with the victims of that system. By contrast, in many ordinary situations of life, you discount the feelings and doubt the judgements of individuals who are in certain positions of benefit and relationship analogous to your own.

It is remarkable that such suggestions of the self-interest of moral feelings are disdained or doubted by those who are familiar with certain institutions of a supposedly fair society – fundamental institutions so constructed as to defeat to some extent such things as self-deceiving responses to groups other than one's own. The institution of the law is the principal one of these. It will be remarkable, too, if such suggestions of self-deception and the like continue to be dismissed by philosophers. No recent work of moral philosophy lacks a device against self-deceiving self-interest in its recommended system of reflection. In some cases, the device is most of the system.

Some may regard some or all of the foregoing eight reflections on distress and violence as ill-judged. This may have to do with a failure to recognise that there are two orders of fact, each of them compelling, each of them terrible. Not to recognise this is to fail in feeling and judgement. Again, there is an inclination to suppose the question of terrorism, like any serious moral question, is one for ourselves as moral judges. That is, it is a question for the moral consciousness or the moral self, or perhaps the conscience. It is not one of which we can rightly treat by bringing in a kind of psychology, propositions about the causes of feeling. This inclination, to my mind, is not one to be encouraged. The moral consciousness, somehow insulated from our attitudes and situations, is a fiction, and not a good one.

PROHIBITED ACTS

There are moral philosophers and the like who say, whether or not they would always do as they say, that there are certain kinds of act which are absolutely prohibited. These are acts about which there can never be a moral question, acts which must never be done whatever the circumstances. Those who express this view, connected with religious tradition, do not have in mind such 'truisms' as this, that an act is prohibited if *all* that is known of it is that it would cause suffering. They have in mind certain familiar acts, identified in quite different ways. One kind may be the killing of another person, an innocent person.

It is unlikely that many people would hesitate if they were faced with a straight and clear choice between killing a man on the one hand, and, on the other, inaction of which they believed with *certainty* that it would give rise to catastrophic consequences, perhaps many deaths. If, as is far from being the case, they were faced with a choice between an act of killing and, on the other hand, inaction taken to involve the near-certainty of catastrophic consequences, many would still choose the killing and would defend their choice. Doctrines about absolute moral prohibition have lost any pervasiveness they may once have had.

Nonetheless, there is no doubt that there exists an inclination, or perhaps something more than that, a conviction, against certain acts and those who perform them. It is not the claim that there is an absolute prohibition, but it is somewhere in the direction of that conclusion. What is in question here, as before, is the idea that an act of killing, say, is somehow wrong in itself, and not that it is wrong because in fact it will be ineffective in securing an end, say the rescuing of a people from degradation. There is thought to be a kind of moral constraint upon us which does not have anything to do with the consequences of action or inaction. It is a constraint which has to do with acts in themselves, and one which sometimes may rightly be effective in preventing individuals from doing what would have the best consequences.

This is the second of the responses to inequality and political violence that I wish to consider in this essay. It may be an unconsidered reaction to acts of violence and to those who perform them, either when lives are taken or endangered, or in other cases as well. Alternatively, it may be more reflective. In both forms, rightly or wrongly, it has been persuasive with many people.

The kind of inclination or conviction in question may of course arise in cases that do not have to do with terrorism. Bernard Williams, in *Utilitarianism: For and Against*, considers the example of a chemist, without a job and hence with his family in difficulty, who is offered work in a laboratory whose research is into chemical and biological warfare.[18] He, unlike his wife, is particularly opposed to such warfare and to the research. However, he understands that if he refuses the job, the research will proceed anyway. More important, he knows that if he refuses the job, it will go to a particular man who is likely to push along the research with greater zeal than he himself would. The chemist none the less refuses the job. It is recommended to us that he has done the right thing. The acute and engrossing argument for this recommendation has to do with two things – integrity, as it is called, and responsibility.

In refusing the job, we are told, the chemist's action flowed from deep attitudes that are fundamental to the person he is. He has not acted as a consequence of the attitudes or actions of another, in such a way as to alienate himself from his own actions, and hence in such a way as to diminish or destroy his own integrity, his integrity in the most literal sense. He would have diminished or destroyed his integrity if he had taken the job, as a consequence of the fact that the other chemist would be more diligent in the research. He would, in that case, have been acting as a consequence of the attitudes and actions of the other man.[19]

To pass on to responsibility, the chemist does take the view, understandably enough, that one of the two possible states of affairs would be better than the other. The better one, of course, is the one in which he himself does take the job and hence the research goes forward more slowly than it would in the hands of the other man. However, the chemist also takes it that it is not his business to engage in this state of affairs. It is not his business to prepare, however less efficiently than someone else might, for chemical and biological warfare. There is a great difference for him between this possible state of affairs and the worse one. Although he himself is involved by his refusal in the coming about of the worse state of affairs, *the other chemist does the job* and hence 'a vital link in the production of the eventual outcome is provided by *someone else's* doing something'.[20]

It is allowed that in refusing to take the job the first chemist is responsible, in some sense of the word, for the fact that the research will go forward more quickly than it might. However, this will only come about through the other man's actions. The first chemist cannot be said to make this happen, and, it is suggested, he rightly does not accept a full responsibility for the outcome.

In all of this we do have an illumination of the common inclination against certain acts. Certainly there is a great deal of difference between the case of the chemist and the case of a man who contemplates an act of terrorism. None the less, any considerations which apply to the chemist also apply to the other man. We may have the inclination that he should be such a man as the chemist. He should be of a certain integrity, and he should maintain that integrity by not engaging in violence, even though he believes that the consequences of his engaging in violence will be, or are likely to be, better than the consequences of his not doing so.

The inclination needs examination, and for several reasons it will be best to proceed by way of the given example of the chemist. There is one preliminary. The inclination to integrity is in conflict with several general attitudes to the effect that we ought always to act in such a way as to produce the best or the least bad state of affairs. One such general attitude is that we ought always to act so as to produce the greatest total of satisfaction. The case of the chemist is indeed offered against this proposition, which is the Principle of Utility in one formulation. However, the inclination also comes into play against the attitude, to speak very quickly indeed, that we should always act in such a way as to do most to rescue those in distress.

This attitude, which has informed some of my earlier remarks, and of which I shall say more, is the fundamental part of the most common of reflective moralities. It, like Utilitarianism, is *consequentialist*. It takes into account only what may be called the consequences of action, although other consequences than are considered in Utilitarianism. It conflicts with the inclination having to do with integrity which has been mentioned. Let us have in mind this particular consequentialist attitude. Let us imagine what is certainly reasonable, that the chemist in refusing the job does something which makes distress or inequality more likely.

The main difficulty about the case, it seems to me, is that of actually finding what consideration or principle it is which can lead us to agree that the chemist's act in refusing the job is right. That consideration or principle is not actually supplied to us. Let us see what, if anything, can be found.

We are told that the chemist preserves his integrity in refusing the job. This may amount to different things. The first of them which must surely be got out of the way is the *matter of fact* that the chemist, in refusing the job, is acting in accordance with deep attitudes of his own. His action is in no sense in conflict with these attitudes, whatever they are. Hence we say, if obscurely, that there exists a unity or a whole. *He* remains whole. Integrity, in a literal sense, is maintained. In this, however, it must seem we have no consideration whatever that might lead us to agree that refusing the job is the right thing to do. It seems obvious enough that there is no connection whatever between the described integrity in itself and right acts. An act of integrity in this sense, given certain imaginable deep attitudes on the part of an agent, will be an act of absolute immorality. Nothing follows about the rightness or wrongness of the act from the fact alone that it is in line with an agent's deep attitudes, which presumably may be of any kind. If this itself is a moral judgement, it is a peculiarly solid one.

To say the chemist preserves his integrity by refusing the job, then, is surely to do something other than state a seemingly morally irrelevant and somewhat obscure matter of fact. It is to approve of him, to commend him. It may be to approve of him or to commend him because, as we may say, he is true to himself. The chemist perseveres in certain deep attitudes. This second speculation about what is said of integrity is of course related to the first, and it faces a similar objection. It is obviously important what the deep attitudes are. Here there is some obscurity, but it may be that the attitudes are to the effect that he himself, with his own hands, should not carry forward research into chemical and biological war. He persists in this attitude even when he sees that it issues in making chemical and biological war more likely. This is how the chemist is true to himself.

There are several related things to be said about this second speculation as to the matter of integrity. One is the general one that there seems to be very little relevant connection between a man being commendable in the given way and his act being right. A man, it seems, can be commendable for the reason that he is true to himself no matter what act he performs, so long as he is himself morally committed to it. All that is required is that he sticks to his moral convictions, whatever they are, having to do with a self-picture or not. An appallingly wrong act, perhaps one of vicious torture, does not move a bit in the direction of being right when we learn that the torturer is being true to himself. What changes, perhaps, is our view of *him*.

There is the possibility of a confusion at this point. Surely, someone may object, we can support a man in his act, to which he is committed, for the reason that things work out better in the end if people are true to themselves. More important, we may sometimes even support a man if we think his act is somehow wrong. Several questions are raised by this objection, but it would be confusion to think that it is an effective one. The objector asserts the value of our being true to ourselves *in order to object to consequentialism*. However, the objection itself *derives from* consequentialism. In part it is that the effects, perhaps in terms of distress, will be better if people are true to themselves. However, what we are trying to find in the case of the chemist is a consideration or a reason of a non-consequentialist kind, a consideration or a reason for doing what is likely not to have the best effects.

The second and lesser thing to be said about commending the chemist is to be distinguished from the point just made that his act may be wrong even if he is true to some commitment. It is that if we are even to commend him, and, more important, if there is to be so much as a question of commending him, we must believe that he does really have something that is distinguishable as a moral attitude or a moral commitment. We cannot commend a man for integrity on the ground that he is, so to speak, true to his selfishness. An absolutely unswerving record of acting in one's own interest does not establish integrity.

What then is the chemist's moral attitude or commitment? As we have noticed already, he does have an attitude: he is opposed to carrying forward research into chemical and biological warfare with his own hands, even though the only alternative is more effective research by someone else. Is that a moral commitment? It will occur to everyone that the chemist, in leaving the job to the man who will do more effective research, is simply engaged in keeping his own hands clean. Better that someone else should make a larger contribution to a terrible eventuality than that he should make a smaller one. Better that chemical and biological war should be slightly more likely than that he himself should have his hands in it. The chemist may be said to be engaged, if one puts the point in Williams's own way, which might be thought to endanger it by overstatement, in 'self-indulgent squeamishness'.[21]

Williams replies that the criticism is not independent of the assertion of a consequentialist morality. If the point were addressed to the chemist, it would necessarily be no more than an invitation to reconsider his decision, and in particular to reconsider it from a consequentialist point of view. The criticism would not consist in an independent argument, which is what is required, but simply a reiteration of the opposed morality.

This reply seems to me partly right and importantly wrong. The criticism is in a certain sense not an argument, but it need not be merely an invitation to reconsider either. It may amount to the suggestion that it is only self-indulgence which can be discovered to explain the chemist's decision. It may amount, again, to a challenge to produce what is persuasively or anyway recognisably a moral explanation or a moral reason. We are indeed told that the unpleasant feelings which the chemist would have if he did the job would be 'emotional expressions of a thought that to accept would be wrong'.[22] However, we are not told the thought, or given to understand anything much about its nature.

What we seem to end with, then, if we look to what is said about 'integrity' in order to find a moral consideration or principle of relevance, is something different, the feeling that the imagined chemist would indeed only be engaged in a kind of self-indulgence. Do we get further on towards finding a consideration or principle if we direct our attention to what is said about responsibility? To recall, it is allowed that the chemist is in some sense responsible for the research going forward more quickly than it might, since that, as he knows, is the upshot of his refusing to do it himself. However, he is said to be less responsible than he would be if he were to do it himself. He is less responsible for the reason that the other man's activity is a vital link.

There is the possibility of having the wrong thing in mind here. Certainly the chemist's responsibility for research done by himself, and, as we can say, *freely chosen*, would be greater than his responsibility for the other man's research. What one should have in mind, presumably, is something else: what the chemist's responsibility would be if he himself went ahead with the research for the strong or indeed coercive reason that otherwise the other man would do it more efficiently. If the chemist did *that*, would he have a lesser responsibility than he has when he refuses the job?

In any case it is far from evident that the rightness of actions has to do with responsibility in such a way that the argument about the chemist is at all persuasive. Let us assume it to be a fact that the chemist in refusing the job is less responsible for the research than if he were to do it himself because of the coercive reason. Let us add in, for what it is worth, that in not taking the job he does not make the other man's research happen. Do we now have a consideration or a principle which might lead us to agree that he does the right thing in refusing the job?

I cannot see that here, or elsewhere, we find such a thing. It is essential to the argument, of course, that the consideration be produced. It would not be enough to suppose that it can be perceived, but not reported, by someone of especially good moral vision. That would just be resort to mystery.

Finally and differently, notice that any moral consideration having to do with integrity or responsibility, supposing it can be found and got clear, is of fairly small importance. In a second example,[23] which involves a man's straight choice between killing one person and acting in such a way that someone else will kill twenty, it is allowed that the man's integrity and responsibility cannot stand in the way of his taking one life in order to save twenty. Consequences matter more.

In the case of the chemist, by the way, we are likely to attribute more weight to some consideration of integrity than we should. That is, if we feel inclined to side with the chemist in his decision, we may too quickly attribute this inclination to a consideration of integrity. This comes about, I think, because the case as described is indeterminate. Different possibilities are left open. This in fact brings it into line with reality, but, as can be seen on reflection, it also makes it indecisive as a proof or persuasion about integrity.

Very briefly, we have been assuming of the case that what the chemist should do, if he is to choose the particular state of affairs most likely to avoid distress or inequality, is to take the job, knowing he will do it less efficiently. But that is not entirely clear. One rightly takes it, in thinking of the situation, that there is only a probability that there will be a chemical and biological war to which the research will contribute. But how small a probability is in question? If we take it, unreflectively, to be very small, so that a war is in fact very improbable, then any inclination we have to side with the chemist may perhaps be explained by our consequential attitudes. That is, we may be moved by the consideration, as people generally are, that a possible upshot very unlikely to obtain must count for less than one which is certain or probable. What is certain or probable, if the chemist takes the job, is that he will be distressed, that he will not have registered a protest, and so on.[24]

It remains to transfer these conclusions from the example of the chemist, where attention is not likely to be led away from the principal question by passion or aversion, back to the subject of terrorism. What I wish to suggest, although I shall return to the subject,[25] is that one response to terrorism and those who engage in it, a response having to do with something other than consequences of actions, is at least unclear, and certainly not something of large moral importance. Whatever is to be said against violence, there appears to be no large argument to be found in suppositions of the kind we have considered, about integrity and responsibility, and hence about certain moral prohibitions.

IRRATIONALITY

Political violence is said to be irrational, and said so often enough that the opinion has a persuasiveness for that fact alone. Let us consider the matter, which is in fact large and ramifying. That it is this, rather than something easily manageable, is much of what I wish to maintain.

Some lesser but bedevilling things need to be noticed before we come to what is of most consequence. First, it at least appears that a good deal of slipshod self-persuasion and perhaps persuasion of others goes forward in this area. Let us look at one example. The philosopher of science and ideologue Karl Popper, near the beginning of his essay 'Utopia and Violence', which has to do with political violence as we have understood it and also with war, writes as follows:

> It ... need not be a vain hope that violence can be reduced, *and brought under the control of reason.*
>
> This is perhaps why I, like many others, believe in reason; why I call myself a rationalist. I am a rationalist because I see in the attitude of reasonableness the only alternative to violence.[26]

Near the end of the essay, there is this observation: 'Reason ... is the precise opposite of an instrument of power and violence.'[27] We are offered an explanation elsewhere in the essay of 'reason' or 'rationality' or 'reasonableness'. It is explained as a certain set of ways of ending disputes, ways which are related at least by the fact that they are all non-violent. They include give-and-take discussion, argument, arbitration, willingness to be convinced, willingness to admit error, and so on.

The sentences quoted may be taken to express sentiments of the right kind. However, they may also be looked at more critically, as indeed they should be. As may be confirmed by reading the essay, they do not have in them propositions which are actually argued for elsewhere. Still, they are not mere bluff declarations that 'reasonableness' is right and violence is wrong. They are more than that, which is not to say, unfortunately, that they have argument in them.

(1) In part they are an instance of the simple enterprise of persuasion-by-naming. That is, one set of ways of ending disputes is given a good name, or rather three good names. Of course, there is some warrant in ordinary language for using the mentioned terms for the defined ways of ending disputes. There is most warrant for naming them the ways of 'reasonableness'. It is a small fact, and of no use in serious reflection. As we shall see in a moment, it is perfectly possible to describe some violence as 'reasonable', 'rational', or as proceeding from 'reason'.

(2) In part, the quoted sentences declare a fundamental opposition between violence and 'reasonableness', which opposition invites one towards a general judgement on violence. However, if one is to take the sentences seriously, one needs to know what opposed features of violence and 'reasonableness' are in question, and why these may be thought to make 'reasonableness' invariably right. These questions are not adequately answered, and so we are left without argument. In the place of adequate answers, there is a remarkably unsupported linking of 'reasonableness' with human equality and violence with inequality, and perhaps one other relevant contribution. However, it can stand by itself for consideration.

(3) That is, one may speculate that the quoted sentences also have in them this piece of persuasion: 'reasonableness', which is give-and-take discussion and so on, is alone rational, the only choice for a rationalist; hence it is always superior to violence, which is never rational. What does the word 'rational' mean there? If we continue to take it to mean something about give-and-take discussion and so on, the proposition that reasonableness is rational is not a premise for the given conclusion or indeed anything much, since it is merely tautological. Give-and-take discussion, etc., is give-and-take discussion, etc. If no different and suitable meaning for 'rational' is given or suggested, we have only rhetoric.

Might the piece of persuasion be turned into something better? Elsewhere in the essay, Popper mentions in passing an entirely familiar and indeed a fundamental conception of rationality. 'An action is rational if it makes the best use of the available means in order to achieve a certain end.'[28] Irrationality thus consists, as we can better say, in the adoption of means which do not in fact serve one's end, or serve it at too great a cost. By the use of these conceptions we can certainly escape tautology.

Is it obvious, however, as it should be in the absence of argument, that 'reasonableness' as defined is always or generally rational, the best means to the end? It is not. Is violence the precise opposite, whatever that may be, of rationality in this sense? Is violence never the best means to the end? That is obviously not obvious. As it happens, indeed, it is maintained by Popper in the essay that a good deal of violence is not irrational in the given sense, but rational.[29] That is, violence against those who are intolerant or threaten violence is defended as the best means. We thus come to a question about political violence, not a generalisation to be used against it.

Before considering this major question, there are three other distractions we may put aside quickly. One, which is also brought to mind by 'Utopia and Violence', is the idea that violence is unreasonable because it is the result of speculation about a Utopia, a transformed society. Such speculation is poor stuff, and the activity which follows from it is therefore ill-founded. One thing to be said here is that it is plainly mistaken to suppose that all political violence has to do with the large goal of a transformed society in the ordinary sense of that term. Most political violence has had smaller or anyway different ends. Most of it has been directed against oppression, often invasion. It is equally mistaken to run together all reflection which does have to do with transformations of society. It is not all of the same quality or kind. For example, not all of it has to do with speculative philosophy of history, as in Hegel and Marx.

The second distracting supposition is that terrorists are figures of irrationality in that they are self-deceived. That is, their actions are in fact not done from motives which have to do with the facts of inequality. Their thoughts, and their protestations, are mistaken. What needs to be said about this is that it would be a remarkable fact, one that would distinguish one kind of human endeavour from all others, if those who engage in violence were never subject to anything but what they themselves take to be their ends. Equally, it would be remarkable if campaigns of violence with supposed political ends were ever wholly the product, or even in large part the product, of desires unrelated to those ends. It is mistaken to suppose that senseless and unrecognised hostility, and like things, never have anything to do with campaigns of political violence, and it is mistaken to suppose that these campaigns have nothing else in them.

The third supposition also has to do with the agents of violence. It is not to be assumed, as often it seems to be, that their own views and defences of their conduct are the only possible views and defences. We do not suppose, generally, that what can be said for or against a line of action is no more than can be said by those persons who are or might be engaged in it. No such requirement survives reflection. No one would deny, certainly, that lines of action and their outcomes are in different ways determined by the beliefs and passions of the agents. Their beliefs and passions, then, must enter into anyone's consideration of the value of their conduct. This granted, it remains mistaken to fix on the agents and to suppose that political violence is to be seen only or precisely as those who are engaged in it see it.

To turn now to the major subject-matter, what may come to mind is something like this question: Is political violence generally irrational in that it gives rise to distress itself and yet is uncertain to achieve its ends? It is all right as a question, but only as a culminating, final question. Something like it none the less appears to be the only question about irrationality which is considered by many philosophers who offer pronouncements. At any rate, they answer only it or something like it. What is certain is that any effective answer to so general and presupposing a question must be supported by explicit answers to quite a number of antecedent questions.

Violence differs considerably in its first effects, and the same is true of its aims. One obvious essential, then, before answering the general question, appears to be a separation of kinds of violence in terms of first effects and aims or ends. Is the kind of terrorism that will almost certainly consist only in damage to property, rather than injury or death, a rational means of pursuing decent lengths of life for millions of people? What of the kind of violence which carries a risk of a relatively small number of injuries or deaths, although it seeks to avoid them, and has the same end? What of the kind of violence, still with the same end, that consists in intentional injury? What of violence, again with the same end, which consists in intentionally causing death? What of the rationality of violence of each of these kinds, but with the different end of that freedom that will be the ending of the violation of a homeland?

There is point in remarking that we can count quite a few questions here, and that more can be added, each of them independent and of importance. Indeed, before considering such additions, each of the questions needs to be replaced by several which are different in that they contain approximate numbers. Certainly such questions will be regarded as offensive by many, but they are far from unknown elsewhere in human life and they are certainly unavoidable. They are often resisted by those who are worried that they will issue in certain conclusions.

Let us in what follows have in mind but one of them: Is violence which causes several thousand injuries or deaths, despite attempts to avoid most of them, a rational means of pursuing equalities in lifetime for a society's worst-off tenth, numbering more than five million people? It will be obvious enough to anyone who hesitates for reflection that we are far from being able to *assume* an answer. This has to do with the fact that the question also raises others.

Let us put aside problems having to do with uncertainty of outcome for a moment. We suppose, that is, that the violence in question would in fact produce the equalities. Would it be worth it? If we are familiar with the existence of such choices, where different kinds of things must be compared, we certainly are not familiar with an effective way of answering them. This is partly a matter of fundamental principles, of which I shall have a bit more to say in the last part of this essay. It is also partly a matter of judging the nature of kinds of human experience. We do not have an effective way of assessing injuries and deaths on the one hand and, on the other hand, the distress in its various kinds. We must judge of such matters if we are to arrive at reasoned conclusions about the rationality of violence. Anyone who argues that some violence is rational must obviously deal with comparative questions of this kind. Anyone arguing that all political violence is irrational must also do so.

To take up what was put aside, the matter of uncertainty of outcome, I have already assumed in these remarks that it may be that some violence is rational even if it is not *certain* to succeed. Although sometimes those who condemn violence seem to suppose that it must always be certain of success in order to be rational, this is a proposition for which argument is needed. There obviously are circumstances in human life where something that is not certain to succeed, or even something that is unlikely to succeed, is rationally attempted. These, of course, are situations of greater or lesser extremity. Very roughly, then, there is the question of how probable it must be that the given violence will be successful if it is to be rational. The answer, which I shall certainly not try to give, will depend in good part on comparisons of the facts of violence and the facts of inequality.

The question will bring to mind yet another, which is prior and as essential. Any view of the rationality of a kind of violence will depend on a factual judgement, or more likely many such judgements, of the actual probability of success, as distinct from the probability necessary for rationality. What is to be said here will have much but not everything to do with the evidence of history. The same applies to the other relevant factual question of probability: How probable is it that given ends of political violence will or would be achieved by non-violent means?

These latter three questions, about uncertainty, are like the others in having presuppositions which must themselves be fixed. What period of time is to be assumed in the last question about achieving ends by non-violent means? That question, if made explicit, must mention a period in which the ends will or would be achieved. The fact of mortality, and hence the length of human lifetimes, suggests a period. I shall not pursue the matter, except to say that it is easier to argue against violence, from a premise about things being better for future generations as a result of non-violent progress, if one's place in a present generation is satisfactory.

Enough has been said to establish that the ready response to political violence that consists in abusing it as irrational is open to question, indeed open to many questions. What has been said, equally, establishes that any unreflective response which consists in the opposite thing, accepting violence as rational, is just as jejune. One's conclusion may have to be that the question is an open one. That is a possibility.

Such a conclusion is likely to give rise to several different although related responses, which I shall not attempt to discuss adequately. One is that violence must be mistaken in that it causes harm or tragedy and its rationality has not been shown. If a general comment is of use here, it is that the choice is not necessarily one between violence, whose rationality is not established, and something else, whose rationality is established. There are the same kinds of difficulty to be faced in considering the alternative to violence: non-violent activity which appears to have a lesser chance of securing an acceptable change in the facts of inequality. Perhaps it does not need saying again that a different view, to the effect that this other political activity is already established as rational, is likely to derive in good part from an insufficient appreciation of the facts of inequality. A relevant generalisation, obviously, is that situations of extremity do call for the consideration of the rationality of terrible means.

One other thing that may come to mind as a consequence of my conclusion about an open question is that accredited members of societies, as they might be called, are more able to guess what should be done about the distress of inequality. Accredited members include governments and their personnel, leaders of traditional political parties, and so on. Whatever one may think in general of the right of governments to take decisions, it may be supposed that they are in a superior position of knowledge, or of ignorance, when compared to those who contemplate or engage in political violence.

When this is a piece of unexamined piety, as often it is, there is room for that familiar jibe that the wars and catastrophes owed to the accredited members of society do not recommend their judgement. If we depart from piety, and from the jibe, we are bound to find difficulty rather than simplicity. Part of it has to do with the connections between power and judgement, or between power and want of judgement.[30]

My general conclusion here, about which I shall have more to say in another essay,[31] is that common responses to terrorism, having to do with its supposed irrationality, are themselves unreasonable. In the end, when the work of inquiry and reflection has been done, it may be that the strongest arguments against much or some political violence will indeed be those having to do with the probabilities of success. No doubt we can conclude, now, that such arguments will sometimes be as conclusive as arguments in this area ever can be. No doubt there are situations in which political violence cannot be justified, because it is sufficiently unlikely to work.

It may also become evident in the end, less comfortingly, that violence *would* be justified in these situations if it worked. That is, it may become evident that in these situations, as in others, violence which *did* end wretchedness would be preferable to no violence and no change. What may be thought to follow from such a proposition is not our concern now.

THE BASIC MORAL PRINCIPLE

Utilitarianism as a basic morality appears to have had its day, and to have remaining to it only a twilight in economic theory. There is no question of our accepting a principle about well-being, satisfaction or happiness that gives us this general instruction: judge the balance of well-being over distress likely to be caused by each possible action or policy, and do the action or adopt the policy likely to have the best *total* – the greatest balance of well-being or the least balance of distress. Following the instruction may very often satisfy our moral convictions, but we can have no guarantee that we will not sometimes act unfairly or unjustly. Sometimes, if we follow the instruction, we may cause great inequality and distress. It may be that the greatest balance of satisfaction can be secured only by way of the victimising of minorities or individuals. For example, it may be that the greatest balance of satisfaction in a society will be produced by certain punishments which are certainly intolerable. This will be so, roughly speaking, when the alternative to the given punishments, although it consisted in a loss of satisfaction or even a great total of dissatisfaction, would be so shared out that it was bearable to particular individuals.

Utilitarians have of course been aware of such objections to their principle, and have been persistent in attempting to rebut them. They have attempted to show that for one subordinate reason or another, it turns out not to be true that the Principle of Utility does ever issue in victimisation. In general, their argument has been that if we take into account long-term consequences and various side-effects of possible courses of action, we shall see that the Principle of Utility does not issue in victimisation. Their argument, which must go without reconsideration here, is not finally persuasive.

There is then the question of what the alternative basic moral principle is to be. What will come to mind, no doubt, partly as a result of what has been said already, is that we must have a principle of equality, fairness or justice. Certainly the defence of minorities and individuals has always been conducted by way of such principles. What we must also have, in addition to the fundamental principle or principles, although this is not our present concern, are subordinate conceptions, rules, and so on. One of these would have to do with forms of government, and others with our obligations to government and with the forms of political activity. Some would pertain to social institutions and others would have to do with private relations between individuals. Such things would be consequences of the fundamental principles.

To announce these needs, however, is to say something less than wonderfully useful. While the conviction that we should have such a fundamental principle is not uncommon, is it actually available? Are we, as some suppose, in so much or such deep difficulty about such a principle that a kind of despair is in place, an acceptance of early defeat in our reflections and of what follows from it?

If one picks up a piece of philosophical writing on equality, there is still a decent chance that it will describe egalitarian thinking, by which I mean the propounding and defending of principles of equality, as lacking a large and defensible principle or as coming to very little in the end. These claims about the feebleness of egalitarianism, if they are right, show that there is nothing of value to be had from this tradition of feeling and thought. A pastiche derived from these philosophical writings on equality, a decently representative one, goes as follows.

Consider the *Principle of Absolute Equality*, which is that everyone is to be treated absolutely equally in every respect. This is absurd. It is absurd because, for example, not everyone can possibly live by the seaside. Also, we cannot think of treating the sick as we treat the healthy. If more needed to be said of the principle, there is the fact that there is no earthly chance of its being realized, and that if it were realized, the resulting dull uniformity would be appalling. Let us, then, be guided by the idea just mentioned, that obviously the sick are not to be treated equally with the well. Indeed the only sensible thinking about equality begins from the observable facts that men are different or unequal in some respects and perhaps the same or equal in other respects. The sensible general idea of equality, in fact, is that those who are in fact equal in a certain respect ought to be treated equally, and those who are in fact unequal ought to be treated unequally. This is the *Principle of Formal Equality*.

If it derives from Aristotle, however, it does not carry us at all far. It gives no direction at all until one has found what actual equalities do exist among men. Clearly men are not equal in intelligence, industry, and a great deal else. Indeed, it seems that they are equal only in having certain basic or fundamental needs and desires, and if one can ever get the matter clear, in being individuals. That is, perhaps, they are such that they should be treated as ends rather than means.

Given the overwhelming natural differences or inequalities between men, and these few equalities, it is merely confusion to suppose that men ought in many respects to be treated equally. Nothing of this kind follows from the Principle of Formal Equality. The most that one can reasonably say is that they ought to be treated equally in such basic ways as these: all should have their fundamental needs and desires satisfied, and none should be deprived of what is called human respect.

We may take this consequence of the second principle and regard it as a principle by itself, that of *Minimal Equality*. It does not require anything like a large redistribution of wealth, or greater participation in social decisions, or an end of social distinctions. It does not require much. What it comes to is something far less than egalitarians have imagined. There is in fact no large and defensible principle of equality.

Egalitarians have also offered many other principles. There is the *Principle of Equal Opportunity* and there is the *Principle of Equality of Wealth*. They have claimed too, if not often, that those who are of equal merit should be treated equally, and that those of equal need should be treated equally. The latter principle, sometimes expressed as 'to each according to his need', implies the existence of unequal needs, and so is not the Principle of Minimal Equality.

These principles taken together are inconsistent. Equal opportunity issues in inequality of wealth. When these inconsistencies are seen, something must in any case be given up, but how is the egalitarian to choose? Moreover, it is quite unclear how these latter principles are related to the previous two, those of Formal Equality and Minimal Equality.

Finally, there is the large attempt by John Rawls to bring a kind of sensible moderation as well as order into egalitarianism. It is, to say no more, based on a kind of argument – a speculation about a merely imaginable social contract – that carries little conviction.

As will be made clearer, it is hard to disagree with at least most of this – Rawls's theory of justice, and in particular his contract argument, will get attention in a later chapter.[32] But is there really no strong and general principle of equality, no unqualified ideal which is fundamental to egalitarian feeling, and which would be acceptable as the basis of a basic morality? Is everything here open to objection and involved in great difficulties? Has what you have heard about equality and distress been based on an illusion of clarity? Does equality come down to sympathetic hopes and bits and pieces of regulation in the liberal society?[33] The question needs consideration. It will get it, beginning in much of the next essay.

2
A Theory of Justice, an Anarchism, and the Obligation to Obey the Law

Just about all of us have the conviction that the members of a society have some obligation to abide by the law. At any rate, there is this obligation if the society is at all tolerable, maybe even if it isn't. Many things are not to be done, for a reason having to do with the fact that they are *illegal*, as distinct from other reasons that may also exist. It is thought by some that this obligation to keep to the laws is at its strongest with respect to the laws prohibiting violence, certainly including political violence. Still, it is unclear from what it is that the general obligation derives, and hence what weight it has. Almost all of us accept the existence of *political obligation*, as it is misleadingly called, partly because it may be thought of as an obligation to the state or to government. Still, if we do accept it, we are likely to grant that there are circumstances even in tolerable and better societies when the obligation is rightly overridden.

Of the long welter of doctrines whose aim has been to minimise or more likely to maximise the fact of political obligation, I should like to consider a radical one and a liberal one, both American. The first, a philosophical anarchism, is partly to the effect that to accept political obligation, understood in a certain way, is in fact to be immoral – it is to go against a certain moral imperative. The second is partly to the effect that political obligation, differently understood, must be recognised as weighty. While one may in extraordinary circumstances be enabled to escape the obligation to the extent of engaging in the mildness of civil disobedience, or in what is called conscientious refusal, anything more is as good as unthinkable.

The first doctrine, owed to Robert Paul Wolff,[1] comes of one of the traditions of thought and feeling that give first place to conscience and individual responsibility, and second place to political obligation and the like. What is said about the immorality of political obligation is taken to have consequences for a particular idea of violence, one called the distinctive political concept of violence. We shall consider that matter, which is intimately related, as well.

The second doctrine, owed to John Rawls, is the outstanding political philosophy in our part of the world as the new millennium begins. It derives from the tradition that has to do with suppositions about a social contract and about obligations that flow from it.[2] However, it is different from all or many of its predecessors. One large difference is that we are offered not only an argument about political obligation, and in particular our obligation not to use terrorism, but also an argument for two basic moral principles for the ordering of societies. We shall, then, consider not only certain specific contentions about a social contract and political obligation, but also the argument for two basic moral principles and then the principles themselves – a theory of justice.

Finally, by way of introduction to these two doctrines, it is to be said that they appear in one respect similar. They are complex, if in different ways. Their complexity, if I am right, is unnecessary. The fundamental argument, in each case, is relatively simple in kind, however compelling or uncompelling. An examination of the two doctrines, then, may serve to engender or strengthen a certain scepticism about The Impressive in political argument. This scepticism, I am sure, in consideration of violence and other matters of seriousness, is an essential. Matters of seriousness call for a certain kind of plainness, and they generally have in them quite enough of true and unavoidable complexity. Certainly this is true of political terrorism.[3]

My intentions in summary, then, are to consider an anarchist rejection of political obligation, a certain theory of justice, the political obligation that flows from it, and, implicitly in all this, the need to be unimpressed by political philosophy. The last intention is not incidental. To try to realise it, I shall linger a bit at points in the discussion rather than press on single-mindedly.

A RIGHT TO OBEDIENCE

Wolff's essay 'On Violence' has to do with the idea, as it may be expressed, and as he does express it, that some governments or states *have authority*. Some governments or states, to put the same thing differently, have a right to be obeyed by their subjects, the members of the relevant societies. This appears to be tantamount to the proposition that is our concern – that the subjects have an obligation to obey the law.

The obligation depends on the existence of law, as already remarked, and hence also on the existence of government and presumably society. The *reason* for the obligation has to do essentially with law, government, and society. Political obligation, so-called mainly on this account, is thus distinct from other obligations. If a man wounds another, in most circumstances, it will be at least possible that he has broken two obligations. One, we may say, is the simple obligation not to wound others. He would have this obligation even in a 'state of nature'. He would have it, that is, even if there were no law, in the ordinary sense, against his action. In addition to this, there is what is relevant to our present reflections – his obligation not to break the law against wounding others.

Political obligation is obviously a kind of *moral* obligation, although not the most familiar kind. This is why its name is misleading. The idea is that the subjects of governments, or some governments, are under some moral obligation to give up all courses of action that are made illegal. There is a moral restraint or prohibition on subjects with respect to these courses of action that are prohibited by the law of the state. Subjects are in some degree constrained to give up the behaviour in question, despite the fact that some of it may be morally desirable in their view.

The idea that subjects have an obligation, that governments have an authority, has been defended in different ways in the history of political thought. A conclusion about authority is accepted today by those of us who are committed, happily or unhappily and more or less completely, to a kind of government described as democratic. The conclusion has been accepted by those who have made use of the notion of a social contract, as we know, by those who have believed in a monarch's divine right to rule, and by those who have found a superiority for a social or an economic class in the wisdom of the class or in what may be called its historical role or mission.

There is a good deal more to be said about the nature of political obligation, but let us now pass on to a second thing in 'On Violence'. The distinctive political concept of violence, like other concepts of violence, is said to be an idea of a use of force to effect decisions against the desires of others. That all concepts of violence have these features seems mistaken, but the matter is not important. The special feature of distinctively political violence is that it is a use of force either prohibited or not authorised (we are offered these two different possibilities) by *a state that has authority*. It is a use of force prohibited, to remain with that possibility, by a state whose subjects are under an obligation to obey its commands.

Let us look, thirdly, at a very different claim that enters into the argument. It is one to which Immanuel Kant gave some attention in his moral philosophy, and it is that a man is under an obligation not to act in a given way unless he himself sees good reason for so doing. The principle part of what is meant here is that a man is obliged not to act on the mere ground that someone has told him to do so. I do not have a reason for action in the bare fact that someone has told me to do whatever it is.

This seems a defensible claim, although it is inexplicit as it stands, and perhaps is in need of qualification. If we were to consider qualification, we should have to look into the possibility that unless we are all to become a good deal more reflective than we are, or more inactive, the range of acts for which good moral reason is needed must be limited. Humming a bit of a song while doddling on the lawn with someone may not seem to be something that requires any reason. Certainly I am not prohibited from doing so by the fact that all I have in the forefront of my mind is that my companion has asked me to do the thing. Or, should we say that one's unconsidered recognition that certain behaviour is inconsequential does provide one with a good reason for the behaviour?

In any case there is also consequential behaviour to consider. If I lack the slightest notion of what will avert some disaster, I am surely permitted to do what I am told by someone who has a gleam of hope in his eye. I am under no obligation not to act. Given these several reflections, it seems that a man can fulfil his obligation and still come pretty close to doing something simply because he has been told to do it. No doubt the ordinary case is different.

Let us now assemble our three pieces, unfinished as they are, and see how they work. There is an obligation just mentioned not to perform many actions, or many actions in certain settings, without what seems to be a good reason. This excludes doing many things simply because one has been told to do them. Well then, no state or government can have authority, the authority mentioned above. There is an obligation borne by everyone which makes it impossible for any state to possess a certain right to a person's obedience. Or rather, to include a qualification to which we shall return, no state that is a practical possibility can ever have the right in question. It is allowed that it might be possessed by a certain ideal democratic state, ideal in that all its policies are considered and voted on by all its citizens and hence have their unanimous support. Such a state is allowed to be a fantasy.

If no state that is practically possible can have the given right to a person's obedience, there are consequences for the distinctive political concept of violence. If violence is taken to be a use of force prohibited by a state with the authority in question, then there is no violence, since there is no such state to prohibit anything. No use of force falls under the distinctive political concept of violence. The concept is empty. In order to get to a still further conclusion that is drawn, that talk of violence of this kind is *incoherent*, one notices the presupposition that the concept does distinguish between uses of force that are violent and uses of force that are not. This is a presupposition of an entirely general kind, present in the use of any concept. However, by the argument just given, the concept we are considering fails to do any such distinguishing. No use of force is violent. Here we have incoherence, presumably related to inconsistency. Given the further argument that I intend, there will be no need for greater precision on this obscure point.

Incidentally, one can also attempt to establish the conclusion about incoherence from the other definition of violence. There, to recall, it is a use of force *not authorised*, as distinct from *prohibited*, by a state with the right kind of authority. In this case, since every use of force is not authorised by such a state, there being no such state, we may try to maintain that *every* use of force, however 'official', is an instance of violence, and also maintain the further conclusion about incoherence. Let us continue to have in mind the other form of the argument, proceeding from the definition of violence as a prohibited use of force.

CLARIFICATIONS

What we now have is less than crystal clear. Still, it is clear enough that the argument so far does not have as its goal a merely conceptual point, a point about the emptiness or incoherence of a concept. To describe the argument in this *recherché* way is entirely misleading. Its goal, rather, is a proposition of morality. The argument so far, at bottom, is something like this:

(1) Each of us is obliged never to act, except perhaps in certain circumstances, on the mere ground that we have been told to do so.

(2) Therefore, it is mistaken to think that any existing government could have a certain right to the obedience of its subjects.

(3) One cannot claim, then, against those who do such things as set bombs, that they are violating a related obligation of obedience.

There is no reason to rewrite this latter conclusion in any less overt way. Consider an analogy. Suppose that one comes to believe, along with those impressed by the privacy of the soul, that it is impossible ever to assess a man's responsibility for an action. Whether he really had a choice must remain obscure. Suppose one believes, too, that it is necessary, if punishing a man is to be morally tolerable, that it be known that he was in fact responsible to some degree for an offence. There follows the conclusion that no one ought to be punished, whatever else we ought to do about criminal behaviour. The conclusion, for all that has been said so far, can be couched differently, by specifying a distinctive concept of justified punishment. Some punishment, we say, is of an offender of whom it is known that he was responsible for his offence. The conclusion of our bit of argument may then be put as this: the concept of a justified punishment applies to nothing and talk that makes use of it is incoherent.

There is in fact no reason to conclude this argument by somewhat obscuring observations on the concept of justified punishment. There is no more reason to conclude the other argument by talk of the distinctive political concept of violence. Some may think that this opinion can be supported by showing that neither the concept of justified punishment nor the given concept of violence is entrenched in ordinary usage or in any other relevant usage. This may be true. A better reason is that the guiding intention of both arguments is not merely to change linguistic usage, supposing such an achievement by itself to be even conceivable, but to contribute to a change in moral attitude, policy, and of course action. Given this, what might be called the standard form for moral judgement is preferable.

Let us then consider the argument in its direct and overt expression, as set out a moment ago. What we have in the first part is that a man is obliged never to act, except perhaps in certain circumstances, simply because someone has told him to do so. The concern of this nostrum is clearly the moral agent or the good man. A good man, we feel, is one who has the trait among others that he does not act *without seeing good reason for doing so*. He acts in accordance with some fact of personal responsibility, a fact that is not to be escaped and that he does not attempt to escape. We must, it seems, accept this first item of the argument.

It is thought to follow from this that governments are not justified in claiming a right of obedience from their subjects. They cannot, we are told, have authority. Does this follow? Well, it depends on how the thing is taken. It seems likely that there is *some* right, *some* authority, which we must agree a government cannot have if we accept the first part of the argument. Let us settle clearly what particular authority it is that suits the argument. Let us see what kind of authority it is that a government cannot have if the first part of the argument is accepted. Again, what right of obedience is it that a government cannot have if we accept that every man has an obligation not to act, anyway in most circumstances, on the mere ground that he has been told to do so?

To proceed a bit indirectly, let us imagine someone who does *not* have the specified trait of the good man or the moral agent. Imagine a man who is wholly law-abiding and who says that he lives as he does only because the law so directs him. That, he says, is good enough for him. If we pester him a bit, he will not assent to various alternative arguments for his living as he does. He will not accept the account that he lives as he does because that is the lawful way and the law expresses his own will. Nor does it matter to him, if it is true, that the law expresses the will of a majority of the members of his society. He will not accept, either, that a justification of his behaviour is that obedience to the law has the recommendation that it avoids greater losses, of whatever kind, than those that may be involved in disobedience. If he did assent to *any* such explanation of his conduct, he would not be the man we want, not a pure case of the obligation of the special kind that we have in mind.

We may suppose, if we want, that our man sometimes thinks there is a good reason for obeying this or that law, a reason other than that it *is* a law. At other times, he thinks there is such a reason for not obeying a law. None of this makes any difference to him. His life, or the part of it with which we are concerned, is governed by the simple fact of his beliefs about legality and illegality. If something is ordered by law, he does it. He is amoral, indeed what we might call the automatic law-abider or, just conceivably, he is a man of *one* moral principle. It is, simply, that one ought to abide by the law, and absolutely. He has no other relevant moral belief. What gives rise to action on his part is the law, and, it must be remembered, this is not to be taken as involving an enthymeme. It is not that obeying the law has this or that further unmentioned recommendation, as people often believe.

It is such a man, and only such a man, who does accord to his government the authority or right to obedience that fits the argument. It is such a man, and only such a man, who accords to his government an authority that runs against the obligation of which Kant speaks. The authority in question, now that it is more explicit, can be seen to be an extremely curious right, not merely to behaviour but to a certain genesis of behaviour. It is a right to unreflective responses or, as one might fairly say, to a certain sort of person.

A CONCESSION AND ITS IMPORTANCE

There remains a good deal of mystery about our man and the related authority that a government might be claimed to have. One would face great troubles in attempting to give a full characterisation of what we can call the unreflectively obedient man. He may indeed be a phantasm of the philosophical imagination. In any case, it does seem necessary to agree, and not merely because of Kant's obligation, that it would be wrong for any government to have the authority in question. It is morally mistaken to think that any government could be justified in claiming this right of obedience from its subjects. The second step of the argument is certainly all right.

Most important, to pass on to the third step of the argument, we may grant without hesitation that there is one thing that *cannot* be said against the man or woman carrying a bomb. It is that he or she has violated an obligation deriving from the government's right to his unreflective obedience. More simply, we cannot condemn him for not having been unreflectively or, as might be said, mindlessly or idiotically obedient. We could only condemn him, it seems, if we took to be praiseworthy, or possibly praiseworthy, a different man: the soldier who kills the peasants without reflecting on what he does and *simply because* his officer has given him a command. We certainly do not regard either the automatic soldier, or the soldier with a single moral principle about obeying all commands, as praiseworthy.[4]

One incidental point is worth a moment before we press on. We were given to understand, before we became clearer about the authority in question, that it *could* be possessed by a government in an ideally democratic state. That is, subjects of that state could accord the authority to their government without infringing their Kantian obligation. This is confusion. What is true, rather, is that it is near enough a logical impossibility that the subjects of this state infringe their Kantian obligation. This is a state where all subjects consider, vote on, and in fact approve of all legislation. Given that, their obedience to law cannot count as unreflective obedience. The fact that I participate in making the laws, and agree to them, does not make it morally tolerable to obey them unreflectively. On the contrary, unless I am a bizarrely divided personality, my participation makes it a logical impossibility. The confusion of thinking otherwise points to a fact to which we shall come.

Our present position is that we have conceded the force of an argument against a supposed obligation of obedience, and hence against a particular claim about a government's authority. There can be no such obligation on the part of those who contemplate violence, and no such authority on the part of a government that attempts to stop them. What is in question, as we have seen, is an authority of a striking kind. How important, then, is this concession?

It is said that people do in fact persist in assigning to the state precisely the authority which we have conceded that it cannot have. They have the belief, it is said, that the state has a right to what we have called unreflective obedience. Is this so? It seems to me impossible to think so. Does *anyone* believe that the state has *this* right? Does anyone believe the state has the right about whose nature we have become clear? Does anyone half-believe it? There is no point, of course, in supposing they have some related belief. A related belief might be acceptable and not be open to rejection by way of Kant's conception of the good man. Hence it would not fit the argument we have been considering.

It may be that many people have had, or indeed now have, attitudes to the state that are consonant with a demand for unreflective obedience, as understood above. Assuredly the state has been made an object of a kind of superstition, has been perceived as having a religious character or something akin to one, and has been offered something like worship. There is also deference, usually silly. These attitudes owe something to the nature of governments. They make laws, and these are not seen as the giving of advice or the offering of reasons for certain conduct. Laws, it seems, are imperatives. One does not get, in a statute, a lot of reflection on why it ought to be obeyed. Hence, some may suppose, the implicit stand or position of governments is as follows: Do this because our enacted law demands it.

Still, it is pretty clear that these attitudes of veneration fall well short of the belief that the state has a right to unreflective obedience, that someone carrying a bomb is behaving wrongly because of this alone, *that he has had some thoughts about his behaviour.* It is therefore difficult to resist this first substantial conclusion of our reflections: the argument we have been considering consists in refuting a quite deplorable belief ascribed to the opponents and condemners of political violence or terrorism, but unlikely ever to have been contemplated by them.

There is another matter, perhaps more important. It may be supposed that whether or not anyone has held to the belief, it nonetheless is essential or important to an argued condemnation of violence. Hence, its failure is crucial. My second substantial conclusion, which I shall support in three ways, is that none of this is correct either. That the belief is deplorable and refutable is something without further consequences. It is not a belief important to an argued opposition to violence.

(1) In recognising one claim about political authority as deplorably mistaken, we do not commit ourselves to any general view about the impossibility of ascribing any authority to the state. We are certainly not committed to thinking that there is no sort of authority or right to obedience that the state can have. We are not committed to thinking that there can be no arguments against violence that rest on the existence of society and government, and on a claim they make.

The idea that as a result of the given argument we cannot ascribe any authority at all to the state, which would be important, might arise from the supposition that to accord someone a right to something, or to grant someone authority with respect to some matter, is to grant an unquestionable power of decision. This is mistaken, as can certainly be shown.

What needs to be pointed out is that there is a notion of authority that is quite different, a notion that is in no way jeopardised by anything conceded so far. It is also clear, and it is what most or many readers will have had in mind at the beginning of this essay. If I think there is a moral argument for complying with most of a government's commands, and I also think that there exist certain kinds of expectation or support, I may with perfect sense talk of the government's right to obedience. The expectation is on the part of the government and society, and is an expectation of obedience to the government's commands. The support, in part, is support for the government in its attempt to enforce obedience to the commands. For the government to have this right is for it to have authority, indeed authority in the most common sense. It is an authority that can be had without its possessor being taken as godlike.

By way of illustration, suppose that I am a democrat in a decent democracy. I do not think that any policy the government may pass into law ought to be complied with, but I do think, for various reasons, that *some* recommendation attaches to supporting any policy that is passed into law, although there may be things against it. My central idea is that supporting the policy is supporting the system, which I take to be the best system of government. Quite often, I will vote for policy A over policy B and think it right to do so. However, if B wins over A, I will conduct myself according to B. Further, I will take the view that there are better reasons for complying with B, as a law, than A, supposing A to be against the law.

Thus there is, in my view, a moral argument for obedience to any democratically enacted law. If others take this view, and if there then exists the expectation and support mentioned above, it will be perfectly reasonable to talk of the government's right to obedience, the government's authority. This, incidentally, will be perfectly compatible with the belief that for some A and some B, there would be better reasons for complying with A, as a policy against the law, than B, supposing it to be the law.

These are perfectly ordinary conceptions of right and authority. It is clear that they need a good deal of attention, that they raise problems of several kinds. Equally clearly, we can anticipate that it in no way follows, from the fact that a government cannot have a right to unreflective obedience, that it cannot have authority at all. Most important, it does not follow that we cannot ever condemn the terrorist as having done something against the law, something prohibited by the government as a matter of right or authority.

Perhaps to put the point in that way is to obscure it, or to obscure it for some. The point does not have to do, fundamentally, with the propriety of talking precisely of rights to obedience and authority. We may feel little inclination to engage in such talk. Indeed, it may be thought that it is talk worth avoiding. The important thing is that there remains open the possibility of argument against violence that depends essentially on the existence of law, society, and government, whether or not this argument mentions authority or rights. It can be argued, from several premises, that it is right or that there is a moral reason for obeying the law, and hence refraining from violence. The fact that talk of rights and authority is in place (since others are likely to agree, and to give support) is of secondary importance.

(2) A related idea about an important loss that we suffer, when we give up the specified argument against violence, has to do with the history of political theory. It does appear to be an assumption in 'On Violence' that traditional political theory has had as its principal object the establishing of a government's right to unreflective obedience.[5] It is assumed, it seems, that those who have maintained theories of a social contract, or those who have developed democratic theory, have been attempting to establish that each of a state's subjects has that obligation of obedience that is in conflict with the moral rule about having good reason for action. Hence, one may be led to the idea that all of traditional political theory has nothing of value to say against violence, since traditional political theory is argument for unreflective obedience, which is indefensible. An arsenal of argument has been shown to be empty.

However, it is a spectacular unlikelihood that John Locke, for example, was concerned to argue for unreflective obedience. He was concerned, rather, to advance a reason for obedience. This should not be confused with anything else and, in particular, not with a reason for giving up reflection on the government's commands. It seems that Locke's contention included nothing whatever to which Kant could object. Precisely the same is true of other doctrines of authority that have places in the history of political thought. It does not matter that some of these doctrines come close to demanding absolute obedience. In fact, to suppose that the traditional political thinkers were struggling towards a proof of the rightness of unreflective obedience is to suppose them pretty well out of touch, or a bit dotty. We must see them as spending a long time giving us reasons for obeying the government, in the hope that we shall forget them.

Scholarship is not required for the main point, however. It is plain that the traditional political doctrines can be used in a certain way. Whatever use may have been made of them, they can be used to argue for a familiar right of government to obedience, a right of the kind mentioned a moment ago, something to be sharply distinguished from the right to unreflective obedience. For example, there are the arguments to the effect that a democratic government is superior in several aspects to a dictatorship. One can proceed, in particular, towards the conclusion that there is much to be said against violence, conceived fundamentally as a use of force that has been prohibited.

(3) There is one other idea that may come to mind in connection with the supposed seriousness of the concession about unreflective

obedience. It is perhaps a more natural idea than either of its pre-decessors. As we have seen, there are a number of arguments that may issue in the conclusion that the state has an authority, a right to obedience, ordinarily conceived. On many occasions, it may be felt, this conclusion will carry the day over any other consideration. Certainly it will often carry the day over a man's sincere conviction that he ought to do what the state forbids, or ought not to do what the state commands. The state is to override conscience. Some may think that what we have in the end, then, in such cases, is in fact an assertion of the state's right to unreflective obedience. Some may think that claims of the ordinary kind about a right to obedience, despite what has been said, do issue in the indefensible assertion of a right of unreflective obedience.

Fortunately, this is confusion. We may indeed assert that the state may force a man to act, as we say, against his conscience. Sometimes doing so appears to raise moral questions and sometimes it does not. In no case, however, does doing so amount to the securing of un-reflective obedience. To be unreflectively obedient is to act, more or less willingly, on the say-so of another. It is to give over one's conscience to another, by not thinking at all or by having one mistaken moral thought. It is not a matter of being *compelled* by another, or by the state, to act in a certain way. A man who is being compelled successfully to keep the law is being obedient, but not unreflectively obedient.

Indeed, one might say that if he is being compelled, it is logically impossible that he is being unreflectively obedient, since behaviour of the latter kind requires that he obey another *only* because of the other's *command*. To assert that the state may often force a man to act against his conscience, then, which may be the upshot of certain arguments about authority, is not to assert that the state ever has a right to unreflective obedience.

In summary of my entire discussion, then, there is a conceivable belief about a government's authority, and hence a conceivable con-demnation of a man who engages in political violence. It is that he is failing in a particular obligation: to obey the law for the reason, merely, that it has been made. Such a condemnation is deplorable, since it presupposes that the man should be morally irresponsible. The argument against it, set out in three parts above, is conclusive. However, it is entirely doubtful that those who oppose violence have ever attempted the given condemnation. It would be mistaken, further, to suppose that this condemnation of violence enters into other things. It is not relevant to other contentions which mention a government's authority. Its wrongfulness does not cast doubt on traditional claims in political theory, and it does not put in question a belief we have that a man may sometimes be forced by the state to go against his conscience.

PRINCIPLES AND PROPOSITIONS

Let us make a fresh start, by considering a fundamental part of Rawls's celebrated book, *A Theory of Justice*. In this part, or these parts, it advances two basic principles for judging or changing societies, and also a number of propositions about political obligation. The argument for the principles is of the same distinctive kind as the arguments for the propositions, and has to do with the idea of a social contract.

However, the basic principles and the propositions about political obligation are connected by more than the fact that they have similar supporting arguments. This is so, as may be guessed, since any claim about political obligation in a society must have a very great deal to do with the acceptability or unacceptability of that society, and hence with correct principles for judging societies. It is hardly too much to say that one's political obligation depends on the goodness or badness of one's society.

Of course, the appraisal of societies comes into one's reflection on political violence where the special matter of political obligation is not in question. For example, there obviously are arguments against violence that do not have to do with obeying the law but do none the less have much to do with the state of societies. One can argue against terrorism, obviously, by citing the tolerable state of a society, and without mentioning the illegality of violence. Basic principles of judgement thus have a general importance. We shall pay full attention both to the two which are offered here and to the particular argument that is offered for them.

In what follows I shall expound in turn the argument having to do with a social contract, then give the principles, and the propositions about political obligation, and then go on to objections and indeed to what I take to be a refutation. One of the two principles has to do with certain traditional liberties and the other with the distribution of socio-economic goods. The propositions have to do with what is called a *natural duty* to obey the law and in general support one's society, and what is called an *obligation* to carry on in much the same way. Violence, given the duty and the obligation, is prohibited, or as good as prohibited.

To begin with what is presented as the fundamental part of the argument before us, we must engage in an activity of imagination. We imagine an assembly of people agreeing on the nature of their coming society. We do not engage in the speculation, rightly dismissed by Hume in his essay on the Social Contract, that they did once exist, or in the bizarre idea that we have inherited obligations from such actual founders of our own societies. We do not suppose, either, that our imagined people in their proceedings serve as a representation of some activity of agreement into which we ourselves enter tacitly by living in a society. None of these things is in question here. We merely conceive of people of a certain kind and in a certain situation agreeing on principles that will govern the society of which they are to be members.

It is of the first importance that our imagined people have particular characteristics and not others, and are in a particular situation.

(1) They are self-interested.

(2) They are equal to one another in their freedom to advance conceptions and principles for consideration.

(3) They are rational. That they are rational is no more than that they choose the best means to their ends, these ends being the possession of 'primary goods', and that they do not suffer from envy.

(4) They know or believe certain things. They are said to have an awareness of general facts of human psychology, society, politics and economics.

(5) It is essential that none of them, however, knows anything of what will be his or her own individual future in the society to come. None of the imagined people knows what his or her own natural assets and abilities will be, or economic and social place, or even his or her own psychology or conception of what is good. They do not know if they will be intelligent or otherwise, rich or poor, with or without prestige, black or white, male or female, and so on.

It is argued that our imagined assembly would agree on two principles as the basis of their coming society. They are principles of distribution, usually referred to in a somewhat question-begging way as principles of justice.

The first, as remarked earlier, is that each member of a society is to have a right to the greatest amount of liberties that is consistent with each other member having the same. The liberties include political rights, freedom of expression, freedom of the person, and the right to hold private property. It is important that the first principle, the Principle of Liberty, has priority over the second. That is, it is to be acted on first if both cannot be acted on together, and there are to be no departures from it at any stage of a society's development in the interest of a benefit in economic or social goods or their distribution. These latter things are the subject of the second principle.

It, the Principle of Difference, specifies allowable differences between social classes in socio-economic goods. The first part of that principle is that 'social and economic inequalities are to be arranged so that they are ... to the greatest benefit of the least advantaged'.[6] What is intended appears to amount to two conditional propositions. The first is that if one class in a society is better off in goods, this must somehow have the effect that the worst-off class in the society is better off than it would be without the inequality. This states a morally necessary condition of an inequality, a necessary condition of the relative positions of the classes. It is a necessary condition of some people being well-off, relatively speaking, that those who are worst-off also benefit. They would be still worse off if the well-off were not exactly as well-off as they are. The second proposition is that if a worst-off class is better off as an effect of another class's being in a better position, the latter class must remain in its fortunate position. This states a morally sufficient condition of the same inequality. It is a sufficient condition of some people being well-off that the worst-off also benefit.

By the first conditional proposition, then, to put the matter another way, we have it that the existence of a better-off class is *permissible* only if something else is true, and by the second proposition we have it that the existence of the better-off class is *obligatory* under the same condition.

As will be seen on reflection, the principle does not by itself tell one what equality or inequality a particular society should have. No inequality is allowable that does not improve the lot of the worst-off. Indeed, if a departure from a state of absolute equality in a particular society were not to make everyone better off, including a worst-off class that would then come into existence, the departure would not be acceptable. The society would have to remain in the state of absolute equality. On the other hand, *any* inequality in a society is obligatory that does improve the lot of a worst-off class. It is therefore a theoretical or logical possibility that the principle be satisfied in a society of no social and economic inequality whatever, in a society of overwhelming inequality, or in any society in between. The principle leads to a particular society only when it is conjoined with certain special propositions about individuals and their behaviour, resources and so on. The principle itself is in a real sense indeterminate.

The particular propositions that are assumed in the doctrine before us, and which lie behind the Difference Principle, are to the effect that some inequality will indeed be required in any society if all of its members, including some who have a lesser amount of social and economic goods, are to be as well off as they can be. Any alternative, a system with less or no inequality, will result in everyone, including the individuals just mentioned, being worse off. All this depends on the familiar reasoning that favourable inequalities are incentives that are necessary for a higher production of goods.

The Principle of Difference, as I have said, has two parts, of which we now have one before us. In its second part, it is to the effect that all members of the society are to have a considerable and equal opportunity to gain any allowable positions of favourable inequality, say wealth or power. This is not an after-thought, of secondary importance. On the contrary, this second part of the second principle has priority over its first part. The society will not improve the lot of a worst-off class if this can be done only by giving some members an unequal opportunity to secure positions of favourable economic and social inequality.

As for priority generally, then, the Principle of Liberty ranks first. Traditional rights, such as the right to vote, come before progress towards equal opportunity and the reduction of poverty. The second part of the Principle of Difference ranks second. Equal opportunity to become as rich as is permitted, for example, comes before the reduction of the poverty of a worst-off class. The first part of the Difference Principle, having to do with a worst-off class, ranks last.

As I have said, it is argued that our imagined assembly would agree on the two principles and also their priority or ranking, which is evidently of fundamental importance. Let us refer to this as the *basic proposition* of the doctrine before us. It appears to be basic, certainly, and it is certainly so regarded by Rawls. It is, to repeat, that the imagined people, people in what is sometimes referred to as the *Original Position*, having the qualities they have and in their prescribed ignorance and belief, would in fact choose the principles and their ranking.

The basic proposition is thought to enter essentially into an argument for the rightness of the two principles, the two principles as ranked, which is always to be understood. It is not that this proposition, that the members of the imagined assembly would agree on the principles, is taken to support the conclusion that these would be the correct principles for *their* coming society, which society we can also imagine. The basic proposition is thought to be part of an argument for the moral superiority of the principles for actual societies.[7] Our own societies are acceptable to the extent that they are informed by these principles rather than others, and this is a conclusion thought to be supported by the basic proposition. More precisely, the two principles are morally superior within the class of principles that have to do with the amount and distribution of goods. The two principles provide the correct answer to what is named the question of distribution or justice. A society governed by the two principles, to look ahead, will be a society in which political violence will be unjustified.

The other part of the argument for the two principles is that the situation in which they allegedly would be chosen, the Original Position, would be a fair one.[8] The conditions under which an agreement on the principles would be reached in the imagined assembly would be fair to all. That is to say or to make the evaluation that no one would be under any disadvantage, or, more explicitly, under any wrongful disadvantage. What is important, and likely to be overlooked, is not that none of them has any disadvantage, where that is to talk simply of matters of fact. Rather, none of them has any disadvantage of which we disapprove. A horse-race illustrates the distinction. None of the horses is at a disadvantage, in the sense of wrongful disadvantage, because some of the horses carry more weight and thus, factually speaking, have a disadvantage.

What is important to the argument is that it is the conditions or the circumstance that would be fair, as distinct from the principles chosen, of which the same might be said. The conditions in question are of course those already mentioned, including the ignorance of the members of the imagined assembly as to their individual futures. The conditions secure that members of the assembly would be prevented from discriminating against any group in the society to come.

The whole argument before us, then, is taken to be this:

(1) the proposition that a certain choosing-circumstance would be a fair one,

(2) the basic proposition, that people in that circumstance would choose the two principles, and

(3) the conclusion that the two principles are justified.

The conclusion, more fully, is that the ordered principles of Liberty and Difference are those by which we are to assess our own societies. To the extent that these basic principles are realised in it, a society is a morally acceptable one. To the extent that a society is not in accord with the principles, it is not morally acceptable. We shall return to the two principles, and to the given argument for them, after we have before us the related propositions about political obligation.

Any proposition about political obligation, as we have already noticed, depends essentially on the state of society. We might then have in mind, in thinking of political obligation, an imagined society that is fully in accord with the two principles we have been considering. This might be of use in developing a theory. We might instead have in mind a society, to describe it quite insufficiently, that comes near to realising the two principles. We might rather have in mind, as in fact we shall, our own societies. It is part of the doctrine we are considering that they have gone some considerable way towards realising the two principles. In speaking of our societies, I mean such as the societies of Britain and America.[9]

The first proposition is that we, the members of these societies, have a natural duty. To express the proposition differently, we ought all to accept that we have a certain natural duty. It has two parts. The first is that we are to comply with, and do our share in, the just or nearly just institutions that are thought already to exist in our societies. A just institution, by specific definition, is one which is in accord with the two principles.

That the institutions are just or nearly just is not the whole argument for the duty. Of course, that the institutions are just or nearly so could naturally be taken on its own as a reason for political obligation. If a society is a good one, then as a matter of logic there is a duty to conform to it and support it, which will principally be a matter of conforming to its law. However, as we shall see in a moment, this reason for political obligation is in fact not all of the argument that is presented.

The natural duty, in its second part, is to assist in the establishing of new arrangements, just or more just, in areas of one's society where they do not yet exist. It is to be noted that the duty, in both its parts, does not derive in any way from our own voluntary acts. It is partly derived, as I have said, from the nature of one's society, but not at all from any act, say of promising or of taking benefit, which one has performed.

It will be clear that we do not have a precise account of this duty. In particular, we do not have a precise understanding of its weight. However, we are certainly to understand that the duty is a very considerable one. Certainly it is to be taken as ruling out acts of political violence. It is a part of our duty not to engage in violence, since we must comply with just institutions and it is accepted as part of the doctrine before us that our institutions of law are tolerably just. Indeed, it appears to be accepted in the doctrine that most or almost all of the institutions of our societies are either just or else decently on the way to it. Their being just, to repeat, is for them to be in accord with the two principles.

To come on to the argument for the natural duty, it is made to depend in part on this proposition: that it would be agreed by an imagined assembly of persons, somewhat different from before, that the members of societies like ours ought to have this duty. Those in the assembly, we suppose, are contemplating the possibility of being members of a society like ours. Hence, they have rather more general knowledge of their future society than those people choosing basic principles whom we imagined a little way back. However, our present assembly is in other respects like the first one. The people in it are self-interested, equal, rational, and quite ignorant of what particular position each will have in the society to come. These things make for fairness.

Hence the whole of the argument for our natural duty, as will be expected, is as follows: a certain imaginable assembly would agree on such a duty for the members of societies like ours, more or less just societies, and this would be an agreement made in a fair situation, or under conditions of fairness. The argument, then, is analagous to the one for the two principles. It is pretty clear, incidentally, that an assembly would agree on the duty if, as we may suppose, it would earlier have agreed on the two principles, although under conditions of somewhat greater ignorance, and if our societies are taken to be decently on the way to implementing the two principles.

The second proposition to be considered is that we have a certain obligation, which is something distinct from the natural duty, to behave in certain ways. Suppose that by our voluntary actions we have gained benefits from an institution in our society, and furthermore, that the institution is a just or nearly just one. Under these conditions we have an obligation to support or to play a part in the institution in question. Thus we have both a natural duty and an obligation to support certain institutions. It appears that the institution of law counts as one of these. We have an obligation, then, as well as a duty, not to engage in political violence.

The whole argument for our having this obligation is of the same kind again. It is in part that the imagined assembly, contemplating membership in a society like ours, would agree on the obligation. In its other part the argument is that this would be an agreement made in a fair situation, one where no one was under a wrongful disadvantage.

THE ARGUMENTS REDUCED

The first of my objections, which will take a bit of time to lay out, has to do with the family of arguments. What I shall have to say pertains to all of them but I shall speak mainly of the first one, for the two principles of justice. That argument, if the repetition is bearable, is taken to be (1) that a certain choosing-circumstance would be a fair one, (2) that people in that circumstance would choose the two principles, and therefore (3) that the principles ought to be accepted by us.

This argument consists of an evaluative or normative premise and a factual premise. It is, then, of a familiar kind. The evaluative premise, that a certain situation of choosing would be a fair one, however much we may be inclined to accept it, is in a certain sense unsupported.[10] No proof of it is offered. We thus have an argument of precisely the kind that has led many philosophers and others to say that the evaluative conclusions that are drawn are without 'justification'. Hence, what might be called the first and traditional enterprise of moral philosophy, to attempt to find firm foundations, is in no way advanced by the argument that includes the basic proposition. These are conclusions about the argument for the two principles as we are given it, and as I have just sketched it. In what follows I shall give a more explicit statement of the argument. As will be apparent, the same judgements can be made on the more explicit argument.

Perhaps, however, no justification of the kind traditionally pursued is possible. It may be that in reflection of this kind we have only lesser possibilities, one of which is to begin with the plain assertion of an unproved evaluative premise. It may even be that this is no worse than beginning from unquestioned 'axioms' in other kinds of inquiry. Let us take up this point of view, which cannot be confident but is surely reasonable enough, without further discussion. That is, let us agree to have some evaluative premise or other whose credentials are simply taken to be acceptable.

Both the evaluative and the factual premise get their detail or indeed their identity from the specification of the imagined assembly. It is necessary, at this point, to recall its features. It is an assembly in which the following conditons are met:

(a) Each person can and does pursue his own interest.

(b) Each person has an equal ability and opportunity to do this.

(c) Each makes a rational or effective choice, one that does in fact serve his ends and does not proceed from envy taken to be a willingness to have one's own position worsened in order to worsen the position of another person who is better off.

(d) Each person has general beliefs about human psychology and about society, politics, and economics. These beliefs are in fact regarded as being true, as being knowledge. It becomes apparent that they are principally beliefs about the paramount importance of liberty in societies and, it seems, the necessity of inequality to general well-being. The latter belief, implied by the Difference Principle, has to do with the familiar doctrine about an incentive system.

(e) Each person is ignorant of any natural capabilities or attributes he or she will have in the society to come – attitudes and moral outlook, wealth or poverty, social position. He does not know his future race, colour, religion, politics, culture, income, or social standing.

The evaluative premise, then, is that an assembly of people satisfying all these conditions, (a) to (e), would constitute a fair choosing-situation, one involving no wrongful disadvantage. However, to come now to my first principal point, it is entirely clear that our acceptance of this premise, assuming that we do accept it, does not come out of thin air. What it comes out of are some moral convictions and some beliefs which we happen to have. As seems plain from a number of passages, Rawls is aware of this fact if he does not state it so clearly, or give it the prominence or repetition that he accords to other facts of the theory.[11]

What are the convictions and beliefs? There can be no mystery about that. They are convictions and beliefs that are given expression or effect by the conditions (a) to (e) mentioned above.

We have the conviction (A) that each member of a society, each member of an actual society, has a right to goods, a rightful claim to what is in his interest. We accept (B) that each member has an equal right to such goods, or, at any rate, that we must pay attention to considerations of equality. We accept (C) that steps must be taken to realise each member's right, but that a man should not be worse off simply in order to reduce the benefits of someone else. We accept (E) that the rights in question do not depend on certain things, which are to be regarded as irrelevant. These will include race, colour, religion, and so on. That is, we have convictions that certain facts about members of our societies ought to be irrelevant, and these are precisely such facts as those about their futures which the members of the imagined assembly are denied.

If our acceptance that the imagined situation would be fair must come out of these convictions, there is also something else from which it derives. We think, presumably, that the entire speculation is in another way acceptable. A fair choosing-situation, obviously, is one in which the people in question are not misled and do not have false beliefs. They are not disadvantaged in that way. Our acceptance of the imagined situation as fair, then, to put the matter briskly, must derive from (D) beliefs that we have about the important place of liberty in societies and also, as importantly, about incentive systems.

It is the work of a moment, I think, to put to rest any doubt about the claim that our acceptance of the imagined choosing-situation as fair, assuming we do accept it, does depend on the given convictions and beliefs. Suppose that we did believe some benighted proposition contrary to (A). That is, suppose we believed that some members of societies, somehow identified, do not have any right to goods. If we did believe this, we would not approve as fair a choosing-situation of such a kind that it gave rise to a society where every member had such a right. Suppose that we believed, contrary to (E), that a man should be paid more simply because he is white-skinned. Suppose that we believed, contrary to (D), that it is just mistaken to give more importance to traditional liberties than to the reduction of poverty. We would then not approve of a choosing-situation which, in a word, does not reflect these beliefs. We would not regard it as a fair one.

The upshot is that the argument we are considering, to make it explicit, really consists in:

(1) some moral convictions and some beliefs, which lead us to accept

(2) that a certain imagined situation for choosing principles would be fair,

(3) the basic supposition that people in such a situation would choose two principles, and

(4) the conclusion that the principles have a recommendation.
This, we can say, is the Contract Argument for the principles.

Some may be inclined to think, at first thought, that the first premise is not logically distinct from the second. The truth is otherwise. One part of the second premise, about fairness, is to the effect that a choosing-situation in which people could not allow the colour of a man's skin to determine his liberties would be in that respect fair. This is evidently distinct from the conviction that a man's skin colour ought to be irrelevant to his liberties.

Some may think, secondly, that to set out the argument in the four steps is to set it out uneconomically. They may feel that it can be set out more efficiently as it was before, in the last section, consisting just in the assertion that a certain choosing-situation would be a fair one, the assertion that people in that situation would choose the two principles, and the conclusion that the principles have a recommendation.

Several things might be pointed out about this. The most important is that what appears in the first part of the four-part argument must in fact occur in any expression of the argument that is complete. It is plain enough where it does occur in the three-part argument. It is bundled into the initial premise, that a certain choosing-situation would be a fair one, one in which no one is at a wrongful disadvantage. To assert this premise, plainly, is partly to assert that the choosing-situation is in accord with certain convictions. The situation, for example, is in accord with the conviction that skin-colour ought to be irrelevant to certain things.

In what follows, then, let us have in mind the four-part form of the Contract Argument. What is to be said for this form, in general, is simply that it is fully explicit. All that I shall have to say of the argument in this form, evidently, will be relevant to other forms of it.

Let us put all aside for a moment and consider a different and common kind of reflection on societies and principles. Suppose someone wishes to arrive at principles for the governance of her actual society. She wishes, that is, to get an answer to the question of distribution or justice. She begins with her convictions and beliefs. They are to the effect that each member of a society is to be regarded as having a right to goods of one kind and another, and that steps are to be taken to secure this right. As it happens, her convictions and beliefs are precisely those sketched a little way back, (A) to (E). Having got them straight, she *advances directly* to the conclusion that the best answer to the question of justice amounts to the two principles of justice of which we know. The principles, of course, as in the case of the Contract Argument, are in good part no more than *generalisations* or *summations* of the convictions, although there is much more that might be said. What she will have done is produce what we shall call an *Ordinary Argument* for the two principles.

The first thing that I wish to point out about the two arguments is that the Ordinary Argument is *as* good as the Contract Argument in giving support to the two principles. From what has been said so far, of course, it is less than clear that either argument is much good. There is an impressive gap, or rather, nothing so clear as a gap, between the premise or the premise-set and the shared conclusion. This summing-up is not just adding. It is arguable, of course, that many principles could not get support from either the single premise of the Ordinary Argument or the set of three premises in the Contract Argument. Racist principles, and principles of discrimination generally, are in this group. However, there are more left over than only the Principles of Liberty and Difference.

Can the Contract Argument be improved? In *A Theory of Justice* a good deal of effort is put into arguing for the truth of the basic proposition: that the assembly would choose the two principles. The argument, in one important part, is that each member of the assembly, in comparing different principles or groups of principles, would realise that all of them, save total equality, would have within them the possibility of different upshots for the member in his future life in the society. He or she might be among the rich or among the poor, for example, and this cannot be known in advance. He or she would, it is suggested, be of such attitudes as to *maximin*: that is, to choose the particular conception whose worst possible upshot for him would be more acceptable than the worst possible upshots of other conceptions. Each member of the assembly would, as a result, be led to favour the Principle of Difference. What this amounts to is in fact a further characterisation of the assembly.

There is another essential matter to be kept in mind if we proceed in this way, giving a further characterisation of the assembly. We must also suppose, to keep the whole doctrine standing, that the enlarged conception persists as a conception of a fair choosing-situation. We must then have certain convictions or beliefs. We must, in short, have a commitment to the maximum principle. We must feel it is a good idea to play safe.

I have suggested that at first sight, or in its first presentation, the Contract Argument is no better than the Ordinary Argument in producing the two principles of justice as conclusion. We now suppose, however, that the Contract Argument can be strengthened. This is done by characterising the imagined assembly more fully and adding the feature just mentioned. If the Contract Argument can be strengthened in this way, however, to come to the main point here, it is necessarily true that the Ordinary Argument can be strengthened to the same extent. One adds one's strengthening conviction to the premise of the Ordinary Argument. One adds the conviction that one should always choose the policy whose worst upshot will be best. In general, whatever is done to the Contract Argument can have a counterpart with respect to the Ordinary Argument. The latter will be as good, bad, or indifferent as the former.[12]

What follows from this, I take it, is the conclusion that the actual grounds implicit in the Contract Argument, however adumbrated, are identical with the grounds in some version of the Ordinary Argument. All that actually gives support to the conclusion in the Contract Argument is the first premise, a certain collection of convictions and beliefs. All that actually gives support to the conclusion is exactly and no more than what supports the conclusion in the Ordinary Argument. What we have called the basic proposition in the Contract Argument is *logically irrelevant* to it. So too is the evaluative proposition that the imagined choosing-situation would be a fair one. The Contract Argument is the Ordinary Argument with two superfluous parts. What is taken to be the foundation of the Contract Argument is in fact no part of the structure. Reflection on the basic proposition, so-called, let alone prolonged reflection, is idle. So too for the proposition about fairness.

(The analogy is incomplete and maybe a bit unfair, but one is put in mind of the sanguine sociologist, say, who comes to some conclusion about the nature of society. He does so only on the basis of certain evidence and by way of certain canons of inquiry. He proceeds to attribute belief in precisely his evidence, as well as acceptance of precisely his canons of inquiry, to an imagined conference of sociologists. He is pleased to discover, and entirely right to discover, that the conference would confirm his conclusion. Someone will have to point out that from the point of view of the logic of the situation, the validity of the argument, the imagined conference is an irrelevancy. The analogy between our contracting assembly and the sociological conference, incidentally, becomes nearer to complete if we make our sociologist a bit odder still. He imagines a conference of sociologists who do not in fact have precisely his evidence and canons, but, for some reason, draw a conclusion as if they had. What leads me to say this, of course, is that the members of the assembly have no moral convictions, but, for reasons we know, they behave as they would if they did have.)

It is worth noticing, in partial explanation of the error of thinking that the basic proposition does have some logical utility, that something like it *does* have utility when it turns up in other speculations about a Social Contract, those traditional ones mentioned some way back in this essay and having to do with actual people and the grounds of political obligation. Suppose that somehow we do tacitly commit ourselves to our societies and their principles. We may, then and afterwards, have convictions that lead us to think the principles are good ones. Thus there is that reason for going along with them. However, our observance of the principles also has this to be said for it: we promised it. This proposition, one that is related to the basic proposition in the doctrine we are considering, provides an independent argument of some strength or other for our observance. At any rate the proposition will do so if it is true.

I should like to anticipate one objection to what has been claimed. The people in the imagined assembly, we have granted, would agree on the principles. This is part of the Contract Argument but not the Ordinary Argument. The objection, which will barely survive being made explicit, is that some recommendation is shown to attach to the principles by the fact that they would be agreed upon by the people.

What recommendation is it? We must not drift into thinking, obviously, that any real person has ever made such an agreement and so acquired an obligation. The Social Contract, in its traditional form, is not our subject. It does not matter if we grant, as we are urged, that 'we' *would* agree to the principles if we were as the people in the Original Position.[13] *We* are different, have never been there, and have made no agreement.

If we stick firmly to the supposition that imagined people would agree on the principles, there is still no recommendation in the bare fact of their agreement. To see this, suppose we imagine an assembly made up of people who know that the coming society will have in it weak and powerful members. Moreover, and more important, each person in the assembly knows where he will turn up, whether he will be weak or powerful. Suppose, then, that the assembly comes to agree on principles which will favour those who will be powerful, and that this comes about essentially as a result of an awareness of that future state of affairs.

We will not suppose that the fact that there would be this agreement would recommend the principles. The mere fact of agreement in an imagined assembly is by itself of no relevance to us. If, incidentally, the example just imagined is taken not to be one of satisfactory or full agreement, but rather an example involving something like coercion, it is easy enough to think of an alternative. There is the assembly with false beliefs, to mention but one.

We thus have the conclusion that what confers relevance, if no more, on an imagined agreement, are the conditions under which it is made. The recommendation of the agreed principles, in that case, rests on the conditions, and then on the convictions that support them. What we have is the Contract Agreement as sketched, with no reliance placed on the bare fact of the agreement.

In any case, talk of agreement in the imagined assembly, like talk of an assembly at all, is quite otiose for a reason so far unmentioned. What we are contemplating, if we are following the instructions, is an assembly for identical persons. At any rate we contemplate them only in so far as they are identical. Each is taken only to have precisely the qualities that have been mentioned. If we set about assigning them other qualities, perhaps various and compensating knowledges of capabilities of judgement, we depart from our instructions. It is not suggested that we are to do this, and if we attempt it, the truth of the basic proposition becomes still more uncertain than it is if we follow our instructions. What we do, then, in short, is imagine identical persons. In this case, all talk of agreement is otiose or pointless. We might as well have imagined a single individual and not an assembly.[14] For this reason alone, an elaborated theory of the kind we are considering verges on the ridiculous.[15]

So much for the structure of the Contract Argument for the two principles. Perhaps, in the confines of this essay, I have attended too much to the structure of the argument. Still, the doctrine about political obligation we are considering is given to us as all of a piece, a piece in which the Contract Argument is fundamental.

Also, there is the larger matter already noticed, having to do with The Impressive in political philosophy. It is worth remarking, in this connection, that it is not as if the structure of the argument were something in every way distinct from the force of the argument, the final worth. Strictly speaking, of course, the final worth of the argument is not affected by the discovery that the structure has redundant parts, parts on which the conclusion does not depend. None the less, many people are likely to think more of the Contract Argument when it is presented to them than they would think of the Ordinary Argument. The structure itself distracts attention from the prime question of whether the two principles are an adequate generalisation and reconciliation of the collection of attitudes and beliefs. One is less likely to see how much a matter of hesitant judgement it must be, rather than a matter of anything like plain logical fact, that the two principles follow as a conclusion from what goes before. One is less likely to see, too, how hesitant one's judgement must be about supposed consequences of the principles, notably those having to do with political violence, whatever else is to be said of it.

To persist with structure for a moment more, there are also the given arguments for the two propositions about political obligation. Again, what is taken to be fundamental is logically irrelevant. There are certain special complexities here, but let us pass them by. What I shall do is merely state, pretty roughly, the actual arguments that are contained in the presented arguments. These actual arguments are analogous, of course, to the Ordinary Argument.

(1) Given certain convictions and beliefs, the same as outlined above for the Ordinary Argument, and given the belief that our societies are decently on the way towards achieving a goal defined by the two principles of justice, it follows that we have a natural duty to support and advance the institutions of our societies. In particular we must abide by the law and refrain from violence.

(2) Given the convictions and beliefs as before, and given that we have chosen to benefit from institutions in our societies that are in accord with the two principles, we have an obligation to play our part in the institutions. In particular, we are obliged to abide by the law and refrain from violence.

THE PRINCIPLES AGAIN

It seems plain enough that the Ordinary Argument does not come near to establishing the two principles in their ordering as the basic principles for the judging and directing of societies. It follows, given what has been said, and perhaps it is evident anyway, that the same is true of the Contract Argument. It may be, further, that nothing so neat and ordered as is suggested by the word 'argument', as usually used, will ever convince one that any basic principles are the right ones. Also, a ramified thing that is larger and looser than an argument, if it does produce a kind of conviction about particular principles, is unlikely to 'establish' them, let alone 'demonstrate' them. It is unrealistic to hope for the neat cogency that the words suggest.

It must be allowed, of course, despite the weakness of the Ordinary Argument and the Contract Argument, that their supposed conclusion is nonetheless correct. That is, it might be that the two principles are indeed the right principles for society. Are they? Something needs to be said, however, partly because of the relation of the two principles to the propositions about duty and obligation, propositions on which we also need to come to some judgement. They also may be better, so to speak, than the given argument for them.

The two principles are mainly compared by Rawls with the Principle of Utility. The latter principle is taken to be the most important alternative, and much argument against it is offered. The argument in the end is fully familiar: the Principle of Utility countenances inequality or unfairness, indeed calls for it, when this happens to maximise the total of satisfaction or minimise the total of dissatisfaction. The two principles are likely to be regarded as superior to the Principle of Utility in that they are in several obvious ways concerned with equality.

The first principle calls for a certain equality in liberties, that particular equality in which everyone has the greatest possible amount of them. The second principle is concerned to improve the lot of the worst-off in terms of socio-economic goods by allowing certain inequalities in terms of such goods. The two principles are like the Principle of Utility, of course, in being consequentialist: they judge practices, institutions, and so on by their consequences. Or, to be more precise about the nature of consequentialism, they judge things in terms of their consequences in felt experience, as distinct for example from such so-called consequences as *the right thing's having been done*.

To grant that the two principles are superior to the Principle of Utility, however, is not to grant all that much. There are other principles that also are superior to Utility. These also have the virtue of giving a place to equality. The one that seems to me right – the Principle of Humanity, to which the next essay is devoted – is indeed suggested by certain criticisms that can be made of the two principles.

(1) By the first principle, that of Liberty, a society is to accord to its members the maximum amount of liberties consistent with all members having the same amount. This principle takes precedence over the second one, the Principle of Difference. Let us consider this precedence, if briefly. It is, in part, that there is to be no infringement of a man's or a group's liberties even if this will serve to raise the socio-economic level of the worst-off class in society. There is this prohibition on interference with liberties at any stage of social progress.

It is not made at all clear in *A Theory of Justice* what we are to have in mind as the liberties in question.[16] This remarkable failure makes discussion frustrating, but not impossible. If a rough description is worthwhile, let us think of those things, including various property-rights, which are commonly mentioned as liberties in our societies. Surely it cannot be acceptable that there should be an absolute pro-hibition on interference with these things. It is not too much to say that social progress in the past now approved by all, say with respect to obstacles to democracy or what we now see to have been vicious deprivations, has *depended* on infringements of such things. Can it be thought that no possible future advancement will be worth an infringement? Decent lengths of life for the worst-off? Is it certain that the present amount of liberties had by each member of our societies is correct? It is nothing like certain. With less of certain liberties, presumably, there would be less socio-economic inequality of the kind that does not help the worst-off. There would be less of wretchedness and other distress.

There is also an objection that has to do with the fact that the liberties are merely rights in a certain standard sense. That is, to have a liberty is not necessarily to have the power to act on it. My right to hold property does not ensure that I own anything whatever. Should we not focus upon powers? Rawls has something to say of the question but hardly enough. My main criticism here, however, is the other one. The place that should be given to some principle about liberties is not the large place given the Principle of Liberty in the doctrine before us.

(2) There is evidently something, indeed a good deal, to be said for this first part of the Principle of Difference, about necessary inequalities in socio-economic goods. Still, there is a large question to be asked about it. Is it an *effective* socio-economic principle? That is, in the main, is it such a form as to be most likely to forward its end? It is given as this proposal: a society can and must have all

the inequalities of whatever size, if only those, that are necessary to make the position of the socio-economically worst-off better than it would otherwise be. Are those the inequalities *demanded* by those who enjoy them? Because of what it strongly implies, the proposal as it stands might reasonably be called defeatist, and can undoubtedly be called cautious.

Although in its concern for the worst-off it derives from a commitment to equality, it is so expressed as to bring into prominence the declaimed need for incentive inequalities. It thus may encourage those who in fact favour socio-economic inequality that is against the interests of the worst-off. The analogy is a loose one, but it is as if the Utilitarians, instead of urging us to maximise total satisfaction, had urged us to pursue the distress, if only the distress, that will serve to maximise satisfaction in the end. Keep on the look-out for useful unhappiness!

It will be said that caution about ending inequalities is required, and that it is a good thing to give it expression in the formulation of the principle. A single sentence cannot despatch this dispute. But it is worth noting that socio-economic history shows no shortage of claims, now falsified, about the necessity of various inequalities. There is a related point. Despite history, there is hardly a more established controversy in economic and political thinking than the one between those who believe in the necessity of much inequality as a means to a good end, and those who believe that much less would suffice, or suffice for a better end. On the other hand, there can be little controversy about the proposal that we should pursue an ideal of equality having to do with the least well-off. If we have an area of agreement, or something like it, and an area of controversy, it is as well to separate them. The Principle of Difference brings together what is best kept apart.

It would be mistaken to take this reflection about effectiveness less seriously because it consists in an objection to the emphasis or style rather than just the propositional content of the Difference Principle. One line of thought can obviously have several different attitudinal embodiments, and hence enter into what it is not silly to count as different principles. What one has in a principle is not only what it states, in some restricted and very literal sense, but also an informing spirit. It is important that what is literally specified by a principle reflects our convictions, but it is quite as important that its style and spirit do so.

(3) There is also the second part of the Principle of Difference. Should all members of society have an equal opportunity to gain any allowable positions of favourable inequality in socio-economic goods? The question becomes more clearly troublesome when it is put this way: Should all members of society, whatever their natural strengths and weaknesses, have *only* an equal opportunity to benefit from the society's resources? The question needs to be answered by way of the reflection that some individuals must have greater shares of things if they are to avoid distresses that other individuals can easily avoid without having such shares.

(4) All of the three points made so far about the principles of Liberty and Difference point towards a more general and fundamental principle. Liberty, it was said, can hardly be allowed to obstruct progress in alleviating distress. What we must have, it was then said, is an *effective* socio-economic principle for the aid of the worst-off. Thirdly, certain kinds of favourable inequality of opportunity are needed by some individuals if they are to avoid certain levels of experience.

The more fundamental and general principle is the Principle of Humanity, towards which we are moving. The Difference Principle in comparison is a principle of generality and blandness. It is, you will remember, about *socio-economic goods* – of which, you may drift into thinking, everybody has some. If those goods and in particular the lack of them had been made explicit, would they include dying young, being in pain, being denied freedom, respect, family relations, a way of life? If these things were in view, would it be so possible to contemplate that it is necessary to a society to have roughly the inequalities that the better-off demand for their contributions?

THE DUTY AND THE OBLIGATION

Just as the Contract Argument for the two principles reduces to the Ordinary Argument, so the subsequent arguments about political obligation and hence violence reduce to analogues of the Ordinary Argument. The first of these in one formulation is that given certain convictions and beliefs, and given that our societies are decently on the way to realising the two principles, it follows that we have a natural duty to support and advance the institutions of our societies. We have a natural duty to obey the law and to refrain from violence.

We may suppose that the conclusion follows from the premises but, as what has been said already clearly suggests, the premises are open to question. The collection of convictions and beliefs is in part at least controversial. For example, there is the belief that certain liberties have an importance greater than anything else. This point was to be anticipated, of course, since the same objection has been made to the summation of the convictions and beliefs in the two principles.

Furthermore, even if we accepted the convictions and beliefs and the two principles with hesitation, there is the question of how far our societies do in fact realise them. Let us give some attention to this, or rather, to the limited question of whether our societies are decently on the way to realising the Principle of Difference, which, despite what has been said against it, is superior to many other socio-economic principles. That our societies are decently on the way to realising the principle is obviously essential to the argument about duty.

To speak particularly of Britain and America, are these societies tolerably well on the way to having only those inequalities that are consistent with the Principle of Liberty and are necessary if a worst-off class is to be better off than otherwise it would be? The question is far from precise. Let us take it to be tantamount to something else, perhaps slightly better: Are these societies so much on the way to having only the specified inequalities that their members have a weighty duty, however 'natural' or 'unnatural', to obey the law? It is allowed, in the doctrine we are considering, that things may seem otherwise. That is, it is allowed that it may seem likely that there is an awful lot of unnecessary inequality. At this point, an additional economic consideration is introduced.[17]

It is that the production of goods depends not only on an incentive system, but on something that in our societies is closely connected with it – real capital accumulation. What we are to understand is that we could, for one or a few generations, reduce the gap between rich and poor, by reducing benefits to the rich, and that we would not pay the price of reducing the state of life of the poorest. However, this would have the effect of reducing real capital accumulation and hence, in the end, the effect of depriving future generations of the poorest of a certain degree of well-being that might otherwise have been theirs. I have stated the argument briefly but not, I hope, unfairly.

One reply, which seems obvious, is that there is only a contingent connection between real capital accumulation and the existence, as we know it, of extreme economic and social inequality. One can hardly ignore the fact that there exist different economies that satisfy an analogous requirement of real capital accumulation and do not do so by lodging the capital with a class of overwhelming privilege. There seems no quick or slow argument to the conclusion that a society *must* do its saving by sustaining the existence of great inequalities. We need not dismay ourselves by the reflection that the economic theory in question is extensive and unsettled. We can rest on the fact that there do exist economies that face futures as secure as those of America and Britain and do not sustain similar systems of inequality. There have been satisfactory economies without the rich.[18]

Two other things are to be said against the idea, which, it will be as well to say, is to me a *wild* idea, that our societies are so far on the way to having only the necessary inequalities that it follows that we have a weighty political obligation. It may well be that there exists some such obligation, of course, somehow grounded. What seems absolutely implausible is that it can be grounded on the proposition about necessary inequalities.

The first point is that to think that we *are* decently on the way to having only necessary inequalities is almost certainly to be out of touch, for one reason or another, with the magnitude of existing inequalities. This is a matter, in part, of that ignorance of the facts of inequality noticed in the first essay in this book. To approach the question of magnitude in one way, it is in no way rhetorical to observe that some large minority of members of our societies, a well-off minority, if their lives were altered in a certain way, would experience them as lives of horror. I have in mind an alteration such that their new existence would be one that *is* in fact the lot of another minority now. If we in the minority of privilege bring to mind, and not for a passing moment, what touches us most closely, perhaps our children and their situation, it must be impossible to think of tolerating the alteration. By way of one example, it includes those existing schools that make our commitment to proper opportunity no more than hypocrisy. They are schools that blight and constrict the entire lives of the children who go to them.

Shall we say that such an existence would carry a distress for us unlike the distress now caused to those who now experience it? No doubt this is in some degree true. Distress in part is a consequence of expectation. Destructive circumstances have a lesser effect on those who have not anticipated anything else. For such reasons there once was, in terms of satisfaction and distress, the possibility of a certain defence of the institution of slavery. (Certainly neither the bare lack of such goods as money and property, nor inequality in them, is *by itself* of importance. What is important is avoidance of the experience of distress, and it *may be* avoided despite the absence of certain goods.) What matters is well-being, which a person might possess despite inequality of some goods.) Certainly the argument of different expectations is a vanishing one. Each slave-class took up, to an increasing extent, the expectations of its masters. Today, oppressed classes in our societies are aware of their situation to a very considerable degree. Their awareness is not yet ours, but that does not make it reasonable to continue to weigh the goods of the world in two sets of scales. Experienced deprivation in our societies is in fact great.

The other remark about necessary inequalities has already been made in another connection. It cannot be in dispute that virtually every major economic and social advance in history, every advance in the direction of well-being for all, has been resisted by an argument about supposedly necessary inequalities. Almost no one takes the view, now, that the inequalities *were* necessary to things of importance. No one takes the view that any losses suffered did outweigh the gains. What we have here, to speak quickly, is an iron inductive argument in favour of scepticism about all claims as to necessary inequalities in our present societies.

What remains is only to draw a conclusion about the argument for our supposed natural duty to obey the law and hence to refrain from violence. It cannot be that we have no duty whatever. We have more of a duty than we would have in a slave-society. It has not been shown, however, to state the proposition as best one can, that there is a weighty duty. Our circumstance is far from an imagined one, also considered by Rawls, where the members of a society are members of an ideal society and so have a weighty and indeed an overwhelming duty to support it.

Let us leave the duty and pass on to the separate obligation which we are thought to have. Given the same convictions and beliefs as before, and given that we have voluntarily acted so as to benefit from institutions in our societies that are in accord with the two principles, we have an obligation to play our part in the institutions. What is to be said against this is partly the same as with the natural duty. The convictions and beliefs are not beyond question. The two principles are not beyond question. Hence even if the institutions of our societies are in accord with the principles, we do not have the simple fact that we have benefited from institutions which are clearly defensible.

We may reflect, however, that there is *something* to be said for, say, the Principle of Difference. Do we then have a resulting weighty obligation? The answer depends, as before, on whether institutions of our society do in fact come near enough to being in accord with the principle, hence having only certain necessary inequalities. I have already suggested that there is no reason for thinking so. It is a dream.

There are further difficulties about the obligation. It is not clear, despite what is said about voluntarily accepting benefits, how the obligation is supposed to come into being. Suppose a man does accept a benefit by invoking the law in order to protect his own property, and then breaks a law for political reasons. In so doing he destroys the property of someone else. In what does the wrongfulness of his act consist? What is the particular wrongfulness which has to do with the fact that he has used the law in his own interest previously? Is it that a consideration of consistency or equality enters into the argument? That is, does the wrongfulness consist in treating identical or similar cases, cases of property-ownership, differently? One of the difficulties in the way of this line of argument is that the two cases, although alike when considered in terms of property ownership, are fundamentally different. To say no more, one is a case of *political* violence.

Alternatively, if it is an alternative, does the wrongfulness of the political act consist in the fact that it is not an acceptance of rightful *debt*? This is suggested by the emphasis on voluntary action in connection with the obligation. Here we have it that by voluntarily benefiting from an institution of his society, the man acquires a certain debt. We can say that certain behaviour on his part is now owed, or called for, or fitting. This behaviour is precisely other than the behaviour of destroying the property of others.

There clearly are replies. First, if the man believed that a minority of his society was being degraded, he rightly might not allow himself to be restrained from violent political action by the single fact that he had been a beneficiary himself. Rather the contrary, perhaps. What is said in explanation and defence of the obligation leaves out of consideration all people other than the man himself and those individuals whose property he may destroy.

Again, assuming that the man does in fact acquire some debt by making use of the law in his own interest, how large is that debt? Could it be that if it exists at all, it is very small indeed? Consider an opposite case. Most people would not feel that a man had gone any way towards justifying the setting of a bomb if he established that he had eschewed, as far as he could, the benefits offered to him by society. He would not do himself much good by pointing out that he had not called the police when his house was broken into. The smallness of his defence indicates the smallness of the accusation that can be made in our primary case, where a man is claimed to have disregarded the debt acquired by voluntarily acting in such a way as to benefit from society.

Our supposed obligation, then, seems a still smaller thing than our natural duty. There may be stronger arguments against political violence that are based on a fact of political obligation, and indeed we shall return again to the question.[19] The present argument is no winner.

Let us finish by recalling the main conclusions of this discussion of *A Theory of Justice*.

The Contract Argument for the Principles of Liberty and Difference as ordered, by which we are to judge our societies, contains parts thought to be basic but which in fact contribute nothing to the strength of the argument. The same is true of the analogous arguments for our supposed natural duty and obligation to obey the law, and hence to refrain from political violence. There is a likelihood, in the case of each argument, that its expendable machinery will distract attention from its value. Its value is no greater than that of the related Ordinary Argument.

If one looks at the two principles directly, or, much the same, looks at the conviction and beliefs which are their source, one finds several grounds for objection. One has to do with the place given to liberties, another with the character of the Principle of Difference. The Principle of Equality is needed.

Objection must also be made to the claims about natural duty and obligation. One large point here is that the arguments for the duty and the obligation, and hence for refraining from violence, presuppose that our societies are decently on the way to realising the Principle of Difference. They are not. They are nowhere near it.

3
The Principle of Humanity

Every political philosophy, ideology, hope of a people, political movement and party creed should begin from a response to the question of what well-being there ought to be, and, whether as means or end, what distress.

Evidently an amount of distress can sometimes be a means, a price that ought to be paid in order to avoid more of it. Some say, differently, in connection with punishment in particular, that others deserve distress: it is to be imposed not as a means to what will then happen, but merely for what has already happened. Also, it may indeed be that to pursue the largest possible amount of well-being for a society and the least of distress would sometimes be to arrive at an unjust or iniquitous sharing of it. Further, it may be true of well-being and distress, as commonly it is taken to be of wealth and income, that the totals are less important than who has it, those who struggle and those who do not, those who produce and those who do not, the inheritors and the unlucky, and so on.

Whatever propositions or complications there are along these lines, it must be that every political philosophy and the like should proceed from an explicit response to the question of the distribution of well-being and distress: who is to have what amounts? Answering takes less time than answering another still larger question, that of actions, campaigns, policies, tactics and institutions – of how to secure and to hang on to the proper distribution. Still, there is the requirement of rationality that the end be given before means are considered, and therefore the question of distribution comes first. This essay considers it, and what seems to be the proper and true response to it.

CATEGORIES OF GREAT DESIRE

For a start, we need to give greater content to the fundamental ideas of well-being and distress. They are to be understood as two kinds of human experience, those in which desires are satisfied and those in which desires are frustrated. They can in fact be identified with the relatively clear ideas of satisfaction and frustration, clear because of their connection with action. There is that test of whether someone is satisfied or not. In a different and secondary usage of a familiar kind, we may speak of degrees of well-being or satisfaction, some of which are in fact distress or frustration, but that will not be our usual procedure.

Desires are to be conceived in so large a way as to include needs, passions, wants, commitments, loyalties and felt obligations, life-plans, and more. They then include what in a more restricted sense of the word are not or might not be desires: certain feelings for others, keeping faith, a determination to preserve one's integrity, being willing to pay a high price to achieve excellence, and so on. Let us proceed in a way which has not enough familiarity, by quickly specifying general categories of desire, in this case six. They have to do with subsistence, further material goods, freedom, respect, personal relations, and culture.[1]

It is not in dispute, despite the existence of those who give up their lives for various ends, that the primary desire is for subsistence, one's own and that of some other persons, often one's partner and children. This is the desire for that minimum of food, shelter, strength, and perhaps satisfactory activity which will sustain a lifetime. A lifetime is to be understood more in terms of an average life-expectancy of 77 years rather than, say, 40. The desire is primary in that there is a wide if limited generalisation to the effect that people, if they must choose, choose to realise this desire rather than any other. With respect to the desires to follow, no serious ranking or ordering is intended.

The second category, for further material goods, can briefly be described as one realised in much of the rich world and frustrated in much of the poor world. It includes desires for income and wealth, unimportant as ends and important as certain means. They are means to the other further material goods: relief from pain, help with disability, a home and a tolerable wider environment, food and drink above the level of subsistence, adequate medical care, material support of several kinds in adversity and misfortune, means of travel and communication, and a good deal more. The category includes items in a small way denigrated only by those who possess them: consumer goods.

Thirdly, we desire freedom and power in several settings. Most important are political and other rights in a self-determining homeland. It would be contentious, in the present discussion, quickly to identify these rights with those realised to some extent in western or liberal democratic states. The question is difficult, but what I have in mind are political and other rights denied by occupying forces, tyrannies, totalitarianisms, imperialisms and hegemonies. We also desire degrees of freedom and power in lesser contexts. Work is perhaps foremost here. There is also the pursuit of one's individual form of private life.

Respect and self-respect, which perhaps are less separable than has sometimes been supposed,[2] constitute the fourth category. We desire standing as individuals, and some standing as groups. The means to this standing are in part the possibilities of achievement, at bottom work. The means are in another part the attitudes of others. It is not enough to have work, and some limited recognition of personal achievements and virtues, if one is the victim of racism, severe class-condescension, denigration for disability, or any other denial of common humanity.

Fifthly, there is the desire for personal and wider human relationships. What comes first here are needs, commitments, and many feelings having to do with the family. There are counterparts in other personal connections. More widely, there are desires having to do with community and fraternity. We want to live lives which give a large place to connection with a few others, a connection of intimacy, protection, support, identity of hope, and many like things. This connection with a few others needs the supplement of association with larger groups, notably one's society.

We desire, finally, the goods of culture. We pursue knowledge, awareness and judgement, and the means to these, of which the principal one is education. No one chooses a general ignorance or incompetence. We want, as well, the experience of art or the lesser but real satisfaction of entertainment. Religion enters here as well, and also other greater or smaller traditions of races, peoples, nations, regions, and places.

These six categories are indeed under-described: what has been said of them catches very little of the richness and wretchedness of human experience. They are given, however, not in the illusion that they do more than fix attention on the real subject of our inquiry. That subject is not caught hold of by way of silent assumption, by any such generic notion as satisfaction or happiness or indeed well-being or distress, taken by itself, or by any abstract account of experience in terms, say, of preference under conditions of risk. Certainly the categories make evident the interdependence of our desires. The first, for subsistence, is necessary to the rest. Kinds of freedom are essential to respect and self-respect, and to certain of the goods of culture. Respect and self-respect themselves play a role in the achievement of the goods of culture. Categories so related do not thereby fail to be categories.

Our question is this: What is to be the distribution of this well-being and distress, or who is to have what amounts? The question presupposes that we can characterise possible lifetimes in terms of well-being and distress as these have now been conceived. Taken naturally, the question presupposes that we can so characterise possible lifetimes in what I shall call a cardinal rather than an ordinal way, which is sometimes doubted. The question presupposes an impossibility if all we can sensibly say about a pair of possible lifetimes is that one would be of *greater* or *lesser* satisfaction and frustration than another. There may be a temptation to transfer scepticisms or resistances from other inquiries to our own, and so to suppose this is all we can say. It seems evident on reflection that it is not.

Consider three possible lifetimes: one cut greatly short since the person fails to come up to the level of subsistence; one where the person comes up to that level and also satisfies the desires of two other categories, perhaps those for further material goods and personal relations; and one involving satisfaction of all six categories of desire: subsistence, further material goods, freedom, respect, personal relations, culture. Are we restricted to saying, with good sense, only that the first possible lifetime involves *less* well-being than the second and third, and the second *less* than the third? It is essential to see how much less we would have to say than we can rightly say, how trivial rather than rightly substantial our judgement of the three lifetimes would be, if this were so.

If we were so restricted, we could reasonably suppose, as rightly we do not, that there was nothing much to choose between the three, and no significant necessity of action, since the differences between the three were insignificant. The three lifetimes might be related in the way of three payments, of $5000.00, $5000.01, and £5000.02, considered only in terms of purchasing power. Again, if we could with good sense make only the ordinal judgement, we should have no reason whatever for thinking it a bad policy to concentrate entirely on aid to the second person. This would in fact be reasonable on the supposition that only a lifetime of the third kind was in fact tolerable, and there was no possibility of making the first life better than the second. Other absurd consequences, all conflicting with what evidently is our situation of judgement, also follow from the supposition that we can characterise lifetimes only ordinally in terms of well-being and distress.

At this juncture it is possible to make a certain mistake, that of identifying judgements of amount, which are essentially cardinal, with judgements only of number. We are all of us in possession of an effective system of non-numerical classification of amounts of distress and well-being. In judging a life to be one of wretchedness, we plainly are not only judging it to be of *less* well-being than a tolerable life or one of abundance. We are judging amount of frustration, and the ordinal proposition is an entailment of small interest. A life in which only the first category of desires is satisfied is one of great frustration, as distinct merely from being a life of greater frustration than others. In fact we have a developed conceptual system for such judgement of possible lifetimes, as of much else that engages our attention. To mention only a few other general conceptions, a possible lifetime may be one of wretchedness, subsistence, pain, being crippled, deprivation, poverty, fear, sorrow, tolerableness, security, satisfaction, fullness, indulgence, or satiety.

That there is a vagueness about these essentially cardinal descriptions, and that we may have recourse to a criterion of action or behaviour to fix amounts of well-being and distress, does not at all establish that all that can sensibly be said about the wretched life of a parent whose children are starving, or the life of a brother or sister dying of Aids, is that it is a life of lesser well-being than the lives of people we know better. The question of well-being, then, does not presuppose what cannot be done. It presupposes, moreover, what is done all the time, in particular by governments in the allocation of resources. The decisions in question are not ordinal and are not dependent on certain small if increasing aids of quantification. That there is a large need for old-age pensions as against a small one for certain roads is not merely the judgement that the first is greater, or has a higher place in an ordinal sequence.

It is less important, but true, that we can to an extent reasonably assign numerical values to possible lifetimes. As remarked, no serious ranking was intended in the listing of the five categories of desire other than subsistence. They can reasonably enough be taken as of equal value. There is no error, and some use, in assigning +1 and –1 to the full satisfaction and full frustration of each of these categories of desire. Greater values, +2 and –2 at least, can reasonably be assigned to the first category. This assignment is not made useless by the existence of some individuals who place different values on, say, art and personal relations, and forgo the latter for the former.

It is a recommendation of fixing attention on the categories of well-being and distress, rather than proceeding in terms of silent assumption, or only generic notions, or preference-systems, that it becomes plain that another problem is not serious. I have in mind interpersonal comparison. It would indeed be absurd to assume of a rich man and a poor, each preferring to have another £100, that their satisfaction in having it would be identical. Here and in some other contexts, it is mistaken to assume that satisfaction is, so to speak, uniform.

However, who will maintain that we cannot usefully inquire into the distribution of well-being since, say, the miserablenesses of two physically alike persons, both having only and exactly the same means to the satisfaction of the subsistence-desire, may be so different as to make the enterprise pointless? Who will maintain that there may be nothing to choose or not enough, in terms of 'intensity of experience', between the life of a weak child who is satisfying only the subsistence desire and the life of a lad satisfied or more or less sure to be satisfied in all of the six categories?

Still, the *assumption* of interpersonal comparability, in connection with well-being and distress, is precisely that: an assumption taken to be defensible and made for a further purpose, in this case inquiry. What is to follow here does not depend on the assumption's being taken as an exceptionless general truth.[3] Such assumptions are ordinary and essential, and we can be justified in acting on them. For example, some minority of people will have their lives worsened, for whatever reason, by being entitled to an old-age pension. This does not put in question the propriety of acting on a certain assumption about need which is close enough to true. Nor, given our resources, would it be right to invest heavily in a procedure for finding the exceptions in order to deny them pensions.

To come to the end of these defences, it is true that the characterisation of the six categories of desire is a matter of decision as well as perception of fact. This is as it must be. The characterisation might properly be said to be arbitrary if it denied that any other categorial description of desires was possible. It does not. What is important is that it be clear and arguable, which I take it to be, and that it be useful, which I trust it will be seen to be. There is in fact no great disagreement, at a certain level of generality, about the goods of human life.

UNSATISFACTORY PRINCIPLES OF WELL-BEING

We might linger over many things, and hence fail to come to our question. Not to linger, but rather to come to it, what are we to aim at in terms of lives of well-being and distress? The most developed answers of a traditional kind are principles of utility, all of which can be stated in terms of the given conception of well-being. On the fundamental one, we must secure the distribution which produces the best balance of well-being over distress. The Utilitarians did not suppose this could have a certain consequence, where the policy producing the best total was such that the well-being went mostly to one minority, class, race, or group, and the distress mostly to another. They did not proceed, either, by thinking of a total population as an entity, a singular possessor of experience, and of its balance of well-being as being decisive. It has long been argued, none the less, as already noted, that Utilitarianism may favour majorities at the expense of minorities, or some minorities at the expense of others.

Utilitarianism has been defended against this by being said to be implicitly egalitarian. I shall not pursue the argument, which has mainly to do with the utility of justice and considerations of decreasing marginal utility. If there were no more than some considerable doubt about the consequences of Utilitarian principles, it would be a good idea to take up something else, about which there is not a doubt. It is not as if we knew in advance that there is some special virtue in Utilitarian principles, not having to do with equality, which cannot be preserved in a more explicit principle.

There is a further consideration. Even if the fundamental principle of utility, say, by way of various true minor premises, did preserve what we want of equality, it would still be unsatisfactory. This has to do with the fact that general answers to the question of well-being cannot be regarded as fully articulated major premises to be connected by tight reasoning with conclusions about particular political, social, and economic policies. In this world as it is, what may be called the merely logical properties of these general answers are not of the first importance.

This is so because there is enough complexity in our situation that the best that can be done is to make judgements *directed* or *guided*, as distinct from strictly entailed, by an answer to the question of well-being. An answer can only be a kind of directive. If all possible precision is important, so is force and emphasis. Principles of utility, as expressed, do not give a good place, let alone prominence, to their supposed egalitarian content. A good flag is not of uncertain colour.

Perhaps understandably, there are no developed answers to the question of well-being in terms of desert or retribution. The question, of course, is wider than that of punishment, or punishment and reward. However, I shall in what follows have something to say of retribution as a maxim of justice. There are doctrines, primarily about what were called actions, tactics, institutions and so on, which bear on the question of well-being, and do have about them some tang of an idea of desert. One, so expressed as to make its bearing clear, is that there ought to be that distribution of well-being which results from a certain principle of liberty, as it is called, about the first-ownership and the transfer of certain fundamental means to well-being, notably material goods and labour.[4] First-ownership should involve a man's mixing his labour with something and in a way not worsening the situation of others, and any transfer should at least in a very weak sense be voluntary.

The doctrine is badly summed up in the maxim 'From each as he chooses, to each as he is chosen'. The tendency of this doctrine, in terms of distribution of well-being, is not entirely clear. Just the actual distribution which now exists is not favoured, since it is in part the result of social and hence governmental interference in what is defined as liberty. The defence made for the favoured distribution is in terms of certain desires in but one of the categories of well-being, the one having to do with freedoms. I shall not discuss the doctrine, but something more of relevance to it will be said.

Are there any developed egalitarian answers to our question? There is nothing to which so much attention has been given as to principles of utility. What will come to mind, although its description as egalitarian can be disputed, and will be here, is that there should be an equal distribution of well-being and distress, perhaps that each individual should have the same balance of well-being over distress. No doubt this has been proposed by some egalitarians, but, if it is not confused with anything else, as it can be, it is unacceptable.[5] The short but sound argument against this – against what can be called the *Principle of Any Equality* – is that an inequality of satisfaction is preferable to an equality of frustration, an inequality at high levels of satisfaction preferable to an equality at a lower level. Nor can we take up the *Principle of Greatest Equal Well-Being*, which is open to the same kind of objection. It is that we should pursue that particular equal distribution in which people have more well-being than in any other equal distribution.

Some will be inclined to say a word in defence of the mentioned equalities as against the inequalities, or at any rate the second equality. They may say that inequality is inimical to self-respect, and hence that an inequality at high levels of satisfaction is not preferable to an equality at a lower level. The reply must be that while there may be a loss of self-respect on the part of those who are least well-off, given the inequality, they remain better off than under the alternative equality. Our subject-matter is well-being, in all of its categories, and not anything else. It is not to the point that an inequality of material goods, at high levels, may not be preferable to an equality of material goods at a lower level, precisely for such reasons as self-respect.

There is also an answer said to be of an egalitarian kind given to our question by Rawls.[6] It is that well-being and distress in a society are to be distributed primarily according to one consideration, then according to a second, and then according to a third. When there is a conflict, as there will be, the first wins over the second and third, the second over the third. The first is the *Principle of Liberty*: each person to have that maximum of rights to liberty consistent with everyone having the same. The second is the *second part* of what is called the *Difference Principle*, that there is to be an equal opportunity to get into any superior positions of socio-economic superiority or difference, as defined by such goods as income and wealth, power and standing. The third consideration is the *first part* of the Difference Principle, that socio-economic goods are to be distributed in the particular way that leaves the worst-off in such goods better off than they would be given any other way of the distribution.

This view is much elaborated and yet for several reasons may be thought to remain indeterminate. There is remarkably little discussion of the given liberties, but, 'roughly speaking', they are 'political liberty (the right to vote and to be eligible for public office) together with freedom of speech and assembly, liberty of conscience and freedom of thought; freedom of the person along with the right to hold (personal) property; and freedom from arbitrary arrest and seizure as defined by the concept of the rule of law'.[7] Presumably also included are other rights before the law. It is not easy to judge the effect of this first-priority principle on the distribution of well-being and distress. This has much to do with the fact that what are in question are indeed rights rather than powers. There has been a long history of argument to the effect that mere rights, unsupported by economic and other resources, are of a limited and uncertain value.

Nor is it, of course, that the second part of the Difference Principle guarantees anything like an economic equality. Conjoined with certain propositions about the need for the incentives of socio-economic inequality, it may issue in striking inequality. Consider then the following description: 'distribution of well-being and distress considerably determined by an equal distribution of rights supported by *one or another distribution* of socio-economic resources'. The description may be thought to pick out nothing definite. It is worth adding that the absence of a specification of 'the right to hold (personal) property' makes by itself for an indeterminateness of considerable consequence.

Rawls's theory of justice, nonetheless, is a kind of culmination of liberal thinking. It raises a question about the nature of that tradition.[8] But let us now consider something else.

THE PROPER PRINCIPLE

The proper response to the question of well-being is at bottom a simple one which has been undeveloped despite being presupposed by many doctrines about tactics and institutions, and which in fact fails to get expression in Rawls's theory of justice. For the reason given in connection with liberties, and others, it is not clear that it is consistent with that theory, even if the theory can be taken out of its given context, which is a single society.

The principle is that we should have actually effective policies whose end is to make well-off those who are badly-off – get them out of distress and into well-being. The principle, which will be more fully stated in due course, and which for a reason to which I shall come will be given the new name of being the *Principle of Humanity* rather than the Principle of Equality, has to do directly with well-being rather than socio-economic goods. Like other responses to the question of well-being, including the Utilitarian, it would have little force if construed in a merely ordinal way. It is not to be confused with the 'negative Utilitarian principle' that we should as far as possible reduce the numbers of badly-off, which was so taken, by a philosopher or two, as absurdly to justify ending their lives.

The population to which the principle applies is that of persons generally, as distinct from persons within a given society or nation.[9] Several future generations must be included, those about which we can make more or less rational predictions. The limitation to such foreseeable generations is essential if the principle is to be at all practical. Needless to say, taking account of the future raises difficulty. It would be wrong to give great weight to any vision of future Utopia, or, for that matter, future ruin. What is obviously necessary is that we follow certain rules, of which a principal one is that a lesser probability of greater distress is to count for only as much as a greater probability of lesser distress. Another is that in general we must assign lesser probabilities to events in the distant as against the nearer future. The upshot is that future generations will count for less.

There is the necessity of reflecting on the restriction of the principle to one species. We should be taken aback by the thought that within a century or two much of our present use of animals may quite generally be regarded with moral disgust. Whether or not this comes about, it seems evident that the lives of animals call for greater regard than we give them. Still, as you will guess, I do not propose that we take the Principle of Humanity to cover more than the human species. One better reason is that other animals have very greatly different capabilities of well-being and distress. What is clearly true, however, is that animals and their distress and well-being must put *some* constraint on the operation of the Principle of Humanity. I shall not attempt to discuss it here.

Taking people generally, of several generations, who are to be regarded as the badly-off?

Certainly to be included are (a) those persons who fail to satisfy even their subsistence desires, and therefore not only desires for further material goods but also to some extent desires in all categories. The latter is necessarily true if, as seems necessary, we take the desires for respect, personal relations, freedom, and culture to be desires for a lifetime's satisfactions of them. The people in question will include individuals of various life-spans, certainly. What they have in common, in terms of length of life, is that they die at one or another premature age.

Also to be included are (b) those who subsist but lack further material goods, and hence are certain to be frustrated in other ways as well, notably with respect to freedom. It also seems to me necessary that we include others in the badly-off. This comes about partly as a consequence of having to pay attention, in a way, to the subject of tactics and institutions. It is not to be supposed, given certain political, psychological, and other realities, that there will or can be a total or even an effective concentration on groups (a) and (b). It seems in accord with the impulse of the Principle of Humanity, taking it to be a principle which has to do with the possible, in a realistic sense, to bring in other groups.

It would be unrealistic and mistaken, given the principle, to object to the endeavours of individuals who choose to concentrate on (c) people badly-off in that they lack the great satisfactions of freedom, say freedom in a homeland. So with concentration on (d) those who lack respect. The same may apply to endeavours in connection with (e) people who subsist but have a minimal degree of satisfaction in all the other categories.

So I take it in what follows that the badly-off or those in degrees of distress, in terms of the population of all persons, are to be understood to be members of the groups (a) to (e). The better-off, those enjoying degrees of well-being, are the remainder of all persons.

It is not inconsistent with the Principle of Humanity, however, to concern oneself with a single nation, indeed one of the nations of the rich world. Again there are relevant political, psychological, and other realities. There are members of group (a) here. Their existence cannot be overlooked. There are also members of (b), including many of the unemployed, and of (c), (d) and (e).

Other groups in the rich societies will come to mind. Here a large majority of people are considerably satisfied in all the six categories, more than minimally satisfied. We make distinctions within this large group. By way of one very general one, there are the poorly-paid and the better-paid. The poorly-paid are not well-satisfied in terms of further material goods, and hence in certain ways and degrees not well-satisfied in freedom and respect. Ought they not to have been included, from the point of view of the Principle of Humanity, as a group who are badly-off? The question is not one to be answered just by discovery, so to speak. We are specifying a principle, and the answer given specifies it further. The principle is to be so understood that this group does *not* count as badly-off. This is not to say that it cannot defensibly make demands of the better-paid, under certain assumptions and by way of different and lesser considerations.

Before considering a bit further the poorly-paid and the better-paid, in connection with the specific policies mentioned in the initial statement of the Principle of Humanity, we need to give further attention to the badly-off as defined by the six categories. The principle is about them and not necessarily about the worst-off in those categories. To proceed quickly, if too abstractly, consider a situation where, say, 999 similar-sized groups of people are very badly-off indeed, and one similarly-sized group is trivially worse-off. Consider a choice between a programme which trivially improves the lot of the single group, and a programme which does not help the single group but very greatly improves the lot of the 999. It is hard to resist the unhappy inclination to prefer the second policy.

It may be that conflicts between the claims of the badly-off and the worst-off do not often occur. In any case, I shall not now say much of how to reach a precise formulation of what seems forced upon us: in part that a large gain for many, say an escape from mere subsistence, may outweigh the abandoning of a few in yet greater distress. We do not actually have a guide until we supply definitions for 'a large gain', 'many', and so on. Are we in this neighbourhood forced to proceed in a piecemeal way, sometimes called intuition-ist, deciding situations as they come up, sometimes being more moved by the situation of many rather than fewer, sometimes not? This sort of procedure is common, and primitive judgements of the kind must occur somewhere in any evaluative system, but it is not satisfactory here.

We can instead construct a certain rule, or at any rate a set of rules for manageably limited problems: a fundamental one would be that of income. Such a rule can serve purposes of an ordinary decision-specifying principle expressed in general terms. It can reflect our convictions, ensure consistency, and allow for its own revision in the event of conflicting and recalcitrant consequences. In short, it will guide action. To construct it we produce a range of paradigmatic possible choice-situations, and give the choice to be made in each, in some in favour of the worst-off and in others in favour of the badly-off. In any actual choice-situation we decide which paradigm is most applicable, and choose accordingly. Such a rule, which has many analogues, can give us what is as satisfactory as a guide of the ordinary kind, expressed in general terms.

It may be rightly anticipated that the proposed response to the question of well-being is not a complete answer to it. It has nothing to say of groups of the better-off *taken by themselves*, say the poorly-paid and the better-paid in rich societies, and their cardinal or ordinal positions. If it were to come about that there were no more of the badly-off, as defined, the principle would have no further use, or rather it would instruct us only to see that no badly-off came into existence.

That the principle has nothing to say of any distributions of well-being, if there are any, that do not affect the badly-off, is a matter of moral concentration. It is a matter of concentration on one human reality, a reality not about to disappear. There is no serious embarrassment in the breadth of the principle, in its being an incomplete answer to the question of well-being. An incomplete answer is not an irrelevant answer. It may be, as in this case, that answer which is taken to be most significant. The conviction here, put quickly, is that what has priority over any other principle for the distribution of things among the better-off is a principle about famine and miserableness and the other kinds of distress.

POLICIES, EQUALITY-PRACTICES

The initial statement of the Principle of Humanity was that we are to have actually effective policies whose end is to make better-off those who are badly-off. What are those policies?

There is the policy to be considered, first, of helping the badly-off without at all affecting the well-being of the better-off. If the pie of well-being can be enlarged by a method which does not at all lessen the shares of the better-off, that is to be done. We must act, if we can, on the familiar instruction to raise up those below rather than drag down those above, to level-up rather than level-down. But could we act effectively by only this policy? Could we, for example, simply increase the various material and other goods, the means to well-being? Alternatively, could we transfer sufficient material goods from the better-off without reducing their well-being?

The first idea supposes that we are in something like a circumstance of realisable abundance or plenitude. The supposition is sufficiently uncertain as to make a reliance on it impossible. The second idea is a reasonable one. The better-off *waste* a great deal. Indeed we waste mountains of means to well-being. Still, it is unclear that we can rely on this alone. We need more than the first policy.

The second possibility to be considered, then, is precisely a policy of transfer of the means of well-being from the better-off to the badly-off, in the knowledge that this *will* reduce the well-being of the better-off. It is maintained by many, of course, that there is a serious question of to what extent we can do this. It is maintained, as it has been for long, that policies which greatly or considerably reduce the means of the better-off will in fact fail to be effective transfer-policies. It is also maintained, differently and extremely, that to subtract *anything* from the means of the better-off will be ineffective. Both claims rest on what is taken to be a fundamental fact of human existence, which is an incentive system's connection with the total pies of means and of well-being, and hence the well-being of the badly-off. The need of the poor is that the rich be rich.

The extreme view, that to subtract any significant amount of the means of the better-off in the world today would necessarily worsen the situation of the badly-off, is of course false. There is only the question of what extent of taking means from the better-off will in fact be successful transfer-policies. What extent of taking from the rich will help the poor? Of the inequalities in means, what fraction of them are in fact not *necessary* inequalities: those of which is it true that they are needed, given attitudes as they are or can become, in order to serve an end of the badly-off?

Something related to this is certainly important enough to stand on its own as a policy, the third one. Indeed it is of great importance. Necessary and unnecessary inequalities in means are in a way relative. That is, a favourable inequality's being necessary is a matter of the attitudes of the person favoured by it. An inequality's being necessary is a matter of its being a necessary incentive, and the latter is a matter of the person's attitudes. He might change, and become less demanding about payment for using his abilities. There is the possibility of practices, not necessarily coercive ones, directed to changing attitudes, so that what are now necessary inequalities cease to be such and can become the subject of effective transfers.

A fourth policy is implicit in what has been said of our fundamental desires, the first and third above all, those for a decent length of life and for freedoms of various kinds. It is also implicit in the policies we already have – policies, in a word, for reducing misery and the like. What the fourth policy comes to, then, is that we of course must strive not to act in a positive way to give rise to misery and the like – we must strive not to attack lives ourselves. So the policy is a prohibition on wounding, killing, torture, sexual violation, threat, intimidation and other violence and near-violence against individuals.

Since this policy cannot possibly be an absolute one, cannot possibly rule out all uses of force by societies against individuals, or rule out an individual's right to try to save his own life by force, the definition of the policy cannot conceivably be easy. It will be clear that it cannot be a prohibition on all terrorism and state-terrorism. It is a policy about which to think more fully not at this moment, but only at the end of such an inquiry as is being taken forward in this book.

A fifth possible policy of the Principle of Humanity, important to some, has to do with envy. It is claimed that some of the distress of the badly-off is owing to their envy of the better-off, and that this can and should change. We can take it that envy is a feeling owed to relative positions of the envious and the better-off, not to the absolute position of either. That is, the envious would persist in that particular part of their unhappiness owed to envy if both they and the better-off went the same distance up (or down) a scale of well-being. Perhaps, since envy also has to do with the means to well-being, the envious would feel in a way better if certain goods or means to the well-being of the better-off were destroyed, as distinct from transferred to the envious. We can, it is supposed, increase the well-being of the badly-off by putting an end to their envy. This fifth policy is related to the first. Both would help the badly-off without affecting at all the well-being of the better-off.

There is a sixth and related possibility, which has to do with condescending pride, to give it a mild name, on the part of the better-off. There is satisfaction owed to relative position, to the fact that others have less of well-being or the means to it. This, like envy, is not a matter of absolute level. Condescending pride perhaps may be said to make some contribution to the situation of the badly-off, partly but not wholly by way of giving rise to envy or reinforcing it. An alteration of this pride, then, would somewhat improve the lot of the badly-off.

Of these six possibilities of improving the lot of the badly-off, the fifth and sixth are not of great significance. It is to be kept in mind that they have to do with one element in one category of well-being, that of respect. The first, at least in part, and the second, third and fourth, are in my view policies that can reasonably be included in the Principle of Humanity.

To say more of the second, about means-transfers that do reduce the well-being of the better-off, should we take it that the Principle of Humanity says nothing, in connection with transferring means to well-being from the better-off, of particular groups of the better-off? Thinking so would not be in accord with the spirit of egalitarianism. It must be that means are to be transferred first from those of the better-off who are better placed than others of the better-off. In terms of the rich societies and the general distinction, effective transfer begins with the better-paid rather than the poorly-paid. What limit is there to the transfer of the means of well-being from the better-off? There is room for choice, but evidently distress must not be increased by the transfer of means. Transfer is not punishment.

It is essential to remain clear about the general goal of the Principle of Humanity. Despite certain possibilities of self-deception and propaganda, the goal is not to lower the absolute well-being of the better-off. The goal is not to level down. That may happen, although the connection between well-being and what we have called the means to it – about which connection not enough has been said – is far from simple. It would be consistent with the spirit of egalitarianism to act only on the first of the five policies if it were anything like sufficient itself, rather than the second. To act on the second policy is then not at all necessarily to be moved by a questionable or base impulse. It is to be moved by the greatest of concerns, that of improving the lot of the badly-off by an effective method. The project remains sufficiently human and proper when the active parties are the would-be beneficiaries. That this method may have the side-effect of reducing the absolute well-being of the better-off is another fact, consistent with the high moral standing of egalitarianism.

A second and related point is that if we act on the second policy our general goal is still not that of changing the relative positions of the well-off and the badly-off. In particular it is mistaken somehow to identify or associate the end with envy. The general goal of the enterprise is not to approximate to or secure an equality, a certain relationship. Certainly to transfer goods is to do something which has the side-effect of tending to equalise both goods and well-being. The hitherto badly-off in well-being will have more of both, and the hitherto better-off will have less of goods and perhaps of well-being. If the goal of the Principle of Humanity were achieved, there would exist as a second side-effect the equality, so to speak, of all people being other than badly-off. Still, none of this is the main end of the enterprise.

It remains true, more important, that changing the relative positions of the better-off and the badly-off is not the main thing when particular campaigns or practices have the specific aim of producing an equality of goods, or approximations to one, as a means to the end of the Principle of Humanity. Such campaigns or practices in certain contexts are the most effective ones. One person one vote is an example. Others, involving material goods, make the correct assumption that a given group of people are in the same need, or roughly equal in their capability to secure well-being from identical shares of resources. Variants of this consideration, that the general goal of the Principle of Humanity is not relative, and of the previous consideration, that the goal is not the dragging down of the better-off, apply to the stipulation that in transferring goods from the better-off, the first to be affected should be those best placed, including the better-paid rather than the poorly-paid in the rich societies.

Does all this need more qualification?[10] I suppose so. In so far as the Principle of Humanity is concerned with freedom and power, it is somehow and necessarily concerned with relative rather than absolute well-being. What freedom and power you have may indeed be a function of how much I have. The very nature of the good of freedom is surely relative. There is a related truth, presumably, about respect and self-respect. Still, the main point stands. The fundamental thing in this morality is not differences between people, but distress and the injustice of it.

The Principle of Humanity can now be more fully stated, as follows:

> Our end must be to make well-off those who are badly off, by way of certain policies: (1) increasing means to well-being and, more surely, transferring means from the better-off that will not affect their well-being, (2) transferring means from the better-off that *will* affect their well-being, those at the higher levels to be affected first, and observing a certain limit, (3) reducing the necessity of inequalities, and (4) allowing only what can be called, without definition for now, necessary violence. Further, these policies are to be pursued in part by way of practices of equality.

HUMANITY AND EQUALITY

The Principle of Humanity, in earlier versions of this essay and earlier editions of this book, was spoken of, rather, as the Principle of Equality. What is more, arguments were advanced for that name. The matter is larger than a merely terminological one. A proper sense of any principle is or should be conveyed by what it is called. It was my idea, in the past, that a proper sense of the thing was given by speaking of it as the Principle of Equality. My reasons were as follows.

The first consisted in several facts mentioned above. These are the two side-effects of concern for the badly-off, these being equalisations or a tendency to them. A second reason, more important, was the noted fact that in many situations and contexts, involving similar need and capability, the most reasonable way of helping the badly-off in well-being is by aiming at an equality of material goods and so on. This is not always true, and that it is not always true is important.

Still, it is true enough to go a good way by itself towards making the principle's name natural.

There was also the third reason that the principle has an excellent claim to be regarded as the principle which has most directed egalitarian struggles throughout history, although these are not too easily defined. It is mistaken to suppose instead that these struggles have been informed by, say, the Principle of Any Equality, or the Principle of Greatest Equal Well-Being. These latter principles, as explained, *are* concerned with relative position, and may have the consequence that the position of the better-off in well-being must be reduced even if this does not improve the absolute position of the poorer-off. These principles may also have the consequence, perhaps intimately connected with the previous one, that certain means to well-being are to be destroyed. These would be means of value to the better-off but for some reason of no use to the poorer-off.

By way of brief support for the proposition that egalitarianism has in fact been informed by the Principle of Humanity rather than these others, let us take egalitarianism to have consisted in struggles identified by demands for (a) giving 'to each according to their needs' or 'equality of welfare', (b) 'equality of opportunity', and (c) 'equal respect for all'. Were the struggles so identified aimed at equality of well-being, *any equality of it*, with the possible consequences just mentioned? Were they instead aimed at helping the badly-off? The answer is plain enough. It is plain despite the fact that egalitarianism, like all other human endeavours and traditions, has often enough fallen into confusion, excess, and absurdity.

Those who have been concerned to satisfy the needs and wants of the impoverished and the degraded have not been aiming at *a relationship* – an equality, any equality. One may be led into supposing so by the truth that they have often had the subordinate aims of which we know, equalities of means to well-being. But there is no reason, to repeat, to confuse their means and their end. They have not had an end which might have been served by *destroying food*, say, or trying to make sickness or poverty or disdain *universal*. They have not sought to have *everyone equally in need*. Nor is it really arguable that they have had the end of the Principle of Greatest Equal Well-Being.

Those who have struggled for equality of opportunity have been motivated by the vision of full lives for those who have not had them because of want of education or the like. Whatever they have demanded about the distribution of educational resources they have in the relevant sense not been levellers. They have not sought *an equality of ignorance*, or *poor education for everyone*. Much the same can be said of those who have been moved by the demand for respect.

My fourth reason for the name the 'Principle of Equality' seemed the strongest. It has to do with the second reason, but certainly is distinct. To use any other name, including 'The Principle of Humanity', would make it more likely, to say the least, that the principal means to the principle's end would not get proper attention. The principal means to the end of helping the badly-off was the means of securing certain equalities of material goods and so on. This, part of the second policy mentioned above, seemed to me fundamental. It was something passed by or resisted. It seemed to me of fundamental importance that the fundamental moral principle, by its name, should convey the essential means to its end, a means which commonly is ignored or obstructed.

Well, I think differently now. The overwhelming reason, as perhaps you will anticipate, is that the great end of the principle, its *raison d'être* so to speak, should not be lost sight of. It sums up a morality of humanity, fellow-feeling or generosity. That is its nature, a concern and determination having to do with people in distress, people with bad lives. Not to have this salient is no service to thinking about the matter. Also, it leaves some of us unclear about the moral imperative of the thing, and enables others of us to avoid it. To repeat something said in another connection, a good flag is not of uncertain colour.

That does not subtract any of the principle's concerns with equality or put into question that it has been fundamental and central to egalitarianism. It must not distract us, either, from the campaigns for equalities of various kinds that are essential. In that connection, it is worth looking at the relation of the Principle of Humanity to familiar principles, rules, maxims, and propositions mentioning equality. If we accept the principle, it follows that some of these are to be accepted, others amended or rejected.

To specify these consequences is to give further content to the principle. It is in part through its own corollaries that so general a principle becomes clearer. My other intention in surveying these consequences is to argue that independently of the Principle of Humanity we, or anyway many of us, are in fact committed to moving towards or inclined to many of them. It appears that we favour or will come to favour things in accord with the principle and not those that conflict with it. Hence my second intention is to provide one basic argument for the principle, that increasingly it reflects ordinary enlightened convictions and feelings.[11]

(1) The day has passed when it could be said that the Principle of Formal Equality, fundamentally that like cases should be treated alike, is the only acceptable upshot of egalitarian reflection. Still, not long ago it was regularly supposed that what egalitarianism comes to is only this, to put it a bit more fully, that no one shall be held to have a claim to better treatment in advance of general grounds being produced. The principle can be realised in a racist society, or indeed in any society which follows rules of any kind. It amounts to an injunction to consistency. The Principle of Formal Equality is consistent with the Principle of Humanity, but cannot be said to amplify it, or to be a consequence or corollary of it.

(2) There are a number of what can be called elitist maxims of equality. One, as the phrase is sometimes understood, is 'to each according to his ability'. A second one, again as sometimes understood, is 'to each according to his capacity to develop'. Others, more likely to go unstated, are 'to each according to his race', or 'his colour' or 'his nationality'. There is the possibility of taking the second maxim differently, in such a way that it may be in accord with the Principle of Humanity. Truly elitist maxims conflict with the Principle, and they also conflict with ordinary and growing attitudes, and indeed with rising institutions.

(3) What of the principle of retributive justice: to each according to his desert? To speak of punishment, it is essential to distinguish between its rules and the principle of retribution. If some people defend the rules, such as the rule that only the guilty are to be punished, by referring to desert, others do so as reasonably by referring to prevention, perhaps deterrence. If we now ask the question of what goals might be served by deterrence, one is obviously the goal of the Principle of Humanity. Certain rules of punishment, then, are in accord with, or indeed follow from, the Principle of Humanity.

There is conflict of a kind between the Principle of Humanity and the principle of retribution, but there is room for a good deal of reflection on the latter. It is arguable that the principle of retribution, on full inquiry, reduces very roughly to this: a man is to have a penalty which (a) exactly satisfies the grievance-desire to which he has given rise, (b) will be in accordance with certain rules of equal treatment, and (c) will cost him less distress than it would someone else who had to undergo it.[12] Given this view, it is possible to argue that the principle of desert is something whose materials testify to the correctness of the egalitarian's conviction that the fundamental thing is the reduction of distress.

It can be argued in any case that ordinary enlightened attitudes about the rules of punishment and about retribution go in the direction of the Principle of Humanity. Particular rules which cannot be seen as serving a tolerable deterrent end are at least suspect. It is not too much to say that the principle of retribution, despite the materials in it, is in decline.

(4) 'To and from each according to his voluntary consents and agreements.' This principle, if taken in some ways, including one which makes it a partial summary of a doctrine mentioned above, does fight with the Principle of Humanity. The central point is that voluntary agreements under a certain loose definition of voluntariness may be agreements which precisely defeat the aim of the Principle of Humanity. They may indeed serve to reduce the well-being of the badly-off. Under other restricted understandings of the quoted principle it is in accord with the Principle of Humanity. It is a part of well-being to have certain agreements protected. If the principle is taken in the first ways, so as to defend distributions of well-being that result from minimally voluntary agreements, as when a man agrees to work for a certain wage when the only alternative is deprivation for his children, there is declining support for it.

(5) There are a number of what can be called weak principles and rules of equality. One is to the effect that we are to pay an equal respect to everyone. No one is to be ignored. Others specify certain absolutely minimal ways in which all people are to be treated. Their 'basic' needs, perhaps what we have identified as subsistence-desires, are to be satisfied. It will be evident that the Principle of Humanity conflicts with such principles, if going far beyond them is taken for conflict. These and other weak principles are no longer ordinarily regarded as sufficient. It is thought by very many that individuals have rights which go well beyond them. There has been a change in attitudes which supports the Principle of Humanity.

(6) There is the matter of equal liberties, with liberties taken in some such way as in connection with Rawls. We have the proposition then that all are to be equal in roughly the legal, political, and intellectual rights defended in Britain and America. As already suggested, equal rights conjoined with unequal socio-economic powers are of limited value, to say the least. It is clear, however, that the Principle of Humanity is at least in accord with equal distribu-

tions of rights supported by like distributions of power. There is a change of attitudes in this direction.

(7) It is said that those who make equal efforts are to be equally rewarded, and still more than those who make lesser efforts. Or, differently, those who not merely try but also succeed are to be rewarded in one way, and those who do not succeed, whether or not they try, are to be less well rewarded. Another related rule has to do with contribution, with or without effort or work. The first two rules, but hardly the third, are sometimes in accordance with the idea that we should have any favourable inequalities of goods and well-being which *in fact* are necessary to the end of the Principle of Humanity.

There is the difficulty that it is far from easy to establish that those who carry forward certain jobs, and hence make larger contributions to the total means of well-being, would not do so without the rewards they are getting. Many jobs and careers bring great satisfaction. It is not surprising that many egalitarians are sceptical about arguments to the effect that company directors, say, must be paid more because of 'the burden of responsibility' which they carry. It may seem that in general this responsibility is not merely bearable but desirable, the proof being that it is much sought after.

Also, to look back to the third of our policies in connection with the Principle of Humanity, it is to be kept in mind that the Principle has the consequence that we should attempt to reduce what is necessary in the way of certain incentives for the given end. It is not possible to say that there now exists some ordinary support for only those rules of effort and productivity which in fact are consonant with the Principle of Humanity. Perhaps there is movement in that direction. Something of the same sort can be said of the desirability of changing incentive-demands.

(8) The Principle of Humanity has informed egalitarian progress, and the latter has included the struggle for equality of opportunity. Still, there is more to be said about the latter, of relevance to a new and more perceptive egalitarian demand. Opportunity may be taken to consist in the use of certain resources, including abilities of other people. If we are to improve the lot of the badly-off, then we shall not always proceed most efficiently by securing equality of opportunity. We shall do so by securing a certain *inequality*.

If we regard well-being as in part a function of opportunity on the one hand and the innate capabilities of individuals on the other, and it is the case that some individuals are less capable than others, we shall sometimes do best by securing that they have *more* opportunity. The Principle of Humanity does not derive from a view of life as simply a curious race where all attention is given to an equal start and no attention to some being lame. There seems little doubt that ordinary moral attitudes are changing in this direction. That is, there is movement towards proper inequalities of opportunity. We are now familiar with the idea of using more resources for the less able in education. There is also reverse discrimination.

(9) If there are circumstances where capabilities and needs are unequal, there are also other circumstances, already emphasised, where given people are roughly equal in a certain capability or need. Here the Principle of Humanity requires that there be a rule of equal distribution of material and other goods. There are many such rules, guiding many practices. The rules have an insufficient acceptance.

(10) Finally, there is the maxim 'To each according to his needs', with needs fully conceived. The maxim may be supplemented by another, 'From each according to his ability', understood in a certain way. Given narrow views of needs, noted above, the first rule falls short of being a version of the Principle of Humanity. Under another reading, the maxim is in fact tantamount to the Principle. It is unique among maxims about equality, and cannot be regarded as merely one among many.

So much for a survey of the consequences of the Principle of Humanity for maxims and other thoughts having to do with equality. There is another possible survey, more difficult but capable of shedding at least as much light on the Principle of Humanity. It takes us in the direction of the question of tactics and institutions mentioned at the beginning, and is of the general political consequences of the Principle of Humanity – political consequences traditionally conceived.

If that Principle is the principle of the Left, or the Right, or the Centre, then it is the principle of the Left.[13] Indeed, the Left in politics is best defined by way of it. It is some parties of the Left, further, that have actually done most for progress toward realisation of the Principle. Certainly the Principle has sometimes been espoused by the Right and the Centre, but typically in conjunction with contradictory or conflicting impulses, among them the impulse to believe that great inequalities in distribution of the means to well-being are required to protect the grim state of the badly-off from being even more grim. The New Labour Party in Britain is an outstanding example, to me an awful one. Still, there can be disagreement about the political consequences of the Principle of

Humanity. More should be said about self-deception in political philosophy, and also the pretence of self-deception, perhaps not only on the Right.

The Principle of Humanity, secondly, at this time as at most times, is the principle not of conservation but of change. That of course is not the same as saying that it is the principle of the Left. The Principle, thirdly, may or may not be the principle of democracy, by which is meant what we now call democracy – once known to others as bourgeois democracy, with some reason. The question is not easy, and certainly not one which allows for brevity. There evidently are many circumstances where the Principle of Humanity issues in democracy. The difficulty is that certain non-democracies can also be seen as in accord with the Principle. Their far greater approximation to economic equality is of great importance. The Principle, fourthly, has sometimes issued in revolution, and it has indeed been behind acts and campaigns of terrorism. It has had to do, fifthly, with provision for free and equal expression of opinion. With the aid of certain suppositions it does provide an argument for some violence. With the aid of other suppositions it provides a more certain argument for free expression.

It will be as well to say a word more on terrorism, and in particular on what can be called *terrorism for humanity*. What it is, by one rough understanding, is terrorism on behalf of humanity, on behalf of people in general who are in distress, all of them. What it is, by another rough understanding, is terrorism out of humanity, terrorism that at least may be owed to that disposition of some of us that is our humanity, generosity or fellow-feeling. Terrorism for humanity, by a third and best understanding, is terrorism directed to the end of the Principle of Humanity or a related end. It is terrorism more or less directed to the end of the Principle of Humanity – reducing wretchedness and other forms of distress. It gets its end from that morality of which I take the Principle of Humanity to be the best statement. You will not need assuring, I hope, that terrorism for humanity so understood is already right – that it is morally defensible by definition. That is no part of the idea.[14]

The Principle of Humanity is not the only conceivable formulation of the morality in question, and it requires enlargement in several ways. But surely it is the proper and true response to the question of well-being. It is, to my mind, the best formulation of the greatest of moralities. That is not so controversial a conclusion as some may too quickly suppose. There remains the other large question, that of tactics and institutions, to which we have latterly approached a bit more closely. There is more room for dispute here. Certainly some 'egalitarian' means to the end of making better-off those who are badly-off are ill-judged. But support for the Principle of Humanity is not to be identified with support for them. Nor should opposition to them give rise to opposition to it.

4
Our Omissions and Their Terrorism

Is there not all the distance in the world between our lives and the lives of such terrorists as those of September 11? Is there not a difference in moral kind between our conduct and theirs? Almost all of us believe something like this. Certainly we are not affected in our having this view, but may be repelled rather than anything else, by talk of terrorism for humanity. We believe that our ordinary conduct in life is right, or right on the whole, or right enough, and thus far away from the conduct of those who kill, maim, and devastate for what they take to be justifying purposes. What they do is wrong, worse than wrong. What would be done by conceivable terrorists with different related aims, perhaps having to do with cut-short but ordinary African lives, would be as wrong.

We may be given pause by the feeling that there is not so great a distance between our lives and the lives of *state-terrorists*, these being most of those who give orders of state and those who obey the orders to engage in violence that is not in accord with international law – or as it may be more realistic to say, international legal norms about which there can be dispute. Still, a little reflection or attention to detail can be salutary. Is there not a gulf between us and those in command of the Israeli soldiers who shoot to death a Palestinian child in the street, or crush to death an American peace activist under an armoured bulldozer? Is there not a gulf between us and the soldiers? That they are official murderers surely cannot close the gap?

But it will be as well not to complicate this inquiry by giving too much attention to state-terrorism, to official rather than unofficial killing. The question can be restricted to our belief that there is a gulf between our lives and the lives of such terrorists as those of September 11 – that what they do is wrong and what we do is more or less right.

This belief is indeed about conduct or actions, not about people. No doubt almost all of us are also confident that we are better persons, morally better, but what I have in mind is a contrast between actions as distinct from actors or agents. Actions are as related but different subject-matter. This is indicated by the simple truths that one can do the right thing for a bad or shameful reason, a reason that lowers or ruins one's standing as a person, perhaps marks one as inhumane. And one can also do the wrong action for a reason or from a feeling that does one credit.

Most of those who engage in unofficial terrorism or contemplate it do not agree with our view of their conduct and ours. This is likely to be true of all of them engaged in freedom-struggles or the like. If we look to what they say in disagreement, what we find may be bound up with an ideology entirely different from our own, or with some history of wrongs done to a people or a group of peoples or a class of people. From each of these things, however, it is possible to take away a general proposition that can be considered on its own, free of certain doubtful presuppositions, of obscurities, encumbering terminologies, and too much of the past. It is that we who are law-abiding, contrary to our common belief, do not live lives that are anything like right on the whole. *Our conduct is wrong.* Our conduct is wrong from some point of view like that of the Principle of Humanity.

The argument for this is that by our ordinary lives we contribute to certain terrible circumstances. We make essential contributions to the shortening of the lifetimes of whole peoples and classes, and to the kinds of distress, including degradation, denials of freedoms, and so on. In fact we *ensure* by our ordinary lives that multitudes of individuals die before time, that families exist in single rooms in awful camps, and that this or that people are powerless in their homeland, subservient in it, or driven from it.

Of course the judgement by actual and possible terrorists and their supporters and sympathisers that our conduct is wrong will be taken as in several ways mistaken, very likely as absurd. At best, it will be said, it is a *tu quoque*, a retort by the guilty that their accusers do wrong. As with *tu quoques* generally, it will get a scornful reply, to the effect that the guilty are trying to divert attention from their conduct, trying to change the subject, perhaps a subject that finally they themselves cannot face. This is too quick. There is a general question about such *tu quoque* retorts and such replies to them. If a *tu quoque* can be established as true, is it none the less to be ruled out of bounds? More particularly, if it can be shown that we all do wrong in our ordinary lives, can this be put aside? Can it be shown that nothing follows about the conduct of terrorists? It may be, rather, that certain things are somehow connected, in logic or in fact. I shall now take this to be true, and in the end say more about it.

There is the prior question, certainly, of whether it actually is true that we do wrong in our ordinary lives. Of course there are replies to this. A principal one of them, which is my subject in this essay, is that our ordinary conduct, even if it does contribute to terrible circumstances, consists in no more than *omission*. It is not as if we *acted* to shorten average lifetimes or to secure other terrible ends. That, of course, *would* be wrong. It may be argued in support of this that there is a certain difference of fact between every act and the related omission, a general difference of fact that issues in a difference of morality. In virtue of the general difference, an omission may be right or at any rate less wrong when a related act would be wrong or more wrong. It may be argued alternatively that there is a limited difference. Some omissions, including the ones in question, differ from the related acts in a factual way, with the given difference having similar moral effects, similar effects with respect to the rightness or wrongness of actions.

But (a) is there really a morally important difference of fact between *every* act and the related omission? And (b) is there a difference of fact between *some* acts and their related omissions, which difference gives rise to a difference in rightness? Rooted beliefs are in question here, but a smallish number of moral philosophers[1] has none the less been inclined to doubt or deny that there is a general difference that will do the required work. Some have also doubted or denied that there is any difference between even some acts and their omissions that makes for a difference in rightness in those cases.

My intentions in this essay are to deal with these two general issues about acts and omissions, and so to arrive at or at any rate come closer to a decision on the judgement of the terrorists and those who think like them that we in our ordinary lives do wrong. The two mentioned issues about acts and omissions are a subject that is wider than that of terrorism, one that has not often been discussed in relation to it and perhaps never at all in what can be called a non-ideological way. It does not begin to follow, of course, that the issues are not relevant to terrorism.

It is true that acts and omissions is a subject in itself. To anyone who feels a reluctance to consider one whole subject in the context of another, it may be worth remarking that in political philosophy as elsewhere one can keep one's nose too much to the grindstone. There is a kind of concentration that defeats its own end, or at any rate does not advance its own end, the end of getting a clear view of something or of fixing its true weight. Given our concern with terrorism and our own moral standing, we might spend time not only on the general question of acts and omissions, but also on war, and on punishment by the state, and on other things. Their relevance to political violence is of several kinds, and it is considerable. If it is true, as it seems to be, that most of the wars of the past ought not to have been fought, and if we were to come to have an understanding of their wrongfulness, we would be more able to judge political violence. So too with punishment by the state, whatever its recommendation or want of recommendation.

POSSIBLE ACTS AND ACTUAL OMISSIONS

The conceivable act of sending a savage militia into refugee camps to kill refugees is not one that it would cross our minds to perform. It did more than cross a general's mind, General Sharon of Israel, later Prime Minister, in the official judgement of an inquiry by his own countrymen, but that does not affect the general point about the rest of us. Nor does it cross our minds to go on a suicide-mission to kill Israelis at a bus-stop, or Americans in an airliner. However, how are these possible acts related to our omitting to give what money we could to such a charity as the Red Cross, or War on Want, or Medical Aid for Palestinians? The result of our omission, isn't it, is that some people lose their lives?

We would not knowingly vote for a political party that actually aimed to secure that the economically worst-off tenth of the population in European and other rich societies continues to have an average of about six years less time to live than the best-off tenth – whatever the political party had to say about the deserts of these people and their betters. How does the conceivable act of voting for such a heinous party stand to our omission in not really working to try to change these average lifetimes?

We would not contemplate infecting others with serious diseases, but we do not try to secure, as we could, that people have equal and more than minimal medical care. We do not try to secure that end for people in our own societies, let alone people generally. We would not remove library books from poor schools, whose pupils can have but the smallest hopes in life. Most of us would not try to increase our private profits by evicting families and hence making them homeless. But we do not work as we might for equal and good education, and we do not work for an end to homelessness. We would not contribute funds to a dictatorship of army generals, or to a minority engaged in denying autonomy to a majority. At any rate most of us would not. However, we do in fact fail to contribute funds to political movements against dictatorships, and to political movements against oppressive minorities.

Some may say that there are more 'realistic' ways of dealing with starvation than by contributing to the Red Cross or the like, and more realistic ways than those mentioned or implied of dealing with curtailed lives, ill health and disease, bad education, homelessness, and oppression. Suppose that there are better ways, perhaps joining this or that political party or forwarding some sort of economic policy, perhaps one of 'self-help'. This will not matter much to our inquiry. Just as we do not contribute what money we could to the Red Cross, we do not do these other things either, whatever is to be said of their worth. We omit these too, thereby as quickly raising the problem of omission.

COMPARISONS

In what ways are acts and omissions the same and different? Let us consider similarities and differences, differences that hold between all acts and their related omissions and also differences that hold between only some of them.

(1) An act is a bodily movement or stillness deriving from intention, or a sequence of movements or of movements and still- nesses. To say this is to move with some speed past a number of philosophical questions, one of them about the nature of the mentioned connection between intention and movement, the connection described by saying the second derives from the first. Still, it surely is no longer the case that the given definition of an act is controversial. Certainly the definition does not make an act into just a movement or stillness. Rather, an act is a movement or stillness with a certain mental ancestry.

What is an omission? One thing to notice is that the term 'omission' can be used in a number of ways. To mention two, it can be used for (a) the omitted action, or what was omitted or not done, and also (b) for the omitting action, or what was done instead. If I omit to turn off the radio at 12 noon, we can use the term 'omission' for what I did not do: turn off the radio at 12 noon. An omission in this sense might be described as an unrealised possibility, or indeed as a mere nothing. Perhaps this conception has had something to do with rather vague scepticism about omissions being morally important. How could a mere nothing be wrong?

Of course, this could not be the only conception we have of an omission. Not all omissions could be mere nothings. This is so, to mention but one reason, since we do often *witness* what we call omissions. These, obviously, are omissions in the second sense, exemplified in the example not by *my turning off the radio at noon* but rather by my *not turning off the radio at noon*. An omission in the second sense, which is the more important one, and the one with which we shall be concerned, is clearly not an unrealised possibility.

How did I not turn off the radio at noon? As it happened, I did not turn off the radio at noon by *staying my hand*, by performing that little action after having made a first move towards turning off the radio. In staying my hand, further, I did not turn off the radio. We can correctly say more than that it was by staying my hand and in staying my hand that I did not turn off the radio at noon. My staying my hand *was* or *was identical with* my not turning off the radio at noon. What we come to, then, is the idea that an omission, in the most important sense of the word, is an action, or, as we may add, a sequence of actions. My not going to Bath over the weekend was my staying in Frome.

We have not got a difference between all omissions in this sense and their related acts, obviously, but a sameness instead. Omissions, like acts, are bodily movements or stillnesses deriving from intention, or sequences of such movements and stillnesses. We might well refer to omissions and acts as negative and positive actions. I shall in fact stick to the familiar terms, 'act' and 'omission' – and use the term 'action', by the way, as against 'act', for either an act or an omission. We shall of course see more of what leads us to regard two actions as being an act and omission, as related in that way. One main thing is that there is the same or a similar or a connected upshot on the whole. Another is that when either the act or the omission is done, the other was possible.

There is of course a great difference between an act, taken as something actual, and an omission in the sense of the 'omitted action', since the latter is not something actual. It is important not to run omissions of the two kinds together. It is possible to do so, and to become a bit mystified, partly because an omission in either sense brings in an omission in the other. If there was an omitted action, there must have been the omitting action, and if there was an omitting action, there was what was not done. It is not necessary, but it will be simplest for us to proceed in terms of omissions in the sense of 'omitting actions'. These, to repeat our first proposition, are like acts in being certain bodily movements or stillnesses, or more likely sequences of these.

(2) Are all omissions simply actions described in a negative way, actions with descriptions that include a 'not' or something like one, while the related acts are described affirmatively? The trouble with this simple idea is that we do not actually get a division into acts and omissions, since each and every action falls under both affirmative and negative descriptions. My not turning off the radio was also my staying of my hand. Another idea is this one: an omission is an action or a sequence of actions that falls under a negative description *for the agent*, while the related possible act would fall under an affirmative description for the agent. That is, the agent describes the omission negatively and would describe the act affirmatively, whatever other people do or would do. This is so because his intention was what it was. We can imagine a doctor, for example, who carries on in a certain way, which does not include giving penicillin to a badly deformed infant to save it from pneumonia, and describes his action as 'not trying to keep the infant alive'. He would describe a related action, perhaps the giving of a lethal injection, as 'killing the infant'.

This common idea is no better at giving us a general distinction between acts and omissions. It does not give us a difference between every act and the related omission. Consider another doctor who also carries on in such a way that a person dies. He too does not give penicillin for pneumonia. However, he describes his behaviour as 'letting the person die', or 'freeing an incurable patient from suffering', or even 'doing what seems to be my duty of compassion'. One of these affirmative descriptions is chosen by him. He may even refuse, for whatever reason, to describe his behaviour as 'not trying to keep the person alive', and also refuse to use any other negative description. This is certainly possible, however unlikely. The plain fact is that this would not stop us from regarding his action, when compared with giving a lethal injection, as an omission. We here have an omission and a related act such that the omission is not negatively described by the agent.

If we return to the six examples given above, we find the same thing. If we compare sending militia to kill refugees and omitting to contribute to the Red Cross or Medical Aid for Palestinians, we shall take the first to be an act and the second an omission, even if the agent prefers to describe the second act affirmatively, as 'buying wine' or 'saving money' or 'looking after my own children'. This is not to say anything of the rightness or wrongness of the actions, of course. In each of the other five examples, the same is true. No matter the description of the agent, the second act of the pair counts as the omission, for reasons to which we will come.

Still, there is something else to be said here. We all have a tendency to describe the acts affirmatively and the omissions negatively. This is the natural thing for both the agents and others, evident enough in what has been said so far in this essay. For what it is worth, then, we here have a difference of fact, our first one, but one between most rather than all acts and omissions.

What is the explanation of this fact that in the case of most acts and omissions, the omissions are described negatively and the acts affirmatively, by both the agent and others? The question is of interest to us for several reasons. It may be suspected that there is some *general* difference of fact concerning acts and omissions that is a part of the explanation of the linguistic tendency, which general difference of fact may give rise to a difference in rightness. (The idea would be that the general difference of fact, for some reason, does not always give rise to negative description of the omission and affirmative description of the act, but it does always affect rightness.) Again, it may be suspected there is a *limited* difference of fact, concerning some acts and omissions, which difference wholly explains our linguistic tendency and gives rise to a difference in rightness in the case of the given acts and omissions.

There is of course an explanation of our linguistic tendency, but, as may be anticipated, it has to do with us rather than with acts and omissions in themselves. That is, it does not have to do with any fundamental properties of some actions but not others, which properties are such as to call out for the word 'not' in their description.

Notice first that it does seem to make sense to say that there are differences between things as affirmatively described and things as negatively described. An affirmative description is such that a thing so described *has a property* and a negative description is such that a thing so described *lacks a property*. An affirmative description, secondly, brings in a single property such as redness, while a negative description brings in a collection of properties, those which are other than redness. Whatever may be thought of these claims, which are a part of the traditional philosophical problem of negation, they do not get us the conclusion that it is a difference in fundamental properties of acts and omissions that explains our tendency to describe acts affirmatively and omissions negatively.

This is so, to repeat an essential point, because any action that falls under an affirmative description also falls under a negative description. In every case there are true affirmative and negative descriptions whether or not we are inclined to use one sort more than the other. Of every action without exception, then, we can say that it has properties of a kind associated with both affirmative and negative description. The explanation of our linguistic tendency does not have to do with there being two separate lots of things, one with one sort of fundamental property only, and the other with the other. All of the things have both sorts.

The true explanation of our linguistic tendency must be otherwise. Let us speculate about what may be part of it. This has to do with an established habit that we carry over from a significantly different kind of situation, but one in which we also talk of what we call omissions. It would in any case have been a good idea to distinguish and set aside this kind of situation and usage. Not to do so would have left open a door to confusion.

In this situation there is no pairing of actions of the kind we have been noticing. To begin with, we speak of an omission but there is no related act: no act with an identical or similar or connected upshot on the whole. On the contrary, there is an opposite upshot. In this kind of situation, secondly, it is more or less generally accepted that the agent had a particular duty to do what he did not do. There is a generally accepted rule, perhaps a law in the ordinary sense. Obviously this is different from the sort of situation and talk that is our main subject-matter. The duty and the rule or law, thirdly, pertain to an individual's special position or role. For this reason, by the way, we can call the omissions in question role-omissions.

Consider a judge, who has a duty to give a certain instruction to a jury, at a fixed point in a trial, so that they will not be prejudiced against the defendant in a certain way. This is specified by law. Suppose the judge says nothing at the given point. We call this an omission, certainly. However, we do not have in mind a certain conceivable act with an identical, similar or connected upshot on the whole. If we did, it would be more or less this: the act of instructing the jury to have or to act on a certain prejudice against the defendant. (We in fact have in mind the action of so instructing the jury as to try to *prevent* prejudice.) We think the judge's omission is wrong not because we have compared it with the conceivable act but because the judge went against his duty, fixed by law, in his act of omission.

It is our established habit to describe an omission of this sort, a role-omission, in a negative way. This is so, presumably, because there is a settled rule that specifies that a person is to do precisely such-and-such. His error, according to the rule, is most precisely or carefully described as not doing such-and-such, and some care and precision are natural in important and more or less formal circumstances. More might be said. Whatever the reason, however, there is the fact of our established habit with role-omissions. To come to the main point, it is fairly certain that it is part of the explanation of our tendency to use negative descriptions for the other omissions, those with acts related to them in the way we know. 'Not's are standard in connection with role-omissions, and so come to be used with the other sort of omissions.

(3) Is the causal connection between an omission and the result different from the connection that would hold between the conceivable act and the result? It is sometimes supposed that it is very different indeed, and significantly so. It has been said that the result, perhaps a harm, would be the result of one's movements in the case of an act, but, in the case of the omission, it is the result of conditions that one omitted to change. These words are not terribly clear, but they manage to suggest that the act would be more efficacious than the omission with respect to the result. An act would somehow be more of a cause than the omission. There is the same suggestion in the related statement that the great difference between an act of mine and an omission of mine is that the result of the omission would have occurred even if I had never been born, but that is not true of the act. The same children who are now deprived of good and equal education would also be deprived of it if I had never existed. On the other hand, the result of my conceivable act of removing library books from poor schools would of course depend on my existence.

Certainly there is a truth in this last point, of whatever significance. One way in which it can fail to happen that I do something is by way of my not existing at all. It is plainly false, however, that my failing to do something, a particular action, is in any way less efficacious with respect to a result than would be my doing something, another action. The omission is precisely as much of a cause as the act would be. Staying my hand at noon, my not working for good and equal education, each does obviously make a difference.

It will be as well, however, to have some details of the causal nature of acts and omissions.

An act in almost every instance would be a necessary condition, in the situation, of a result. That is, the result would not happen in the situation without the act. Also, the act would be part of a causal circumstance, a set of things sufficient to produce the result. That is, it would be part of something that necessitates the result, which would not obtain without being followed by the result. Indeed, the act would complete the causal circumstance: the other things would already be on hand. Sending militia into the refugee camps would be a necessary condition, in a certain situation, of certain deaths: the deaths would not happen without the sending. The act would be a part of a causal circumstance that was sufficient for the deaths. It would complete it.

We can say near-enough the same things of an omission of mine, say the action by which I got rid of £500. Suppose I bought a chaise-longue. It would be mistaken or misleading to suppose that doing exactly that was a necessary condition of the death of a starving person. Still we can suppose that a necessary condition of the death was that in one way or another I omitted to contribute £500 to the Red Cross. By my action I did supply the necessary condition. That fact is not put in question by the fact that I might have supplied it another way. Furthermore, my omission was part of a causal circumstance sufficient for the death. It completed that circumstance. Given all this, it is certainly mistaken to think that the act of sending militia into the camps would be more efficacious, more of a cause, than the omission. Similar comments, although not exactly the same ones, are in place with our other five examples of act and omission.

It is clear enough that very often the causal circumstance in connection with omission and result is in another way different from the circumstance in connection with act and result. In the case of the omission, the rest of the causal circumstance for the result is likely to include the omissions of other people, perhaps many other people. Consider the result that is the particular loss which may be said to result from my failing to work for equal and more than minimal medical care. The omissions of many other people are also parts of the causal circumstance for that result. If we turn to the conceivable act, my intentionally infecting people, there is at least the possibility that my act would be the only action in the causal circumstance for the result. Related remarks apply to all but the second of our six examples, the one having to do with voting for the appalling political party.

It would also be misleading to describe this difference in connections by saying the omissions usually are lesser causes than the related acts would be. They have much the same causal features, those enumerated a moment ago. There is only the difference here that it is usually true that actions of others, perhaps many others, enter into the causal circumstance for the result in the case of omissions, and this would not be so in the case of the related acts. There is the related small fact that it is generally true that if I act, intending to cause a harm, there is a small possibility for others to prevent the harm, but if I omit to act, thereby not myself preventing the harm, there is a larger possibility. I leave more scope for good works and self-improvement by others if I omit to act. There is not much to be made of this, of course, unless one brings in certain religious ideas which are now of the past, and which surely were never sufficient to their tasks.

There may also be other differences having to do with causation between acts and omissions. Often but not always the causal chain or causal sequence in the case of acts would be shorter or 'simpler' than in the case of omissions. Clearly enough a causal circumstance is not less efficacious simply because its linkage to the upshot is of either of these kinds. It is true that certain other features sometimes go with shorter as against longer, and 'simpler' as against 'more complex', causal chains, and we shall notice these features in due course.

(4) If we consider omissions from the point of view of the intentions of the agents, we can make a very rough division into three categories. It has to do, in part, with the fact that any action, as an omission, has what we can call a certain nature or character and a certain effect. One of my omissions is 'not contributing money to political movements against dictatorships by army generals'. That description gives the nature of the omission. The effect is that the given political movements are to a degree weaker. It is the agent's relation to the character or the effect of his action that determines, as we can say, whether his omission was fully intentional, partly intentional, or unintentional.

Fully intentional omissions are taken to occur in medical contexts. Consider the doctor who continues his ward-round during a certain time. To do this is to perform a certain omission, failing to give penicillin to a patient for pneumonia. This has as its effect the death of the patient. If the character of his actions or their effect, as we can say, was the intention of the doctor, then the omission was fully intentional. To put it differently, if the actions derived from an intention which the doctor would characterise to himself as the intention not to give penicillin to the patient for pneumonia, or the intention to bring about the death of the patient, then his actions were a fully intentional omission.

It is worth noting that the intentions that issue in fully intentional omissions are in all respects like the intentions that issue in fully intentional acts. Some are impressive, as we might say, since they involve internal resolutions or declarations to do such-and-such, and some are not. Some are such as to take up or occupy the whole attention of their agents, and some are not. Some are formed under higher-order intentions and some are not. Some are, so to speak, something like the whole story of what the agent is thinking and feeling, and some, no doubt most, are not.

Partly intentional omissions are connected with *earlier* actions and their intentions. The earlier intentions are more important than the *immediate* intentions of the omissions, those that just precede or accompany the omissions. Out of bloody-mindedness, I do not write down a note of an unpromising engagement when asked. I have it in mind that I may forget. There is the result, given my general forgetfulness, that I do forget and do not turn up. My not turning up is one example of a partly intentional omission. Here is another. I look away from the War on Want advertisement in my newspaper, including the photo of the starving child, my intention being not to be troubled or got at by it, and indeed not to have to face a moral challenge and to give money. There is the result of this action and a multitude of related ones, that I later buy wine without thinking that doing so is in fact not contributing to War on Want. A partly intentional omission, then, does not in fact derive from an immediate intention which specifies its character or effect, for the reason, roughly speaking, that the agent has so acted earlier that it will not. A partly intentional omission does derive in part from an earlier intention which does have in it something of the character or effect of the later action. The earlier intention has something of the later omission in it. Needless to say, the characterisation is very vague. Needless to say, as well, there are many sorts and varieties of what have been labelled partly intentional actions. In fact, my main argument has not much need of greater detail, but I shall say a bit more later in other connections.

Unintentional omissions, finally, are those whose characters and effects are not intended by the agent, and it is not the case either that this is so because of earlier activity of his. He did not so act or plan or contrive at an earlier time to have the omission out of mind when he performed it. If the idea of an unintentional omission comes to anyone as a surprise, this may partly be because of the fact that there is a tendency to think of all 'omissions' as blameable. There is also the fact that role-omissions, as they were earlier called, are very unlikely to be unintentional and are pretty well always blameable. As we are conceiving omissions, and as they will be defined in due course, it is possible that they be unintentional. Nothing much hangs on this decision, however.

This three-part division of intentions certainly does not apply to the acts that we compare with omissions. This is a considerable difference between act and omission. This may also come as a surprise, and indeed the surprise derives from a truth. If one takes any of the acts in our examples, say removing library books from poor schools, it is possible at least to imagine a related partly intentional action, and a related unintentional action. That is one fact. Another, however, is that our comparisons of act and omission invariably involve only fully intentional acts. That is our practice, how we go on. One difference between acts and omissions as we have them, then, is that the conceivable acts are fully intentional ones, and the omissions *may* be fully intentional, partly intentional or unintentional.

I trust there will be no suspicion that this distinction between acts and omissions is somehow arbitrary, or that it will have the effect of begging some question. It is a distinction between acts and omissions as we have them, between the actions that we relate as act and omission. In fact, as will become apparent, my conclusions do not depend greatly on the fact that all acts, unlike most of their related omissions, are fully intentional. More precisely, it is not greatly important to my conclusions that there are possible actions that in fact we do not consider but which stand to acts as partly intentional and unintentional omissions stand to fully intentional omissions.

(5) There is a related way in which some acts and omissions differ, having to do with the natures of their intentions. The intentions that would issue in the conceivable acts in the six examples are horrific, inhuman, vicious, grasping or uncaring in the extreme. Let us give a moment or two to details of this intentionality. The agent, in the case of any of the conceivable acts, would be aware that there were victims of his act, persons at least badly affected by it. He would be aware that victims existed. In the case of some of the conceivable acts, the

agent's awareness would derive from the fact that he would have to bring himself into the neighbourhood of the person or persons affected by his act. In the case of other acts the agent would necessarily have a lively awareness of the existence of victims without actually coming into their neighbourhood. This is true of sending the militia and, in different ways, of voting for the appalling party, evicting people for greater profits and contributing funds to a dictatorship.

It is worth noticing separately that in the conceivable acts the victims would be *individuated* by the agent. One way in which a victim is individuated, we can say, is by the agent knowing such individual features of the victim that the victim, for the agent, *is a person*. We might spend time making this notion more precise but it is not necessary. We can also allow another way of individuation, whereby groups of victims are known to the agent by shared features, perhaps connected with membership of a social class, which again makes them *persons* for the agent. As will be plain enough, individuation is something over and above just the awareness that victims do exist. There would be individuation in the case of all our six conceivable acts.

Let us compare this with the natures of the intentions in the case of the omissions or, more precisely, in the three cases of omissions. We must obviously distinguish between unintentional, partly intentional and fully intentional omissions.

Unintentional omissions, as we know, are actions such that neither the agent's immediate nor his earlier intentions involved the character or effect of his action taken as an omission. His intentions, then, are in no way suggested by this action taken as an omission. His immediate intention will have to do with his action taken as something other than the omission, perhaps buying a car or putting his money into a building society. It may be an intention of an ordinary or of course a good kind. In unintentional omission, there is no awareness of the existence of victims, no individuation of them.

To pass on to the nature of fully intentional omissions, there is unlikely to be an instance of any of the omissions in our six examples being performed in a fully intentional way. This is so, at least, if we take certain more precise versions of the examples. It is unlikely to happen that because of some extraordinary situation, a man fully believes that his omitting to contribute a certain sum to the Red Cross on a particular day will result in the deaths of several people known to him, and he does do something or other rather than contribute, and he does this in the desire that the people die. That is, he has the intention of their deaths in the way that the related intention is had by the general who sends the militia into the refugee camp. The omitter may not have it in mind to support his family or to do any such thing by his action. Such an omission would in fact derive from an intention about as horrific as the intention in the case of the related act. There would also be a similarity of intention in our other five examples. That is, the intention in the omission if it were fully intentional would be bad, and about as bad as the intention in the conceivable act.

There is a traditional problem about the nature of the intentions in partly intentional omissions, and the goodness or badness or whatever else of the agents. What has been said here so far, not very usefully, is that the omissions derive in part from earlier intentions, which intentions have in them something of the character or effect of the omissions, in our examples a black character and effect.

We rightly feel that there is more, perhaps a good deal more, to be said against the man whose failure to contribute to the Red Cross is partly intentional, as against the man whose failure is unintentional. There is, it seems, a very great deal less to be said against the man whose failure is partly intentional, as against the man whose failure is fully intentional. Still, how exactly are we to judge partly intentional omission? Reflection on the question leads in several directions. It does seem settled that there is a great difference between the earlier intentions and activity in the case of partly intentional omission, and the intentions in either the related fully intentional omissions or of course the related acts. There is nothing less than a gap between not reading a newspaper account of a famine, albeit out of a certain selfish impulse to avoid the matter, and sending militia to kill refugees or performing a certain conceivable omission with full intention. One can say that almost all partly intentional omissions reflect better or less badly on the agents than the related fully intentional omissions or the acts. This is partly a matter of the degree of awareness in the earlier intention of the existence of victims of the possible future omission. There is also a point to be made about individuation.

We shall later spend some more time on the subject of partly intentional omissions. For now, we have the comparison that in many cases of act and omission, the conceivable act would derive from a horrible, appalling or at least bad intention, while the omission, if it is partly intentional, derives from intentions that do not throw so bad a light on the agent. The comparisons with the fully intentional and the unintentional omissions are of less interest.

It is to be remembered, by the way, that not all cases of act and omission are like the six with which we began, where the intention in the act is as bad as in fully intentional omission, worse than in partly intentional and unintentional omission. Consider the three possible versions of an omission of a kind mentioned above, a doctor's not giving penicillin to an old, dying, suffering, and incurable person. It may be that neither the omission, if fully intentional, nor the related act of killing, comes from anything like a bad intention. Partly intentional omission would here be worse and indeed unthinkable, and unintentional omission worse and no doubt culpable. There are also other conceivable cases of act and omission that are different from our six.

(6) Let us turn from intentions and agents to customary morality, to ordinary judgements about the rightness or wrongness of actions. In the case not of all but of many acts, including all those in our six examples, there is a general acceptance that the act would be wrong, or worse than just wrong. There would also be a general acceptance that the related fully intentional omissions would be wrong. The same thing, whatever we are to make of the fact, is not true of the related partly intentional omissions.

The acts and the fully intentional omissions would be taken to offend against one or more rules, principles or laws. The act of contributing to a military dictatorship would offend against fairly ordinary sorts of political principles, and no doubt against international declarations of human rights. So with the related fully intentional omission. The same and more is to be said of the conceivable act of voting for the appalling political party with the intention of keeping the lives of some people shorter. So with the related fully intentional omission. Removing library books from poor schools, and evicting families for private profit, and the related omissions, would offend at least against standards of ordinary decency or humanity. Infecting people would go against both ordinary morality and law, as with the related omission. The act of sending the militia into the refugee camps would outrage anything recognisable as a decent morality, of course including decent Jewish morality, and also be against ordinary law. So with the related fully intentional omission.

Whatever view we ourselves in this inquiry come to have of the rightness or wrongness of the related partly intentional omissions, then, they are not now accepted as wrong. It is not as if they go against ordinary political principles, or standards of ordinary decency, or ordinary morality, or ordinary law. What I have in mind is a matter of the non-existence of certain conceivable attitudes, practices, and institutions, just as it is a matter of fact that the related actions and fully intentional omissions are accepted as somehow prohibited. Far from being prohibited, many of the omissions may well be accepted as required or obligatory. If I were to increase my contribution to a charity to the point where my children lived poorly, in comparison with certain other children in my society, I would run afoul of an established outlook. That outlook requires that I fulfil certain ordinary obligations that I have, and act on certain loyalties, and, in order to do such things, that I omit various other things.

There remain the unintentional versions of our six omissions. Ordinary morality obviously does not take them to be wrong. They are hardly distinguished from the partly intentional omissions.

DIFFERENT COMPARISONS

The following comparisons between act and omission, as we shall see, have another importance.

(7) Acts and omissions give rise to what we have so far called results or effects, and might more precisely call main effects. These are usually the events or states mentioned or implied in the description of the action. In the six examples, they are the deaths of some people, shorter average lifetimes of some people, the states of health of certain people, poor education of certain children, homelessness of some families, and political oppression.

In general the main effects in question with acts and omissions are harms and benefits. Harms so-called are to be taken as including awfulnesses and catastrophes. The problem we are considering arises mainly from the fact that some harms arise from omissions, and so raise a question about whether the omissions are as wrong as certain terrible acts that would have similar or identical, similar or connected effects. There is also the problem, not illustrated by our six examples, that some benefits are as much the issue of terrible acts as they are of omissions, and so raise the question of whether the acts are right. The cases of killing or letting-die are central here.

Not much needs to be said of the nature of harms and benefits. It can be assumed that there is some fairly wide agreement about what states of affairs are to be avoided or prevented, if we can, and what states of affairs are to be secured, if we can. Such an agreement was assumed, of course, in my listing a moment ago of the harms involved in the six examples. There has been thought to be a considerable problem, certainly, of what general and systematic summary can be given of such events or states. The answer that I favour is that benefits are states or events for which there is something to be said if one is committed to the well-being of everyone without exception, and to something of a related kind for other sentient things. Harms are characterised in terms of conflict with the same ideal. My answer, that is, is in terms of the Principle of Humanity. However, we can agree for the most part on what things are harms and what things are benefits without agreeing on the general systematic summary.

The principal point to be made about main effects has already been in view. It is that the main effect of an act may or may not be the very same as the main effect of the related omission. A comparison as to effects may produce a sameness or a difference between an act and the related omission. It is more likely that there will be a difference. This remains so even when the effect of the act can be described in the same words as the effect of the omission. Generally, of course, there is some similarity between the two main effects, which similarity leads to the two actions being brought together as act and omission. Occasionally, there is connection in main effect, not identity or similarity, as in a situation where a man's act will be the killing of one man and his omission will for some reason result in someone else's killing of twenty.

Main effects, to repeat, are states or events mentioned or implied in the descriptions of actions. They are not to be taken as including effects on agents themselves unless this is specified. Nor do main effects include what may be called side-effects. We shall notice both these things separately.

(8) Some acts make it more or less certain that main effects, whether harms or benefits, will occur. So with some omissions. For the most part, however, there is less than certainty. There is only probability, something in between zero and one. The principal fact to be noted, however, is that it may or may not be true that the probability of a main effect, given an act, is the same as the probability of a main effect, given the related omission. Usually the probability of the two possible effects is not the same. If the probability of an effect given an action is sometimes close enough to be indistinguishable from the probability of a similar or identical effect given the

omission, the ordinary case is otherwise. A moment's attention to the examples indicates this. Again, it is a simple but important fact.

(9) Connected with things already noticed, but distinct from them, are what we can call experiential effects on the agent. An act or an omission is within the experience of the agent, and hence has effects on him at the time and thereafter. These are likely to be different as between act and omission. The different emotional concomitants of killing as against letting-die may come to mind. One relevant fact in connection with the difference in experiential effects has to do with responses already mentioned having to do with attack and the like. However rational it may be, we have a *livelier* experience of attacking than of not-saving. A larger relevant fact is that our customary moralities, as we know, include prohibitions of many acts, and so give rise to accusation and self-accusation. What we feel when we remember our partly intentional omissions is different from what we would feel if we were to remember that we had performed the related acts. The difference in experiential effects, of course, will be different in the case of fully intentional as against partly intentional omissions, and so on.

(10) In addition to main effects, and experiential effects on agents, there are side-effects. These may be effects on victims, other than main effects, or they may be effects on third parties. Any of our examples can be used to illustrate the fact that the side-effects of an omission are likely to be different from the side-effects of a possible act. There are, for example, the side-effects on others in my life if I increase very greatly my contribution to the Red Cross. These would be different, certainly, from side-effects of the conceivable act. In the second example there would be the side-effects on the economically worst-off tenths of there being a political party with the aim of keeping their average lifetimes shorter. There are possible economic side-effects to be taken into account with respect to our ordinary activities in omitting to work for a change in average lifetimes. So with our omissions and conceivable acts in connection with health, education, homelessness, and political oppression.

The side-effects of a possible act, then, may be roughly the same as, but are likely to be different from, the side-effects of the omission. It is to be added, as in the case of main effects and experiential effects, that we are likely to have a situation of probabilities, and of course different probabilities.

(11) An agent who did act, rather than omit partly intentionally or unintentionally, would almost certainly put himself in a position

different from the positions of others, partly in terms of experiential effects, partly in other ways. The others in question may be members of large classes, such as the class of adult and responsible members of a society, or smaller and better-defined classes, such as that of doctors. Omission of the unintentional and partly intentional kinds is the normal thing. The agent who acts thereby makes himself different, in particular in so far as experiential effects are concerned. He may, for example, take upon himself an unequal amount of guilt, however rational or irrational, if guilt is ever rational. The situation is quite different, incidentally, with role-omissions. There, not acting is abnormal and unexpected, rather than acting, and it is omitters rather than doers who stand out. Our eleventh comparison, then, comes to this: those who act, as against those who omit, almost certainly make themselves different or unequal in some class or classes of persons. The examples illustrate this.

SUMMARY OF COMPARISONS
(1)   Act and omission both actions.
(2)   Omission likely to be described negatively, act affirmatively.
(3)   Omission as causally efficacious as act, although other persons likely to contribute to main effect of omission.
(4)   Act fully intentional; omission any of fully intentional, partly intentional or unintentional.
(5)   Intentions in many acts appalling; intentions in related partly intentional omissions tolerable.
(6)   Most acts and fully intentional omissions customarily accepted as somehow wrong; not so the related partly intentional and unintentional omissions.

---

(7)   Main effects of act and omission likely different.
(8)   Probabilities of main effects likely different.
(9)   Experiential effects likely different, and of different probabilities.
(10)   Side-effects likely different, and of different probabilities.
(11)   Agent's situation likely unequal to that of others after act as against omission.

WHAT MAKES FOR RIGHTNESS

We can now characterise an act and an omission of the kind with which we are concerned as (a) a pair of possible actions (b) taken as identical or similar in main effect, or at any rate connected, and such that (c) the act is fully intentional while the omission can be fully intentional, partly intentional, or unintentional, and (d) the intentions in the two actions may be greatly different in nature. We might add something which has been assumed and which will be of a bit of importance later, that (e) the omission (which we are taking to be the omitting action, or what was done) must not involve less expenditure of energy or whatever than the omitted action, what was not done, would have. The omitting action of reading the newspaper at breakfast cannot count as the writing of a whole book.

Our first issue is whether *every* act and omission are factually different in a single way that makes for rightness. It seems that we can now settle that issue fairly quickly. Our inquiry, a pretty exhaustive one, has turned up *no* single difference of fact which holds between every act and omission without exception. The truth seems to be that when people consider two actions with related main effects, and distinguish them as act and omission, they sometimes do so on the basis of some criteria and sometimes on the basis of other criteria. There is no single general criterion. This is not all that unusual in conceptual and indeed practical life. We might describe the situation differently and with the appearance of greater neatness, of course. That is, we might choose to specify several different senses or sorts of act-and-omission, each tied to certain criteria only. There is not much to be gained by doing so.

Our inquiry has of course produced important differences holding between some or many acts and their related omissions, but, before proceeding to them, can we conclude more generally that there is no general difference of fact that gives rise to a general difference in rightness? Can we conclude that we have not missed anything?

The first of three things to be said about this is that no supporter of the idea that there is some general factual difference, one of moral relevance, has ever made clear what that difference is. This is telling. We are not examining a matter that is essentially obscure. What we are examining, once we have got rid of such light ideas as that we are dealing with an act on the one hand and a puzzling nothing on the other, or anyway an act and something greatly more indeterminate, what we are examining is two plainish things: two actions or action-sequences. Certainly they may raise great problems having to do with their main effects, experiential effects, side-effects and equality-effects, and they may be baffling or mysterious in these respects. Still, we know what sort of thing is in question in these respects. If there is another sort of thing on hand, why is it not produced? As David Hume may have remarked of philosophical circumstances like this one, a challenge unmet may come close enough to a proof.

A second consideration is one that should not escape the attention of anyone who thinks of a decently wide range of examples of act and omission. We are looking for a general difference between acts and omissions that supports a difference in rightness. One can look for such a thing with more hope if one supposes, very forgetfully, that there is at least *moral uniformity*, as we can call it, about acts and omissions: for example, at least a presumption of some kind that all omissions are better, somehow, than their acts. This is a non-starter. It sometimes seems to be half-forgotten that there are more cases of act and omission than just problematic ones.

The fact of the matter is that some conceivable acts are unquestionably better than some omissions. Whatever one's reluctance, it would unquestionably be better to act, where the act is the killing of one man oneself, if it really were true that the only alternative, one's not shooting, would have the *certain* effect that someone else will shoot twenty men. This is so in terms of the Principle of Humanity, but certainly not only that morality. It follows that while we are looking for a general difference between acts and omissions, it is not one that is always morally conclusive, in the way of making omissions better. We are looking for a general difference that is of an uncertain moral effect. Such a thing is conceivable, but not much more.

There is one final consideration which I shall postpone for a bit, until after we have considered the non-general differences between acts and omissions. With the aid of that final consideration we shall conclude that there is in fact no entirely general difference between acts and omissions that gives rise to a difference in rightness.

Let us now consider the limited factual differences between acts and omissions that we came upon in our inquiry. Some of these give rise to differences in rightness, but which are they?

The first limited difference (2) was that there is a tendency for omissions to be described negatively and acts to be described affirmatively. It is unthinkable that this linguistic difference in itself is such as to make an action right or wrong, or more right or more wrong. The presence of a 'not' or something like it in a description cannot itself be of moral relevance. One may feel that the linguistic fact is somehow relevant to the matter in hand. This comes about, presumably, not only because of its connection with role-omissions, but because it is connected with non-linguistic facts, to which we shall come, which are of relevance to rightness.

The next limited difference we came upon (3) was basically that while each of an omission and an act is a necessary condition of its respective effect, it is usually the case that the omissions of other people are also necessary conditions of the omission's effect. Not only I but also others must fail to contribute to the Red Cross in order for some persons to die. It cannot be, however, that my action can be made right, let us say, by the existence of others like it. There might be excuse for me in the fact of numbers, but it can hardly be that what I do, my action, is made right or better by it. By way of analogy, torturing would not be better if there were more torturers. Nor, by the way, does there seem any force in another mentioned aspect of connections between the actions and their results. If an action of mine could have prevented great distress, and did not, it cannot be that its status is improved by the fact that the distress would have occurred had I not existed.

What of (4) the fact that the acts would be fully intentional and the omissions may be fully intentional, partly intentional or unintentional? Let us have in mind the particular comparison between acts and partly intentional omissions. These omissions are plainly of most relevance to us.

There are those who think, confusedly to my mind, that an act's being fully intentional and an omission's being partly intentional is of importance to the rightness or wrongness of the act and the omission. The kind or degree of intentionality makes the omission not wrong, or less wrong. There is a long tradition of commitment to such views and related ones, its greatest figure being Immanuel Kant. No doubt the tradition has things of value in it, but its central ideas are certainly not ours. That much can be shown, I think, simply by making some distinctions.

Our concern in all of this inquiry, as remarked at the start, is the rightness and wrongness of actions. Our concern, at any rate fundamentally, is with kinds of conduct, not kinds of people. What is it for an action to be right? According to a very widely-shared moral view, it is for it to be the action, of those that are possible, that can rationally be expected to give rise to the best state of affairs. Again, it is the action that would be selected by someone of judgement and knowledge as likely to give rise to the best state of affairs. More might be said of such a man, but there is no possibility of giving a determinate account of his state of knowledge or his capability of judgement. The idea, roughly, is that his capability of judgement is the best available, and his knowledge is as great as is humanly available at the time. In certain cases little knowledge will be available and the best judgement must be tentative or even hazardous.

As for the matter of good states of affairs, they can be as well or better described as states of experience, states involving amounts and distributions of experience. They do not have to do with any 'values' which are not such facts of experience, the experience of the agent and also others affected at the time and thereafter by his action. It may be wondered what 'values' are left out. If there is a fact about an action that in itself is not any fact of distress or satisfaction, such a fact is not in itself of relevance to the rightness of actions. The bare facts, taken as without effects in experience, that an action is according to a rule, or that it is thought of in a certain way by the agent, or of course preserves the agent's integrity,[2] are not of relevance.

As you will know, my conception of good states of affairs is the one that enters into the Principle of Humanity. Good states of affairs are the ones we all desire fundamentally. They have to do with a decent length of life, material goods that have a certain necessity, freedom and power, and so on. You do not have to sign up as a supporter of the Principle of Humanity, however, to go forward with the argument. You can agree with its conclusions on the basis of a somewhat different morality.

What we have, to return to the main point, is that an action's rightness or wrongness is independent of the kind or degree of intentionality from which it issued. That an action was partly intentional, or fully intentional, or indeed unintentional, does not matter. It makes no difference to its rightness or wrongness. It is not that an omission as compared with an act is right or less wrong because the omission is partly intentional while the act would be fully intentional. There is a bit more to be said, however, and it will be best to proceed by considering at the same time our next limited difference.

It was (5) that the intentions in many conceivable acts would be appalling, while those in the related partly intentional omissions are something like tolerable. The intentions in the case of the conceivable acts in our examples would be horrific, inhuman, vicious, grasping, or something of the sort. The intentions in the case of the related partly intentional omissions are not of these kinds. On the contrary, the *immediate* intentions may be good ones, such as the intention to safeguard the future of one's own children. The *earlier* intentions, whatever else is to be said of them, are greatly different in nature from the intentions in the case of the conceivable acts. They involve a lesser grasp of the effects of the relevant omissions.

According to a widely shared and fundamental moral conviction, none of this matters either to the question of rightness. As remarked at the start, an action can be right, one action that ought to have been done, although it was done from the wrong motive, and an action can be wrong, something that ought not to have been done, although it was done out of a good intention.

Consider a member of the House of Commons who voted for the establishment of the National Health Service. We suppose that he did the right thing, that his action was right, even if he was in fact opposed to the idea on principle and voted for the Health Service only out of a completely self-serving intention to gain re-election. Or rather, as needs to be allowed, there are two propositions that can be expressed by saying that he did the right thing. The main one amounts to the proposition that his action was right, understood on the lines already suggested. It is true. The other is to the effect that he was true to his principles, and so on. It is false. If we are in fact concerned with his action's being right, however we may express this, his self-serving intention and his going against his principles is irrelevant.

It would be mistaken, of course, to suggest that the subject of agents and intentions is unimportant. On the contrary, if it is of secondary importance, it is nonetheless of great importance. It is of great importance to us since we want to have such people as will do the right thing. We are with every reason interested in the goodness or badness of people, as indicated by kind and nature of intentionality, since we are concerned with their future actions. The goodness, humanity, and so on of a person is our best guide to his future conduct.

This, however, should not be confused with the idea that what makes an action right is even partly its actual intentionality, the kind and nature of intentionality actually involved. The fact that we have a great concern with how intentional a man's action was and what his intention was, because of our concern about future actions, should not be confused with the mistake that what makes an action right is the intentionality behind it. That question, the rightness of the action, is not touched by the agent's intentions having been what they were, although the action will no doubt indicate at least something about his intentions, and his intentions will tell us something about his likely future behaviour. It is irrelevant to the question of the rightness of the MP's action in voting for the National Health Service that his action, taken with a knowledge of his principles, tells us something of his actual intentions, and that those tell us something of his likely future activity.

It may be wondered for a moment if I am really describing *the action that turned out best*, and misappropriating the term 'right action' for it, while the right action is in fact the action done from a good intention and so on. Some will say that the correct description of the situation is that the MP did the wrong thing, or acted wrongly, and, as it happened, this turned out well. There is nothing unusual in that, they will say.

I am not in fact confusing the right action with what turned out best. The right action, to repeat, is the one which at the time would rationally have been judged as the one giving rise to the best state of affairs. It is obvious, then, that the right action is not necessarily the action that turns out best in fact, even in the short run. Nor is there any reason to think that our common notion of the right action can somehow be reduced to that. Even knowledgeable judges make mistakes.

What has been said in definition of right actions does bring into view another indubitable connection between the conception of a right action and that of intention. It too needs to be seen clearly for what it is and for what it is not. Given what has been said, the very definition of a right action brings in a notion of intention. That is, to rewrite a bit, the right action is the one that would be favoured by a knowing judge *with a certain intention*: the intention to secure the best state of affairs. There is no doubt about that. There remains the different and essential point that it does not follow that a man's act is right, or wrong, if *he* acted out of this or that intention. The MP's act was right in that it would have been favoured by a knowing judge with a certain intention. It does not follow, as we know, that it was wrong because the MP did not have an identical intention. If, on the contrary, the MP had had an identical intention, and acted as he did, that fact of *his* intention would not have made his act right either, as in fact it was.

One final remark. It may be allowed that a clear enough conception has been suggested, and that we can indeed consider the question of whether actions are right or wrong in the given way. But it may be wondered if this question is the fundamental question in morality, or indeed in life. The reply must be that there is no forcing anyone to be most concerned with what is right, with what ought to happen. Most of us are primarily so concerned, rather than with the question of an agent's actual intention taken by itself, or his moral standing taken by itself, or any other moral question. That is as much as can be said, and of course it is enough.

We were considering two questions. One was the question of whether our actual partly intentional omissions can be regarded as better than certain conceivable wrong acts because those acts would be fully intentional. The answer is no. The kind or degree of intentionality of an action makes no difference to its rightness or wrongness. Nor, to turn to the second question, does the nature of intentions matter. Whatever is to be said of the agent, an act is not made right by a good intention or wrong by a bad one. If it appears that these conclusions can be overturned – moral propositions though they are[3] – this will surely be no more than appearance, since it will be owed to giving a different definition or sense to 'the right action', 'what ought to be done' and so on. This is possible, certainly, but the resulting subject-matter or concern is not ours, and not the fundamental subject-matter or concern in moral and political reflection, whether carried on in books or in the rest of life.

The next difference between some acts and omissions (6) has to do with accepted or ordinary morality. There, there is a distinction between the conceivable acts and fully intentional omissions on the one hand, and, on the other hand, the partly intentional and the unintentional omissions. The former are wrong, the latter not so. In particular, our ordinary failure to contribute to famine relief, or to political movements against dictatorships, is not wrong, but our related conceivable acts would be wrong. One point here is that it would just beg the question with which we are concerned if ordinary morality were taken without reflection to be correct. Certainly we are in no way forced to follow ordinary morality. It in no way follows from something's being generally accepted at a time that it is right. It does not follow from there being an accepted prohibition of the acts but not of the omissions that the omissions are better than the acts. What one needs to do, if one is doubtful about this proposition, is to think of the history of morality. It is a history of what we cannot take to be other than mistakes, a history of beliefs that were both mistaken and generally accepted.

We can allow, perhaps, that something or other is to be said for a generally accepted view, but it is certainly obscure what it is.[4] It is certain that we shall not find a very important recommendation. The obscure recommendation of ordinary morality is not enough to put into question our conclusion that ordinary morality is mistaken in the matter of the connection between intentionality and the worth of omissions and acts. We can also allow a second thing. It is that if people do have certain moral attitudes, however right or wrong those attitudes are, denials of them may result in hurts and distresses. If I believe that you ought to do something for me, the fact that I am mistaken does not stop my being hurt or distressed by your not doing the thing. This sort of thing is sometimes of some importance. It is not of much importance here. Things are different with all the remaining comparisons on our list, all of them involving limited differences between acts and omissions. All of these comparisons are of clear importance to the rightness or wrongness of actions.

It is inescapable (7) that the harms and benefits that may result from acts and omissions are of importance to the moral assessment of those actions. This follows directly from what has been said about rightness. If considerations of death, distress, and inequality do not enter into the judgement of the rightness or wrongness of acts and omissions, then nothing does. Some have tried to avoid the conclusion that follows, that *differences* in harms and benefits must therefore give rise to differences in rightness and wrongness between acts and omissions. They have tried to avoid the conclusion that it is more wrong to have two people suffering to a given extent, or indeed a thousand, than one person suffering to just that extent. Obviously there is no avoiding it. Great tragedies are more terrible than small, and still more to be avoided. We can say, in connection with this seventh comparison, that when other things are equal we are justified in omission rather than action if the omission involves the lesser harm or the greater benefit, and vice versa.

The eighth comparison is a relevant one. An act carrying a high probability of harm, other things being equal, is worse than an omission carrying a lower probability of an identical harm, and vice versa. There are a number of related propositions about probability. An omission carrying a certain low probability of a certain greater harm may be worse than an act carrying a certain high probability of a certain lesser harm, and so on.

The ninth fact of acts and omissions, their experiential effects, is also morally relevant. In certain instances these effects may be of decisive moral importance. In other instances, perhaps more, they are less important than other things. Side-effects, the subject of our tenth comparison, are also morally relevant, and perhaps likely to be more important than experiential effects. Finally, it is clear enough that the eleventh comparison, having to do with the position of the agent in some class of comparison, is of relevance. There are some actions that a man might contemplate, and which it would be wrong for him to do because of the extent to which he would be made unequal as a result.

CONCLUSION

We now have a grasp of the comparisons between acts and omissions. Let us turn back to the particular omissions and conceivable acts with which we began. Would the acts be worse than the omissions are? Would they be no worse? We should now be able to decide. If they would be no worse, the violent have truth on their side in the claim that our ordinary law-abiding conduct is wrong. Their *tu quoque*, whatever is to be said of the relevance of such retorts, is not to be put aside as a falsehood or a mistake. Let us get the answer to our question.

We have spoken of 'the omission of not sending what money we could to the Red Cross or another charity' and the conceivable act of 'sending a militia into refugee camps to kill people in them'. There was also the omission in which we 'fail to contribute funds to political movements against dictatorships', and the conceivable act in which we 'contribute funds to a dictatorship'. These easy phrasings may lead one to overlook what has not been overlooked in our survey, that omissions and acts can differ in main effects. They can differ, as already remarked, even when two different main effects fall under the same piece of language, the same description. Certainly that is clear enough when one stops to think. On the other hand it is possible that omissions and acts be identical in main effects. There is precisely the same situation with the other important comparisons (8 to 11) between acts and omissions. There can be difference or sameness with respect to probability of main effect, and with respect to experiential effects, side-effects, equality-effects and the probabilities of each of these.

There is another fact, a connected one, which is fundamental. *We can choose what conceivable actions to compare with our actual omissions.* Given an actual omission, the related conceivable act is not thereby determined. There is not one conceivable action that is the act for that omission. In fact there is no fixed answer, or rather, there is no answer, to this question: What is the conceivable act that stands to a particular omission? Habit, customary examples, and simple situations may lead us to suppose that there is an answer, but they mislead us. We choose which possible act goes with an omission, what to compare with what. We can vary examples in order to find things out. We have a freedom of inquiry.

Perhaps the tendency of my argument will now be anticipated. We tend to think that conceivable acts would be worse than our omissions because we have in mind *certain of those conceivable acts rather than others*. If we think of others, there is the plain conclusion that our omissions are as wrong as those acts. Those acts would be terribly wrong.

Consider once again the first of the six examples as it was given. In thinking of it, we are very likely indeed to have in mind several ideas. One is that sending in the militia in question would not merely probably, but rather almost certainly, have a terrible main effect – deaths that otherwise would not happen; while not contributing to the Red Cross would probably have some terrible main effect – some number of deaths that otherwise would not happen, not necessarily the same number of like deaths. Here there is a difference in main effects, and also in their probabilities. As for the remaining three comparisons, we are likely to think of worse experiential effects for the agent in the case of the conceivable act, worse side-effects, and a worse equality situation. There can then be no surprise in the fact that we have a strong inclination to think of the conceivable act as worse than our actual omission.

There is another comparison. Let us fix in our minds a conservative estimate of the whole upshot of an actual omission, and then conceive of an act of the same upshot. How much could I contribute to the Red Cross next year? Let us say £4000. Suppose I do not give the money. It is a secure judgement, surely, that my not doing so will have at least two deaths as its very probable main effect. Let us say, for purposes of argument, that the probability is 75 per cent. The experiential effects on me of not doing so will be, very probably, small. My own equality-situation, vis-à-vis those of people like me in my society, will be pretty well unaffected by my omission. The side-effects of my omission will be considerable: they will include the effects of what I do instead with the £4000, and also the effects of the two deaths. Suppose, for purposes of argument, that the money will be spent on improving the life of myself and my family. These improvements, by way of certain comparisons between societies, will provide what indubitably must count as indulgences and luxuries for myself and my family. The effects on people related to the two who die will be very different of course.

It is conceivable that I arrange to perform a certain act, perhaps send some killers, carrying a 75 per cent probability of the deaths of two persons. If I were to do so freely, the experiential effects on me might very probably be small, not different from those of my actual omission. Let us have precisely this possibility as to experiential effects in mind. I would not then be the person I now am, of course, subject to certain feelings of guilt and so on. Let us suppose also that the side-effects by way of the two deaths would be the same as before. That is, we suppose it is by my act that I and my family have £4000 worth of indulgences, and that there are the same side effects as before by way of the deaths of the victims. Let us suppose finally, for reasons which we can conceive, that my own equality-situation in my life would be the same as in the case of my actual omission. Certainly we have now conceived of an entirely extraordinary situation, one that is certain never to obtain. That does not matter at all for the argument. What matters is the likeness of this merely conceivable act to my actual omission, and what we say about the conceivable act.

What we must say, of course, is that my conceivable act would be wrong, and thus we come to the conclusion that my omission next year will be precisely as wrong. We come to the general conclusion that our ordinary lives consist in omissions as wrong as certain conceivable terrible acts. Only quite different conduct, of a kind sometimes mistakenly put aside as something for saints, would be right.[5] It is to be allowed, of course, that my spending the £4000 on myself and my family will only be as wrong as the one conceivable act. It is not that it will be as wrong as some multitude of conceivable acts each similar in upshot to one of the multitude of omissions I will perform in spending the £4,000 as I shall. It does not follow from the fact that my doing A was also not doing a thousand other things. That I could have done the thousand things. That does not much reduce the gravity of our general conclusion.

Is it reduced, incidentally, by the objection that my omission will be only about half as wrong as the conceivable act since the conceivable act would also be something else: an omission to contribute? My spending £4000 on myself and my family, it may be objected, is only harmful as an omission, but the act of sending the militia would be harmful both as that act and also as an omission, the omission of not contributing money to the Red Cross. The act of sending the killers would be about twice as wrong.

There are possible situations in which an objection of this kind is in place, not that its conclusion is greatly reassuring. (The omission in those situations, it might be replied to the objector, is fully half as wrong as some terrible act.) The objection is in fact not relevant to our argument. This is so for the reason that the act of sending the killers would not necessarily count as a relevant omission. It would not count, for example, as omitting to contribute £4000 to the charity. This follows from our conception of acts and omissions. An action is a given omission only if what was not done could have been done with no greater expenditure of energy, resources and so on than that expended in what was done. My reading a newspaper for a few moments cannot count as omitting to write a book. My conceivable act with respect to the militia, to return to that, would not necessarily be anything at all like omitting to contribute £4000 to the Red Cross.

The conclusion that our ordinary omissions are terribly wrong depends on there being no differences between acts and omissions other than those already listed. It depends on its being true, more particularly, that there is no general factual difference between acts and omissions. Two arguments were given against there being such a thing, and a third promised. It can now be provided.

If the factual difference exists, then even if it escapes our detection or description, we ought to be able to feel its moral effect. We ought to be aware of its effect in terms of the rightness or wrongness of actions. Such responses could not possibly be a matter of the special capabilities of only certain persons. Morality is not ESP. The difficulty, of course, is that we have to be sure, about any example, that we are not in fact responding to relevant differences of the kinds we now know, such as difference in probability of main effect.

We can devise certain examples, in areas less controversial than those we have been considering, and hence where we are less likely to go wrong, and with these examples it is impossible to have any feeling of difference in rightness between act and omission. The examples, of course, will be such that there is no difference of the kinds so far allowed to be relevant. We can proceed by way of a euthanasia example. There is the possible act, which might be a doctor's turning off a tap in a blood transfusion tube. The patient, who is incurable and in torment, dies. There is the possible omission, which might again be not providing penicillin for pneumonia. Again the patient would die. If we hold the act and omission identical in the relevant ways of which we know, it will surely be impossible to achieve any sense of difference in rightness between the two actions.

Certainly it is not hard to drift into the feeling that there is more to be said for the omission. It seems invariably true that if this is done at all reflectively, it is done by changing the example: that is, by not holding the two actions identical in the five relevant ways of which we know. The temptation, if that is what it is, seems near to irresistible. In my view all recent philosophers who have tried to claim a special moral difference between acts and omissions have fallen prey to the temptation, or anyway not taken good care to have their examples satisfy the condition of having act and omission alike in the given ways. If the two actions are really held identical in the given ways, I propose, we cannot achieve any real sense of moral difference between them.

Some will suppose there is another way of resisting the general conclusion that in our ordinary omissions we do wrong to a terrible extent. They will suppose that the conclusion can be refuted or put into question by this argument: if the conclusion were true, we would be moral monsters; the wrongfulness of our actions would surely support this conclusion about ourselves; we are not moral monsters; indeed, it would not make sense to claim this of all of us; therefore the conclusion that we all do wrong to a terrible extent is mistaken or somehow in question.

The issues raised are large ones, and I shall do no more than quickly suggest reasons for thinking that the objection fails.

It has already been remarked that it does not follow directly from an action's being right that it preserves the agent's moral standing. Nor does it follow directly from an action's being wrong that it reduces or destroys the agent's moral standing. Still, from an act's being wrong together with certain other facts it does follow that the agent is open to question, or worse than that. What can be said in the case of our omissions?

It is to be kept in mind, first, that few if any of us omit to contribute to the Red Cross in anything remotely like the fully intentional way. We do not aim at causing death. There are no such monsters. Secondly, are there only a few people, as may be thought, whose omissions are of the opposite kind, wholly unintentional? Are there only a few, that is, who have not earlier taken avoiding action? There are more of these innocents than might be supposed, at least if one gives a certain characterisation of what is required for partly intentional omission.

It is reasonable to say that for something to count as an earlier intention-to-avoid, the person in question needs to have had more than fragmentary ideas in mind for a moment, more than a flicker of images. The person in question needs to have had a decent awareness of the relevant effects of the later omission. Also, he needs to have had a decent awareness of what he might do instead in the future. There are many people who have too small a conception of what might be called their world of possible effectiveness. They do not suppose, for example, that they can do anything to contribute to less inequality in average lifetimes. Nor can they be censured for their weak grasp of their possibilities of action. There are therefore more of the innocent, the unintentional, than might be supposed.

Consider now the moral standing of the partly intentional. Putting something out of mind in the required sense is likely to require self-deception. This cannot consist, as some philosophers seem to believe, in successfully lying to oneself, and therefore in believing both *p* and *not*-p together. Self-deception, at any rate when it is nonpathological, consists rather in an avoidance of evidence, or of pointers or clues, with the aim of avoiding belief. It consists in persisting with a question, which is better than getting a particular answer. Part of what enters into putting something out of mind, then, is the fact that we have kept a good distance from places of evidence, perhaps evidence about average lifetimes in societies, or the state of education in certain sorts of school. (I have not said enough, of course, to give the reality of all this. There are many ways and styles of avoiding evidence.) To come to the essential claim, there is some exculpation possible for typical self-deceivers. If I have the belief that a terrible state of affairs exists, about which I could do something, that is different from my in fact having a question about such a state of affairs.

There is something else to be said of partly intentional omission. Omitting to contribute to the Red Cross, to the extent that one is in a state of belief, is likely to involve beliefs as to *distant* awfulness. It cannot be true that an act or omission is right or wrong because of its *spatial* relation to its result. It cannot be that our moral obligations are in any way a function, simply, of mileage. But the questions of acts is not the question of agents, and the question of agents is not easy. What about the relevance of distance, in the ordinary sense and also others, to our standing as moral agents or as human? It seems to be true that those who drop bombs are less morally revolting, if those are the right words, than those who do the close work of hand-to-hand killing. Again, one would feel differently about a family, say, who let a man starve to death in their own flat, as against a family who failed to send food to a man known by them to be dying in another country. What I want to suggest, then, is that the fact that the victims of omissions are distant does have some exculpating effect with respect to agents.

Further and finally, with respect to partly intentional omission, it is safe to say that *in ordinary morality* it is as if there were some great difference of fact between acts and partly intentional omissions. This is a common belief or conviction. In ordinary morality, further, there is no awareness of the great wrongfulness of our ordinary omissions. These are both mistakes, I think, but they are not mistakes to which moral blame attaches. It is not a general requirement of being a good person, now, that one does not make these mistakes.

I take it that these various considerations go some considerable way towards exculpating many people. Or, to come to safer ground, and all the ground I need, it seems that the considerations do the lesser thing of absolving most people from being moral monsters. Whether exculpation, or the lesser absolving, it is partly something that is true at this time in human history. It is dependent on a certain general awareness at this time. It is not an exculpation or absolving that will persist, as it is, into the future. One may wonder, of course, whether it may apply *now* to oneself, but that is something else.

We were considering the argument that if we in our omissions do wrong to a terrible extent, we are moral monsters; and we are not such, and so it cannot be that we do wrong to a terrible extent. The reply has been that for various reasons a general and substantial proposition about overwhelming guilt on the part of many people does not follow from, and hence cannot endanger, the conclusion about the great wrongfulness of our omissions. It is not entirely clear that the conclusion would in fact be endangered if it did carry the given large consequence, but I leave the matter there.

TU QUOQUE

By our ordinary omissions we do as wrong as we might by certain awful acts. Some of us or indeed most of us will pay this conclusion no serious attention. Perhaps it is true that no one will take it so seriously as to act upon it. Such results are dispiriting only to those who are unaware of the history of political philosophy, of serious

moral protest, and of like things. Virtually every outlook or institution or practice that is now venerated did in fact begin life as a silly
proposition upon which no one acted. It began life as such a proposition although in fact there was enough argument for it, and not
enough against it.

What we must accept, to look back to the beginning of our inquiry,
is that those who engage in terrorism for humanity have a truth on
their side when they respond to the charge that they do wrong with
the retort that we do wrong. What is to be said of this *tu quoque*? I
supposed in the beginning that it cannot be put aside, and promised
to return to the matter.

Overstatement is possible. Some of the politically violent will say
that in fact they are not limited to the *tu quoque*, whatever it comes
to. There is more. They will say that our ordinary contribution to
the frightful circumstances of shorter lifetimes, miseries, and the
want of freedoms does not issue only in the judgement that we do
wrong, and whatever follows from that, but also in the judgement
that our ordinary condemnation of terrorism for humanity is
incoherent. If this is not neatly expressed by those who defend their
terrorism, that is in a way not unusual, and in a way not essential.
It is not unusual for those who act in certain causes to be unable to
do well in arguing for those causes; their being unable to do so is not
essential to those causes being defensible ones. Policemen and
soldiers should come to mind.

The claim by terrorists for humanity that our condemnation of
their action is incoherent proceeds as follows. We judge our kind of
conduct to be right, and the terrorism to be wrong, but the two kinds
of conduct are alike in a certain fact, and this fact of likeness is all-
important. Each kind of conduct consists in the denial of the greatest
human desires, in the causing of terrible distress. On the one hand
these things are denied to the primary victims of acts of terrorism,
and also in part to secondary victims, principally the families of
primary victims. Whatever else is added, this much must be allowed.
On the other hand, as has just been said, there are the innumerable
victims of those of us who live ordinary law-abiding lives. These
victims live less long, and live badly, and live without full freedom
and so on.

On each hand, then, there is the denial of human living-time and
other goods. It is also true that while the two kinds of conduct are
alike in the given fact, there is no relevant way in which our ordinary
conduct is different from that of the terrorists, no difference which

makes our conduct right and theirs wrong. We know there is no such difference in the fact that our ordinary conduct consists of omissions and the conduct of the terrorists consists of acts. There is the result that our ordinary condemnation of violence is incoherent, that we fail to make what can count as judgements at all. Our utterances are as insubstantial as those of a man who 'describes' an object in a certain way, perhaps as being of a certain colour, simply and solely because it has a quality to which he points, and then gives a contradictory description of another object with precisely the same quality. He has, in the most important sense of the words, said nothing at all.

Certainly the argument does not work, and in fact it overlooks plain things established in our reflections on acts and omissions. We have found that there are conceivable acts which are factually like our own omissions in all the relevant ways. Our omissions, therefore, are on a level of wrongness with these acts. None of that, however, goes any way towards establishing that our omissions are in the relevant ways like the acts of the violent. That is another matter. There is in fact no likelihood that our omissions can be shown to be like acts of the violent in main effect, or probability of it, or side-effects and their probability, and so on. The claim of incoherence can in fact be defeated by pointing out that it is just mistaken to say that our ordinary conduct is in no relevant ways different from terrorism. It is different in ways in which omissions may differ from acts.

The terrorists, then, have only their *tu quoque*, and not the claim of incoherence. But is there something, perhaps much, to be said for the *tu quoque*?

The terrorists, when they are taxed with what will be called the irrelevance of their claim that our ordinary conduct is wrong, can maintain the strong truth that our two kinds of conduct are connected. It is not that the terrible circumstances of misery and injustice, against which violence is directed, come about by chance. They have not come about through historical passages in which we and our predecessors have played no particular part. The circumstances of distress of every kind, rather, are as good as our own work. We contribute to them essentially by our wrongful conduct. It is not that there is no connection between violence and our omissions, but rather that there is the connection that our omissions are essential contributions to the misery and injustice against which terrorism for humanity is directed.

More can be said along these lines, but all of it may get the reply that it is nothing to the point. Our ordinary omissions, it will be said, are not the subject-matter. The subject-matter is terrorism and what is to be said for and against it. It may be that there is the claimed connection between our omissions and terrorism, and, for purposes of argument, it can be granted that our conduct is wrong. It is none the less true that the subject-matter is what it is, and that it is not our omissions.

There is only one proper judgement on this dispute. It is that there is no ordained subject-matter. There is never an ordained subject-matter. At bottom the criterion of relevance for any discussion is fixed by the demands of those who are taking part in it. If they cannot agree, they cannot discuss. No doubt anything that is one discussion remains within some wide boundary. No doubt it is true, too, that fact and logic impose requirements of appositeness on answers to particular questions, replies to particular claims. There is no fact of the world, however, and no consideration of logic, that stands in the way of the demand of the violent to bring our omissions into the discussion. It is not an absurd demand. What can stand in the way of it is only an opposed demand.

My own determination will by now be clear enough. It is that the discussion be the wider one. My first reason is that it seems possible that we proceed in too simple a way if we declare that the wrongfulness of terrorism is in no way diminished by the wrongfulness of our omissions. No doubt it is worth someone's while to say that two wrongs do not make a right. It may also be worth saying that there is reason to be sceptical, or perhaps it would be better to say that there is reason for some reserve, in a certain kind of situation. It is the kind of situation where we have one man's judgement on another's conduct, and the first man may be influenced by an unhappy perception of his own relation to the other's conduct. More particularly, we have some awareness that we make our necessary contributions to the circumstances that have led and continue to lead to terrorism. It seems to me a likelihood that this awareness affects our condemnations. Our condemnations, although condemnations still, are likely to be different if we are more aware of our own conduct and its wrongfulness.

There are two more reasons for the wider discussion. One is that it is in fact more important that we change our ways than it is that the violent change theirs. We do greatly more damage. Another lesser but good reason for the wider discussion is that it may do a little to diminish violence. The narrower discussion, rightly, has less chance.

5
On Democratic Terrorism

If we look at contemporary and recent writing on terrorism in the hope of finding really cogent arguments against all of it or nearly all of it, and if we are not too disposed to take a side or impassioned, we are unlikely to be satisfied. This disappointment certainly does not derive only from the several pieces of writing looked at in the earlier essays of this book. In the works of Sartre and Fanon, their commitment to the oppressed issues in their judgement that terrorism is not only permissible but obligatory. That some men are made less than men, that they have their stature taken from them, appears to be taken as an adequate ground for their terrorism, terrorism that is to change them. 'To shoot down a European', we are told, 'is to kill two birds with one stone, to destroy an oppressor and the man he oppresses at the same time.'[1]

It is not hard to find questions about the argument or to be repelled by it, even given some understanding, and not merely an awareness of facts about colonial oppression and personality. Most of us, to pass on to but one other example, will be as reluctant to suppose that the 'historical calculus' offered to us by Marcuse can be shown to issue in the conclusion that political violence of the Left generally has a justification.[2] Can there be anything more than metaphor in talk of the rules given us by history?

Some, of course, will find scepticism about Sartre, Fanon, and Marcuse congenial, but not scepticism about others. It is, for me, difficult to see this as other than a result of being too disposed to take a side. To look back, no one should be reassured by Popper on the subject of rationality and irrationality.[3] To return for a moment to Rawls, we should be as reluctant to take up his equally resolute conclusions.[4] It really cannot be that it is economic *necessity* that principally explains the fact that our societies are still subject to wide and destructive inequalities, dragged down by misery and other distress. It cannot be that the intransigence of privileged classes is not a principal part of the explanation. If so, we must at least think about Rawls's prohibition on political violence, based largely on the idea that our societies come about as close to decency as can be fairly asked.

It remains obscure what total of things will enter into really effective argumentation, if it is possible, either for or against terrorism. Certainly some basic principle or principles must be fundamental, as will the facts of distress and the facts of violence. Presumably some complete assessment of claims about political obligation will have a place. There will be no avoiding judgements about responses to terrorism, reactions justified or unjustified on the part of states, privileged classes and others – reponses of both war and state-terrorism. There can be no avoiding judgements on the rationality of engaging in violence.

There is also something else that cuts across some of these subjects. It will be valuable, and I suspect essential, in any effective argumentation to consider how violence is related to other practices, relevant practices about which we have clearer judgements. One of these, perhaps the most important, is democracy.

Many of those who condemn terrorism do so on the ground that it is undemocratic. Many of its apologists are in some agreement with those who condemn it. Their endeavour is to find higher reasons for what they accept, implicitly or explicitly, to be undemocratic. My first purposes in the present essay are to see clearly how terrorism stands to the practice and the rules of democracy, and to the arguments for the practice and the rules. The latter relationship, between some terrorism and the arguments for democracy, will then enter into a characterisation of one important type of terrorism. In the end, we shall be further on the way to having an adequately reasoned conclusion about the morality of violence.

DEMOCRACY

We must first recollect and perhaps become clearer about the nature of democracy, or rather democracy as acceptably conceived in the last few decades of the tradition with which most of us are familiar. It is *a practice in which the people choose and then influence those who do govern the nation and direct its relations of war and peace.* This is but a rubric, and a rubric that might stand at the head of different texts. Even so, since we shall be concerned with such systems of government as those in Britain and America, it provides us with a conception that is more apposite than certain alternatives. I have in mind, for example, the alternative and plain wrong idea of government actually *by* the people. Whatever they do, the people do not govern.

We can clarify our conception of democracy by prising apart three groups of features, which will also serve as criteria for the assessment of existing systems. None of this will be amazingly novel stuff, for good reason. Also, while we shall fill out the conception, in so far as it can be done very quickly, we shall certainly not arrive at as precise a conception as might be required in other endeavours than our own. There is no way of setting out the criteria, incidentally, that will bring together in a particular group all and only those criteria that may be seen as alike from all reasonable standpoints. In what follows, those that are alike from a standpoint other than mine may turn up in different groups.[5] It is also to be noted that a criterion, in the intended sense, may be more or less satisfied by an existent system of government, or, we may say, not satisfied at all.

(1) *Uncoerced choosing and influencing.* In the practice of democracy, to begin with certain considerations relating particularly to pre-election periods, the politics of the electors are not forced upon them. That is to say, roughly, that their attitudes, wants, demands and choices, both interested and in a way disinterested, are of their own making. It cannot be, certainly, that in its politics the electorate is coerced by a minority of its members, that its position is like that of a man deliberately and entirely misled or confused. The matter is one of some complication, however, and we shall return to it.

It is also essential, essential to the freedom of electors to act on their politics, that there is no substantial limitation in law, or as a matter of entrenched principle, on which citizens can be candidates for office. The overwhelming majority can put themselves forward. In addition to this, again in order to secure the freedom of electors, there are no legal or conventionally established obstacles to campaigning. One must add that these possibilities of candidacy and campaigning are possibilities in more than law and general acceptance. They are to some extent generally available options, not privileges that can be exercised only by a minority, perhaps by the wealthy or by a group of men united in ideology who are the instruments of the wealthy.

Finally, again principally for the reason having to do with the freedom of electors to act on their politics, there is an effective prohibition on the coercion of candidates. The politics of candidates are not, in a certain sense, forced upon them.

To come now to elections, they are regular in democracies, and the electors make choices that are not coerced. The latter is partly secured through the institution of free voting: electors are able to register, can come to vote without apprehension, and, since we are not yet in John Stuart Mill's better world, can vote secretly. Their choices, one may add, are made in a tolerably rational fashion. They do not individuate candidates without reference to the politics of candidates, merely engaging in habitual responses of a kind suggested in certain 'realist' theories of political behaviour.

After an election the government is encouraged or restrained, but hardly controlled, not only by the evidence of the past election but also by the continuing articulation, by rising candidates and others, of popular attitudes and responses. These have an effect, partly, because they are indications of possible outcomes of the next election. Again there is the requirement that the electorate is not coerced. Its attitudes and responses are not forced upon it.

All of these features of the democratic practice, having to do with the politics of the electorate, candidacy and campaigning, with electoral choice, and with the exercise of influence after an election, make for what we may label as the *uncoerced choosing and influencing of government*. The label is attached to a group of criteria and is not to be construed as a description that might be applied to systems of government that do not in some degree satisfy the criteria. By the criteria as intended, our conception of democracy excludes the remaining Communist states, whatever their recommendations, and also certain conceivable states that as yet are a matter of hopeful or fearful speculation.

(2) *Approximate equality*. To turn now to the second group of criteria, we must recall first that democracy gives to each of almost all adults the possibility of one vote in the choice of a government, and the possibility of some part, not wholly out of line with the parts of others, in the influencing of government. The second test is distressingly vague but we shall have to get along with it as stated. Here and elsewhere, this essay can be merely a precis. It is to be noticed that we do not require that each citizen can exercise the same influence, but only what might be called a tolerably similar one.[6] Were we to do so, our conception would be remote from actual political systems, and inapposite for the discussion of them. The conception, as one can conclude from the fact of its appositeness, is also a relatively ordinary one, and hence has other advantages that typically go with ordinary conceptions.

In democracy, further, as might have been left implicit in what has been said, a system obtains whereby numbers of votes issue in an affinitive government: that is, an affinitive representative or number of representatives. The term 'affinitive representation' is preferable to what is more usual, 'proportionate representation'. It is a familiar fact that in our actual political systems a party may legitimately take power despite the fact that it has got less of the popular vote than an opposing party. There are other and more common facts of what can only be called 'disproportion'. Things are different in the case of complete systems of Proportional Representation. In order to avoid a conception remote from actuality, let us speak of affinitive representation. Representation is affinitive, we may cursorily say, if it results from a procedure that gives to each vote an approximately equal weight.

We need not speak of a system of influence, a system for giving effect to popular attitudes between elections, that would be a counterpart of the system just mentioned for translating votes into representation. We can perhaps imagine possibilities in this area that would lead us to attempt to specify a safeguarding criterion.

We may bring together the criteria we have – pertaining mainly to 'one person, one vote', to the derivation of representation from votes, and to a similar influence on government of the wants and opinions of individuals between elections – under the label of *approximate equality of opportunity in the choosing and influencing of government*. The criteria have the consequence, which might once have affronted a cultural piety, that the Greek polis was not a democracy because of the exclusion of slaves and women from the franchise. There is also the consequence that contemporary military regimes are non-democratic states.

(3) *Effective majority decision.* To come to criteria of the third group, the first of them requires that elected representatives take decisions of government as a result of majority vote. Hence there are many procedures of importance having to do with the business of elected assemblies and changes in government. It is of importance, secondly, that governmental decisions, like the politics and actions of candidates and electors, are not coerced. Minorities in the society do not force decisions upon government. To use a familiar analogy, and in anticipation of certain reflections about coercion to which we shall come, the government does not have a gun at its head.

It is to be noticed that satisfaction of the first condition obviously allows the possibility that there exists in society a 'permanent' minority. That is, there may be a group in society, united by race, religion or politics, whose representatives have no significant possibility of entering into coalition and hence majority. The condition may also be satisfied despite the existence of certain constitutional restraints on the majority. What are excluded by the requirement in question are certain powers of veto, effective control by non-elective upper houses, and so on.

In the third place, we require of democracy that the decisions of representatives be translated into fact. A system may be a lesser approximation of democracy because of obstruction on the part of a bureaucracy or the courts. Again, a system may fail to be democratic, or fully democratic, because to some extent the rule of law does not prevail. The requirement of rule of law may be pitched so high that all the most likely political systems would, at certain times, fail to qualify as democracies. The requirement may also be pitched so low that something close to anarchy, in a true sense of that wildly abused word, would qualify. I intend to exclude both of these possibilities.

Our third group of criteria, about the procedures of elected assemblies and the efficacy of their decisions, may be labelled as criteria having to do with *effective majority decision by government.*

This, then, is an impression, if not much more than that, of the practice I shall have in mind in speaking of democracy. The conception in question, which will be clarified in some respects in the discussion that follows, is of use in discussing such systems of government as those in Britain and America. It is not, as I have said, utopian, a conception of an ideal democracy, but neither is it a conception that is fully satisfied in Britain or America or like societies. Certainly it does not describe the best conceivable practice of government. Some may say that its full realisation, or the full realisation of a similar but higher conception of democracy, is the best we can hope for in actual political systems.

TERRORISM DEFINED

Let us now spend a bit more time on what was considered earlier[7] – the definition of terrorism or political violence. The question of definition, or what is too loosely called that, has been the subject of a bit of controversy, more than it is worth. In part, the controversy has been concerned with the kind of difficulties that beset any attempt to provide an analytical definition. That is, there have been the problems that arise in any attempt to capture, with respect to something, the definition of it which is implicit in ordinary usage and belief.[8] Some have asked if the definition of violence should be so couched as to capture certain acts of speech.

In a second part, the controversy has had to do with attempts to press a definition wider than those that stand in some tolerable relation to ordinary usage and belief. We have been told that policemen, landlords, employers, shopkeepers, and indeed whole social classes and the state itself, engage in violence as a matter of course.[9] The fundamental suggestion, which has a considerable history, is not that policemen use more than the force allowed by their legal powers, that landlords send round thugs, or that the state engages in war and will use its army against revolution. Rather, it is that policemen, landlords, and the state, in what most people regard as their peaceful conduct, are engaging in violence.

This dispute is not essentially factual in character. It is not about established usage. We are given definitions issuing from political intention and required for simple *tu quoque* argument, whatever it may be worth. Such definitions enable the man who sets a bomb to reply to those who condemn him that they, too, engage in violence, perhaps the 'violence' that others of us might describe as unfairness, deprivation, distress, wretchedness, inhumanity and the like.

In the third part, the so-called definitional controversy has to do with more idiosyncratic suggestions. It has been suggested by Robert Paul Wolff, as we have seen,[10] that the 'distinctively political concept of violence' is to be eschewed because it is incoherent. It is so because of its connection with the notion of what a government or a state cannot morally have, a certain right to obedience. Again, the dispute is not essentially factual. The point stands, certainly, despite complications in the distinction between the factual and the evaluative.

Whatever sympathies one may have with the political intentions implicit in the second and third parts of the controversy, one may decline to take up the recommended usage or to be bound by the intended prohibition. If one sets out only to find a clear and unimpeding definition of violence, one which does not allow spurious victories to either Left or Right or this or that country, there is relatively little difficulty.

Let us then, as earlier in this book,[11] define terrorism or political violence as a use of physical force that injures, damages, violates or destroys people or things, with a political and social intention, and whether or not intended to put people in general in fear, and raising a question of its moral justification – either illegal violence within a society or smaller-scale violence than war between states and societies and not according to international law.

The definition covers such things as race riots, the destruction by fire and bomb of homes, kidnapping, hijacking, injuring, maiming, torture, rape, killing and massacres. It also encompasses revolutionary violence of the past and also state-terrorism of the past and present. In specifying that the physical force has a political and social intention, it does not require that the agents of violence have in view highly specific aims of change. Riots may count as political violence despite the absence of well-articulated intentions of the given kind, and also despite their non-rational momentum.

PRACTICE AND RULES OF DEMOCRACY

The first of the two questions raised at the beginning of this essay was that of how terrorism is related to the practice of democracy. That is, can one have a political system that can be said to satisfy the conception of democracy in some reasonable degree even though terrorism, including state-terrorism, occurs in the given society? The question depends for its sense, obviously, on the level of violence that is presupposed. The latter, in good part, is a matter of numbers of injuries and deaths, amount of damage and destruction. Let us have in mind only political violence at about the level of the violence in America, South America, Europe and the Middle East over the past decade. Our question, although large, is not a difficult one. It will be advantageous in several ways, as I shall explain, to have a tolerably clear answer. In effect, what we shall come to have will be answers to a number of smaller questions. They will be more useful than any summation.

To find our smaller questions, let us look to the criteria of democracy, beginning with the first group, those pertaining to the uncoerced choosing and influencing of government. Terrorism need not stand in the way of candidacy and campaigning, regular elections and free voting. Terrorism, although it has brought appalling personal tragedy, does not in general impede or prevent these things. What of the requirements that electors and candidates are not coerced? The requirements about coercion remain unclear and more will be said of them. However, it seems evident enough that they must be so defined that political violence is excluded. In a situation where violence has forms of popular support, as it commonly does, it may certainly influence, direct, or suborn electors. It must be regarded as conflicting with the criterion of democracy that electors are not coerced. It must also be granted that violence conflicts with the criterion pertaining to the non-coercion of candidates. We may conclude that violence at a certain level stands in the way of a system's greater satisfaction of the given criteria of democracy.

Consider now the requirements having to do with approximate equality of opportunity in the choosing and influencing of government. We may put aside, as not in conflict with violence, the requirement that numbers of votes produce affinitive representation. One of the other two requirements in this group is that each citizen has one vote. If we look at this with only an eye like the lens of a camera, it seems clear enough that violence is not in conflict with it. That is, terrorism is not often a substantial impediment to each man's putting his ballot paper in the box or using the voting machine. To put this matter aside for a moment, there is the third criterion, to the effect that there is for each citizen a decently similar possibility of influencing the government, where that is principally a matter of giving evidence of political attitudes and inclinations.

It seems true, or at any rate arguable, that political violence stands in the way of the adequate realisation of this possibility. The possibility, looked at realistically, depends not only on such things as money for lobbying but also on the capability, preparedness and willingness of individuals to engage in certain lines of conduct. If a majority are in fact prevented, even if self-prevented, from engaging in acts of violence, then their possibility of influence is different from, and too much less than, that of a minority. Here, too, there is more to be said.

Let us look again at 'one person, one vote'. What is secured by this requirement? It is that each citizen has an equal role in that procedure, an election, which in a society without terrorism has a certain large importance for governmental decisions. Equal roles in the procedure recommend themselves because of the effectiveness of the procedure. The criterion of democracy that each citizen has one vote is important only because we assume something about the efficacy of the election. It is not unreasonable to conclude, perhaps, that a certain level of violence in a society, since it somewhat reduces the relative efficacy of voting, is in some conflict with the criterion of 'one person, one vote'. I do not mean to suggest that in recent experience the efficacy of elections has been much reduced.

Finally, there is the third group of criteria, having to do with effective majority decision by government. Terrorism does not conflict with the first in this group, that representative assemblies take decisions by majority vote. As for the second, that governmental decisions are not coerced, terrorism clearly does stand in the way of its fuller satisfaction. The last criterion of the group is that governmental decisions are effective, and hence that the rule of law prevails. Here, it is even more difficult to judge precisely. The principal difficulty is that of setting an upper limit on violence, beyond which it is in substantial conflict with democracy. What can be said with assurance, but not very usefully, is that any system is less democratic in the given respect if there is such an incidence of violence as that with which we have become familiar in the past decade.

So much for one approach to our questions. Another must be made if we are to reach anything like a judicious view of how terrorism affects democracy. Other things also impede a fuller realisation of the practice. We must be aware of them, and take them into account in a comparative view of the effect of violence. In this connection, it is clear enough that some uses of economic power ensure that systems of democracy only partially satisfy the criteria of democracy. Democracy has long been distinguished from plutocracy and the like, in their several guises, and rightly so.

There can be no doubt that wealth, in itself and through its concomitants, makes for a coercion of electorate and candidates in their politics. The ways of this coercion are various and often covert. Constraining ideology, to mention only that, is not just a feature of systems elsewhere. Secondly, it is clear enough that political uses of the power wielded by wealth prevent a fuller realisation of the criteria having to do with equality of opportunity in the choosing and influencing of government. Dahl observed, of but one aspect of the American system, that 'if it could be quantified I suppose that Mr Henry Luce has a thousand or ten thousand times greater control over the alternatives scheduled for debate and tentative decision at a national election than I do'.[12] Mr Luce, of course, was a newspaper magnate.

Thirdly, much the same situation exists in connection with the criteria of effective majority decision. The rule of law has in effect been broken through the systematic avoidance by businesses and individuals of the intended effects of legislation. In general, it is at least arguable that in every recent decade economic power has been greatly more effective than violence in keeping the British and American systems from being fuller realisations of democracy.

It still remains true, however balanced one's judgement, that terrorism does render such systems considerably less democratic than otherwise they might be. This involves the criteria concerned with ways of affecting the politics and actions of electorates and governments, with equality of opportunity in the choosing and influencing of governments, and with the rule of law.

My principal reason for clarifying this factual proposition, that violence does render systems less democratic, is to avoid a certain vagueness and confusion. We all believe that democracy and terrorism somehow conflict. It is important, however, to know exactly where they do conflict and where they do not, and not to confuse these places. We have one clear conflict before us. As I shall explain later, we must not make too much of this conclusion. It would be mistaken to make it decisive in the judgement of all terrorism without exception in democratic systems.

A lesser reason for clarifying the factual proposition about the practice of democracy and violence is to establish the weakness of unreflective and extravagant claims to the effect that acts of violence themselves *destroy* democracy. In general, they do not. They do less to make systems undemocratic than do acts of economic power

It is also unreflective, incidentally, to succumb to the related generalisation that terrorism always poses a significant threat to the continuation of a democratic system of government. The supposition here is that violence, however it may conflict at some moment with this or that part of the system, always carries the significant threat of an unpredictable sequence of events ending in the destruction of the system. I shall have more to say that is relevant to this supposition. It represents, typically, an unconsidered attempt at restraint rather than a considered judgement. Indeed the generalisation that violence always threatens the existence of a democratic system is at about the level of clarity and credibility of the generalisation that a democratic system always threatens its own existence. Collapses of democratic systems have as often been brought about by their own passivities as by political violence.

Let us now turn to the question raised at the beginning of this essay about the rules of democracy. How does terrorism stand in relation to them? We can deal with the matter quickly, partly for the reason that we already have the rules of democracy before us. They have emerged in the description of the democratic practice, since the most economical way of describing it is principally by way of its rules. Also, the question of terrorism and the rules of democracy is in a way more tractable than that of terrorism and the ongoing reality of democracy. Many of the rules of democracy, as we have conceived it, are not determinate. Still, it is easier to conclude that behaviour counts as an infraction of a rule than to decide, as a result of certain behaviour, how far one must qualify a general description of a system that is a complex structure of rules, and indeed more than that.

Guided by our findings about political violence and systems, we can conclude about political violence that it breaks the rule of democracy that electors and candidates are not to be coerced, and also the rule that each citizen is to have one vote, where that is understood to require equal participation in a fundamental procedure that gives rise to political decisions. Violence may be said to break the latter rule because the relative efficacy of the procedure is reduced. In addition, violence may be said to break the rule of democracy that each citizen is to have an approximately equal role in the influencing of governments, where what is in question is something other than voting. Lastly, violence breaks the rule of democracy that governmental decisions are to be taken as binding, that the rule of law is to prevail.

We thus have a second clear conflict between violence and democracy. Violence breaks rules of the practice. This is unaffected by another fact, whatever else may be thought of it, and however it may enter into different arguments, that non-violent infractions of the rules of democracy have been more substantial than violent infractions. Non-violent infractions deriving from wealth and from class ascendancies have been greatly more numerous and effective than violent infractions. It is worth remarking, too, that acts of violence break rules of which there is in fact some observance. It is not as if they 'broke' rules that have been *destroyed* by infractions deriving from economic power, or rules that can be said to have always been circumvented by oppressing classes.[13]

As in the case of the first conflict, our conclusion here must not be taken for too much. It is clear that there is no direct and unquestionable passage from the premise of something's being against a rule to the conclusion that it is wrong. That is a part of what we must now consider.

ARGUMENTS AND ENDS

The rules of democracy are no more than rules, and they do not give one what they imperfectly imply, the arguments for democracy. If one wants to know what is to be said for democracy, and how that is related to other things, one must look elsewhere than the rules. In part they are no more than means for securing ends which are cited in the arguments. The situation is familiar. If one wants to know what is to be said for keeping one's promise, one does not find it, except inchoately, in the rules of promising. The overall rule that one must do as one promises does not give a justification for doing as one promises. That has to do with the effects of the rule.

The arguments for democracy are sometimes collected into a disorder. Here we are offered the traditional liberties or the rule of law or the virtues of the democratic personality, there the efficiency of free-enterprise economies, here governmental stability, and there the progress of science. Better can be done, I think, and without the distortion that sometimes results from a kind of reductionism. There appear to be two fundamental grounds for the practice and rules of democracy. They both have to do in several ways with the Principle of Humanity and hence the goal of well-being for all.

Arguments from both these grounds have to do with the democratic practice itself, and also with consequences of the practice, whether or not they are also consequences of other practices. It is no doubt a mistake to attempt to define the democratic practice by means of rights, policies, customs and benefits that generally go with it but are logically distinct from it. But, although such things are connected with the practice only contingently, they do enter into its justification. If democracies invariably, or even very often, went along with continual economic failure or a denial of non-political rights, we would have very much less to say for democracies.

One principal argument for democracy is that, compared to certain other practices, it gives less freedom to any individual or minority in determining the policies of a society. Most important, it gives less to that minority that is made up of the governing representatives. To accept this, we need not depend on such supports as Plato's taxonomy of political systems, but on the evident nature of recent alternatives to democracy. As a consequence of reasonable argument having to do with such things as the 'intra-party democracy' that existed in the Soviet Union, we may be made to hesitate. We may be made to hesitate, too, by those many accusations, including the Marxist one, concerning privileged classes and minorities in our democracies. Indeed, we must amend a great deal of received doctrine. But it remains clear enough that the practice of democracy gives less freedom to any individual or minority than do alternative forms of government.

It is to be noticed that democracy is not being recommended as denying the mentioned freedom to an individual or a minority and giving it to ordinary people who make up the society. Such a claim is patently at odds with the facts. The people do not rule, and they never have. Democracy gives to citizens only something that can best be described briefly in a negative way: a circumstance in which no individual or minority has as much freedom, with respect to major policies of the society, as have individuals or minorities in other political practices. It gives to citizens not any freedom of power but rather a freedom *from* power. The practice does this as a consequence of certain of its features enumerated at the beginning of this essay. I shall not attempt to relate this general contention, about the general absence of a freedom in major policies, to many related praisings of democracy, some of which are wonderfully inflated.

We have so far considered only a possible freedom which is a power to determine the policies of a society. In a democracy, no individual or minority has it. There are, however, other possible autonomies that in fact are realised in a democracy, or realised to some extent. These are smaller and yet enter importantly into the present fundamental argument for democracy. The argument has to do with the satisfaction and the distress of individuals, in a considerable part the satisfaction of freedom and the distress of a want of freedom.

Some of these smaller freedoms are integral to the practice, as defined, and are secured by what are known as the political rights. How a man will vote is within his decision, and his satisfaction in its being so is real. Others of these smaller autonomies are consequences rather than integral parts of the democratic practice, although not invariably so, and are in part secured by non-political rights. Here we have freedoms of culture, including religion, and freedom in the use of law. Also among the consequences of democracy are certain individual possibilities for the possession and use of natural and produced goods, both materials and otherwise. This recommendation, having to do with a kind of production, is not one that is peculiar to democracy, as some of our economists have so long suggested. It seems a probability that the Soviet Union could have come to have something very like it, and as probable that its not having had it cannot be quickly explained by the non-democratic nature of its political system. Still, the existence of these possibilities for the possession and use of goods is a fact about democratic societies, and hence a recommendation of them.

One fundamental argument for democracy, then, is that is secures to citizens a freedom from a certain possible power, and also secures or allows to them an array of lesser freedoms. They exercise small powers and realise certain possibilities of possession and use. This we may speak of as *the argument of freedom*. It is related to the other fundamental ground of support for democracy, but the two are logically distinct in important ways.

One can advance the argument of freedom, correctly, on behalf of a society disfigured by extreme disparities in individual powers and possibilities. Necessarily, if the argument can be used reasonably, the society is not any form of tyranny. That is, its major policies are not within the decision of an individual ruler or a minority of rulers. None the less, there is no difficulty about supposing that the society in question, while it can be said to accord the lesser possibilities and powers to all, in fact distributes them in a grossly unequal way. Obviously enough, a man may truly be said to have freedoms without its being true, by some comparative test, that he has enough of them. There are situations where for two men to have a certain freedom, it must be that each has as much as the other. This is not always so, and it is not so in the case of freedoms of the kind we are considering.

The second argument for democracy, as may be anticipated, is *the argument of equalities*. It is that in a democracy one gets certain approximations to equality. Some of them are greater approximations than in non-democratic societies, others are lesser approximations. These approaches to equality, full realisations of equality in several instances, are to be found in the democratic practice itself and also in its customary consequences.

With respect to the practice, it is a necessary truth that if no individual or minority has freedom with respect to the society's policies, then all have equal freedom from such freedom. In this case, evidently, there does exist a logical connection between a freedom and its equal distribution. Even here, for good reason, we may distinguish between freedom and an equal sharing in it.

In the case of lesser freedoms that are also integral to the democratic practice, there is a closer approximation to equality than in the case of whatever analogous freedoms exist in alternative practices. In this case, the equalities in question are not entailed by the very existence of the freedoms. About this and other comparisons with alternative practices of government, incidentally, it is worth remarking that there is good reason to concentrate on those practices that have been realised and whose nature is known. There is good reason for the common reluctance to give as much attention to those alternatives that as yet are no more than objects of speculation.

The argument of equalities, as noted, also concerns the freedoms that are not integral to the practice of democracy. Some of them have been more equally distributed in non-democratic than in democratic societies. I have in mind approximations to economic and social equality, and all that goes with those approximations. This is a large fact, and indeed it provides an argument against democratic societies that cannot be much diminished. It is nevertheless not an argument that carries the day. No single argument can. In the case of certain other freedoms not integral to democracy – freedoms of culture and law – democracy does better than its alternatives.

These, then, are the two fundamental arguments for the practice of democracy. We shall have to leave unconsidered what appears to be the virtue of taking freedom and equality as grounds of democracy, rather than beginning from principles of justice.[14] We shall also leave untouched, as I have already implied, the relationship of the two arguments to a number of traditional and derivative defences of democracy.[15]

The remaining question raised at the beginning of this essay was that of how political violence stands to the arguments for democracy. More particularly, how does it stand to the ends presupposed in these arguments? These are political and related freedoms, and equalities in these things. While democratic systems do usually make for some realisation of the specified ends, they do not always do so. Historically speaking, democratic systems have not always advanced progress towards these elements of well-being. They have sometimes impeded that progress. This has had to do, in part, with permanent minorities, non-accredited groups in pluralist systems, and the failure of democratic governments to respond to the intensity of distress, as distinct from its extent. It is an obvious fact that democracy has not always served progress towards the ends of blacks in America and Catholics in the province of Ulster, or of course Palestinians in Israel. This has been a question of some of the forms of freedom and some of the forms of equality. Also, of course, considerable impediments to progress have been raised up by undemocratic means.

I do not mean to suggest, however, that democratic systems have failed only in certain very isolated instances to serve these two large objectives. If one turns one's attention away from political and civil rights and the like, and thinks of the distribution of the material means to well-being and the avoidance of distress, and the consequences of that distribution, one encounters larger facts, general facts of inequality and suffering. The whole of the record of democratic systems is dark.

There inevitably is the proposition, then, that precisely the ends of the arguments for the practice of democracy can also be used to support departures from it. The ends that are thought to be served by the rules of democracy are at least sometimes served by the breaking of the rules. This is as plain as the fact that one sometimes serves the ultimate ends of making a promise by not doing what one has promised to do.

There is a further point. It can be argued that in some cases the only infractions that do effectively serve the ends of democracy are acts of terrorism. The argument is in part that nothing else will work, or that nothing else will work in a reasonable time. A morally insupportable distance between indulgence and misery will not be appreciably reduced in one lifetime, or two, by a commitment to only certain ways of affecting electorates, to 'one person, one vote', to an approximate equality in the influencing of government, and to the rule of law.

Will anyone persist in thinking that if the argument of freedom and the argument of equalities do give support to democracy, it cannot be that the ends presupposed by those arguments can enter into an argument for violent infraction of the rules of democracy? There is no reason for thinking so, no inconsistency. If one considers other practices, small and large, it is evident enough that sometimes their justifying purposes are served by departing from them. Kindness in personal relations is usually but certainly not always done by sticking to certain rules of conduct. It is familiar that certain rules do generally serve ends of fairness, but that occasions arise when precisely the ends of fairness are to be achieved only by making an exception to the rules.

DEMOCRATIC TERRORISM

It could not be the intention of any sane person to suggest a general justification of terrorism. It would be as irrational to do so as to offer a general justification of all uses of force by the state, against its own subjects or others. I do not contemplate, either, any general acceptance of terrorism for humanity. What seems to me true, although beyond being shown here, is that there is a justification of some political violence – some of what falls into the category of terrorism for humanity. There is, most relevantly, a moral justification for some of what can have the name of democratic terrorism. Any terrorism so named is to be understood as having certain characteristics, and these will play a considerable part in any justification it may have. They need full consideration.

One of these characteristics has just been given. It can be said for some political violence that it serves large ends of freedom and equality. One may argue for, although not necessarily justify, such terrorism as serving the ends that are also the ends of the practice of democracy, a practice that by definition is non-violent. Thus the fundamental arguments for the practice of democracy may also be used in defence of some terrorism. Other types of violence that cannot call upon these arguments include violence of the Right, and very likely all state-violence. The proposition that terrorism does as a matter of fact promote progress towards freedom and equality in some circumstances can hardly be questioned. The nostrum that nothing is gained by violence does not survive a moment's reflection. It is remarkable, despite its service to entrenched interests, and to the *amour propre* of democratic politicians, that it persists at all, at any rate in books.

The fact about ends is a considerable one, partly because the ends in question are not external to the democratic practice but internal to it. They inform the practice and are fundamental to its character. Furthermore, although the question is a large one, it may be argued that it is uniquely the democratic practice that is effectively directed towards both these ends. It is not as if some violence were directed towards ends of democracy, but not ends that are of the very nature of democracy, or directed to ends of democracy clearly shared with other practices of government.

None the less, we have in the fact about ends only one characteristic of democratic terrorism, one of five. We have, as well, only a necessary condition of the reasonableness of naming some terrorism as democratic. The argument does not depend on nomenclature, but if no more could be said, there would be justice in the reply that once again a term of honour was being misappropriated. More can be said.

A part of it has to do with a notion that has so far been used in this essay but hardly examined. We have seen that the democratic practice, in several ways, excludes coercion. A part of what is excluded, as we have granted, is terrorism. Let us put this aside for a moment and consider a general and fundamental separation of kinds of coercion. These may be called the coercion of force and the coercion of persuasion.

The coercion of force is exemplified by (a) my remaining in a room because I am bound and gagged, (b) my giving up my wallet in the street at the point of a gun, and (c) my injuring a man rather than allowing a number of men to be tortured or to die. In the first case talk of my *acting*, and my *doing* anything, is out of place, but the case is relevant to our concerns none the less. It is true in an important way, in all three cases, although for different reasons, that I am not left room for effectual reflection and judgement about what I do.

This is so in the first case because only one thing, not even an action, is physically possible. It is true in the second case because only one action is possible, given a limit on human capability that we all accept. I could try to keep my wallet, but only at a risk which I am not expected to take. I am left no room for effectual judgement in the third case either. Only one action is possible, at least if the situation is not complicated in certain ways, given a moral prohibition that has quite general acceptance.

It is evident enough that these three cases differ in a certain respect. The first involves a single physical possibility, the second a single human possibility, and the third a single moral possibility. They are alike in that they offer but a single possibility, and hence that there is no room for effectual reflection and judgement. As a consequence of this, although the fact is of secondary importance to us, I am absolved from a certain responsibility in each case. I may be responsible for an act that gave rise to any of the situations, but that is irrelevant. The third case raises various questions, but it is surely true, in an important sense, that I would not be held responsible for injuring the man.

The coercion of persuasion can be illustrated by my giving an unwilling donation to a dubious charity when I believe that the collector will mention a refusal to my employer, who is in favour of the charity. Another example of the coercion of persuasion is my not intervening in a man's denigrating talk about my friend since I believe the man has just been upset by a personal affront. I am restrained, not willingly, by my belief about his state of mind. My restraint may or may not appear to me to have a moral ground. In both cases, I am left room for effectual reflection and judgement.

I do not wish to assert that there is a distinction of a certain kind between the coercion of force and the coercion of persuasion. That is, I do not wish to assert that there is a criterion such that all instances of coercion fall clearly into one category or the other. It would be surprising if this were true. Many instances do fall into one category or the other, and this is sufficient for my argument. I do not suppose either, of course, that the two coercions have been fully analysed or all questions about them answered.

To return to the relevant criteria of democracy, it is evident that they require that the electorate as a whole not be subject to the coercion of force. If an electorate is subject to the coercion of force, the system of government in question is necessarily a tyranny. It is, indeed, principally because of the obvious need to distinguish democracy from tyranny that the criteria of democracy pertaining to coercion appear to be, as they are, unquestionable.

However, are the criteria to be understood in such a way that the electorate in a democracy cannot be subject to the coercion of persuasion, in any form? If they are so understood, then no existing system of government is within sight of satisfying the criteria, and none ever has been. The practice of democracy is such that it is possible for minorities and interest-groups to exert pressure on the electorate. These pressures sometimes stand in analogy with those persuasions of individuals mentioned above. They sometimes evoke moral responses and sometimes evoke responses of prudence, but not what we may call enforced prudence. It is hardly too much to say that the democratic practice has at its bottom the coercion of persuasion. The electorate is restrained or constrained, but in such a way that it is left room for reflection. The same is true for candidates and governments.

It may be supposed, at this point, that terrorism conflicts with democracy, as we have seen it does, because it consists, always, in the coercion of force. It does not. Some terrorism consists in the coercion of persuasion.

Governments, to speak first of them, are left room for effectual reflection and decision in the face of this terrorism. The American government was not *forced* by acts of violence to enter into a more vigorous policy against racial discrimination and racism. It was certainly not forced by violence, although the point takes us out of the area of our primary concern, to change its policy of war in Vietnam. The British government was not forced to take seriously the demands of the oppressed minority in Ulster. The Israeli government is not forced by suicide bombers to join what are sometimes called the civilised states. A man whose shop is destroyed by a fire or a bomb, or a man who abandons his shop in the face of the direct threat of fire or bomb, *is* subjected to the coercion of force. Such facts, and also the facts of injury and death, must enter into reflection and count against violence. It remains true that governments are not subjected to the coercion of force by such acts. The case is similar with electorates and with candidates. With few exceptions, they are not forced into their politics by violence or forced into particular political behaviour.

We have it, then, that while violence is excluded by the criteria of democracy having to do with coercion, it cannot be that these criteria exclude the coercion of persuasion. It follows, then, that violence is not excluded on account of being coercion of persuasion. The exact ground is different, and not now important to us.

To come to the principal point, some terrorism shares an attribute with procedures allowed by the criteria of democracy, procedures that are basic to democratic systems. Some terrorism is a matter of the coercion of persuasion. It is fundamentally different from behaviour that leaves no option to electorates, candidates, and governments. The second feature of democratic terrorism, then, is just this, that it consists only in the coercion of persuasion, and so shares an attribute with activity that is integral to the democratic practice.[16]

The third characteristic of democratic terrorism has to do with equalities. It has been granted that political violence conflicts with the criteria of democratic practice that require an approximation to equality of influence for all citizens. Violence may give to individuals who engage in it a greater degree of influence than is enjoyed by some of the majority of individuals who do not engage in it. It was granted, too, that violence breaks other equality-rules of the democratic practice.

Still, there is another consideration. Of the individuals who do not engage in violence, as we have noticed, there are some who enjoy very great inequalities of influence. That is, wealth and position give to some considerable number of individuals a far greater influence than is had by almost all of those individuals who are without wealth or position. Let us compare, then, the group of the violent and the group of the privileged. It is plain enough that the violent may be seen as attempting to secure an influence equal to others, or something like it. For the most part, they do not succeed.

It must be admitted that the violent are securing or attempting to secure a favourable inequality when compared with a majority of the citizens of their society. This proposition is a ground for our conclusions concerning criteria and rules. It will be of some importance, too, in any final assessment of violence. At the same time, it is entirely relevant that violence by another comparison may be an attempt to secure *equality* of influence, or an approximation of it.

All of this, needless to say, is of a schematic character and could do with improvement of several kinds. The result of a more extended examination, I suggest, will be a conclusion of the kind we have. It is that some violence has an affinity with a feature of the democratic practice. A criterion of that practice is that there is an approximation to equality of influence. Some violence, by one important comparison, is an attempt to approximate more closely to an equality of influence.

A fourth characteristic of democratic terrorism is that it is not directed to the destruction of a democratic system. This is true of most of the violence with which we are familiar. It is not revolutionary in reality, whatever the accompanying rhetoric. That is, it does not have as its object the establishment of a radically different system, one that is non-democratic. In this respect, it is similar to almost all civil disobedience. To suppose that all violence is revolutionary, and that all violence in democratic systems is aimed at the overthrow of those systems, is to fly in the face of the evidence of the present and the past.

There is also a fifth characteristic, related to the fourth. It is not merely that terrorism of the kind I have in mind is not directed to the destruction of democratic systems, but that its effects are likely to be that the systems in question become fuller realisations of democracy in certain respects. That this has been the consequence of terrorism in the historical development of a number of governmental systems is as established a fact as that democratic systems have had their beginnings in revolutionary violence.

Terrorism, then, may serve the ends that are fundamental to the democratic practice. Second, it may, as coercion, share an attribute with procedures that are intrinsic to democratic systems. It cannot be said without dismay and apprehension, but it is to be said that some bombs are like votes. Third, this terrorism is by one comparison an attempt to gain equality of influence. Fourth, it is not directed to the ending of democratic systems. It may, finally, lead to their becoming more democratic.

JUSTIFICATION

To review the entire course of this essay, we began with the practice of democracy and with terrorism, and passed on to a number of propositions. (1) Terrorism renders the system of government of a society less democratic, as to a greater extent do certain uses of economic power. This is one conflict between democracy and terrorism. (2) Terrorism conflicts with certain of the rules of democracy. Although the same is true of economic power, we here have a second conflict between democracy and terrorism. (3) Some terrorism, as we have just seen, may serve the very ends of the fundamental arguments for the practice of democracy. Here, it is mistaken to find conflict. Some of the terrorism in question, further, has other features of as much importance. It may be named democratic violence.

This latter part of this exercise, in particular, has relevance to the general question of the justification of terrorism. That is, I have not pointed to similarity between the democratic practice and one kind of political violence, democratic violence, only in order to establish the fact of similarity. Rather, it has been my intention to bring into clearer view something that will make less difficult our judgement of political violence. It seems true that in considering problematic behaviour, it is a great advantage if we can see clearly its relations to unproblematic behaviour. If in personal relations a man acts in an ambiguous way, and his action requires some kind of appraisal, that appraisal will be facilitated by our seeing to what extent his action has the character of a threat, say, or a warning. It is when his action cannot be assimilated to anything which already has been the subject of reflection and judgement that there is the greatest difficulty.

Some terrorism has features that are shared with the practice of democracy, and that practice, for all that can be said against it, has a large recommendation. These are facts of which we are morally obliged to take account. We have in them one reasoned connection between facts about our societies, the facts of wretchedness and other distress, and substantial conclusions about terrorism.

I have said that it seems to me that at least some political violence has a moral justification, but I have not shown this. It will be clear, I trust, that I do not suppose that the proposition that some violence has a justification can be easily or quickly derived from the fact that it is in the given sense democratic. To think terrorism can be justified this way is as mistaken as taking a policy to be justified just by the fact that the policy issues from the democratic practice. If some bombs are like votes, they also maim and kill. The wretchedness and other distress that call up violence must not be absent from thought and feeling, and not so present in them as to obscure other terrible realities.

Let us keep both realities in mind in an attempt to come to further conclusions.

6

Doctrines and Commitments, and Four Conclusions About Terrorism for Humanity

It is a terrible fact of this time, not much lessened by there having been similar facts in the past and the certainty of more in the future, that men and women make use of violence against persons and things, violence directed to changing societies but condemned by national law and what there is of international law. Some of this terrorism, if very likely none of it by national states, can be regarded as directed to the end of getting people out of wretchedness and other distress, the end of the Principle of Humanity. My purpose in this essay is to make some final responses, in good part sceptical ones, to the general moral question of what is to be said against and for such violence.

DOCTRINES OF POLITICAL OBLIGATION

Political obligation, of which we know something already,[1] is a supposed moral obligation to act legally, a moral obligation to act in accordance with ordinary law, the law of the United States, the United Kingdom, Germany, France or the like. More precisely, members of a society are morally obliged to act in certain ways for a reason involving the fact that these are the legal ways. Members of a society ought to act so as to obey the laws of the society for a reason having to do in some way or other with the existence of the laws. They are not to act in other ways for a reason having to do with their illegality.

This is distinct from any reason for not acting in those ways that does not have to do with the law, such as the plain reasons that to act in those ways may in itself and directly cause pointless suffering or be vicious, this having nothing to do with illegality. It is important that political obligation, so-called, be distinguished from other moral obligations bearing on the same legal or illegal conduct, obligations that would exist in the absence of ordinary law, and hence if the conduct were neither legal nor illegal.

Some seem to think, still, that the general moral question of political violence can be settled by citing a doctrine of political obligation. It provides an effective argument. Let us consider something more of this, but in the main because it is a means to something else, what will be called *judging between alternatives*. Certainly there are large propositions about political obligation in the history of political philosophy, they have been paid much attention, and they are still relied on. There is not much that is more relied on.

Thomas Hobbes may be taken to say that we ought not to break the law, and certainly ought not to contemplate acts of terrorism, because of the great danger of doing so, which he describes as a state of war. A decent existence depends on accepting the restraints of legality. Breaking the law carries the danger of leading to a state of war. He may be taken to say, further, that as a result of the threat of this alternative, members of a society must consent among themselves to give an absolute monopoly of force to the state, and in fact all of us have entered into such a covenant, or anyway find ourselves in one willy-nilly. That is, we are in a covenant to obey the law, the state's law. The state's enjoyment of its monopoly is not conditional on its ruling in accordance with any agreed terms. It is not a party to the covenant, which is among us members of the society.[2]

From John Locke there is the different doctrine that the members of certain societies, those that are not subject to tyranny, ought to keep the laws of the societies, and certainly not resort to violence, since the alternative, if not necessarily so bad as Hobbes's state of war, is a lesser good, some hurt to the general interest, some reduction in the benefits of civil society. In fact we members of such societies do give our tacit consent to forswear violence and all illegality. The state, for its part, must respect and protect our natural rights.[3] In the writings of Jean-Jacques Rousseau, perhaps, there are similar arguments. However, like others of his thoughts, they are obscured in his grand vision of society, its past, present and future.[4]

What we have, in Hobbes and Locke at least, are two arguments for the existence of an obligation to obey the law. One is of a Utilitarian or other consequentialist sort, that illegality will bring in its train some catastrophe or some loss of goods. To break the law is to endanger a beneficial order. The other argument is that we have made a contract or covenant to obey the law, or that we have given our consent. Let us first look at this second sort of argument. In considering it, of course, we shall not contemplate any merely imaginable or hypothetical contract, any contract other than an actual one. Rawls's method of argument for two principles of justice, and for political obligation,[5] includes an imaginable contract. Merely imagined contracts, whatever use they may be in inquiry into moral and political principles, and into non-contractual obligation, clearly give rise to no actual contractual obligations whatever on our part. That is, they do not give rise to anything like an obligation deriving from the making of an agreement.

Let us examine the possibility of there being a contract between individuals and their state or society. What any contract comes to, at bottom, is that offers were made and were accepted by the two parties to the agreement. But (1) how does an individual offer, to the society in which he lives and to the state under which he lives, to obey the law? (2) How do the society and state accept his offer? (3) How do they offer, and (4) how does he accept, whatever it is that they offer to him, presumably the common goods of civil society?

The principal question of these four is the first one, about an individual's offer to his society and state. An answer derived from Locke comes to this: that an individual's tacit offer consisted in the accepting of social goods. Whatever else may be said of this, one clear obstacle to it is that the act of accepting something, in and by itself, is not an offer of any kind, tacit or otherwise. Nothing will turn an act of accepting, by itself, into the making of an offer. Any doubt about this can be put to rest by imagining acts of accepting something, say a gift or a payment, in various other contexts.

Can we get any further ahead by considering not acts of accepting, but acts of participating in government, or related acts, say voting in a democratic election? Let us think of just the latter, voting, that has sometimes been taken as akin to offering.[6] Voting, evidently, is expressing a preference for one of a small number of general policies for a society, or, better, one of a number of would-be governments. One thing to be said of this, as of accepting something, is that in and by itself it is not offering. To express a preference is not in and by itself to make an offer. This simple truth, like the other one, has too often gone unstated and perhaps unnoticed.

Certainly it is possible, in special contexts, for an accepting of goods or the casting of a vote (or just moving one's fingers, or doing a job, or standing still) to count as something else as well, such as an offer. This depends, as we all know, on there being a certain prior understanding. More particularly, the fact of an offer depends on a prior act or activity by the agent, perhaps an utterance, precisely to the effect that the subsequent accepting or voting is also to count as something else. It is just possible for there to be argument, I suppose, to the conclusion that each of us has acted in such a way as to convey that our acceptings of social goods, or our votings, are to count as offers to obey the law. Any such argument or speculation will surely be weak stuff.

I shall not consider any, but simply make a proposal that may have the virtue of conceding what needs to be conceded, if anything at all is to be saved of the sorry history of doctrines about an actual social contract. Also, it goes a good way towards explaining that history. (If no explanation could be offered of the history, incidentally, one would of course have a reason for suspecting that one had missed a good argument in it that kept it going, or anyway an argument.) The proposal has to do with a general expectation rather than an agreement, and hence it has to do with something that has often been confused with an agreement. This is so since agreements, among other things, do certainly create expectations.

Members of societies make many offers that certainly are related to the supposed offer on their part that is required by the Contract Argument, as we may call it, for political obligation. Many prospective employees offer, in addition to their work, a certain general conduct, more or less in line with legality. In modern societies, further, a good many of the people in question are prospective employees of the state. The offer is an unquestionable and ordinary one, part of a legal contract. So with the offers of individuals who enter into contracts having to do with the hiring of property. There are also related offers made in connection with memberships of various kinds, and with such things as travel.

What we have in all this is a large fact. It is that we make many offers of good behaviour or better. These ordinary offers of ours, and to a lesser extent our acceptings of social goods, and to a still lesser extent our votings, contribute to a *general expectation*: the expectation on the part of our fellows that we will obey the law. It is fortified by a yet larger thing, the plain fact of our customary behaviour where that does not have to do with offers, acceptings and votings. No one will think, I trust, that to create an expectation that one will do a thing is always somehow to *agree* to do it. One can create an expectation without its being true that doing it depends on an accepted conventional procedure to be gone through by two parties.

In this general expectation and its possible frustration, particularly by acts of violence, we have something clear in support of the idea that we have an obligation to obey the law. This is pretty well the residue of the prolonged speculation about a social contract. The best description of our situation is not in part that we have made what counts as an offer, on which some of us may go back, but that we have contributed to a general expectation, which some of us may defeat.

This residue is not nothing, but perhaps it comes to very little. It may be a small thing when compared with others, some of which are also arguments against violence, and some of which are arguments in favour of violence. To approach my main point by way of an analogy, there is the simple truism that the prospective frustration of a class of slave-owners, when their general expectation that the slaves will not rise is defeated, places no noticeable obligation on the slaves not to rise. It is a general truth that what the frustration of any expectation counts for is a matter of what else is on hand. There may be such larger things on hand as misery, exploitation or injustice. Obligations having to do with these larger things will then defeat or overwhelm the obligation not to give frustration. To this point can be added another one, that there may be obligations that do not conflict with, but need no support from, the given obligation having to do with expectation. They are, so to speak, greater forces in the same direction, against violence. They too may have to do with misery, exploitation or injustice.

Let us leave the Contract Argument for a time and consider quickly the other reason for political obligation derived from Hobbes and Locke. It is, in one form, that the illegality of an act, as distinct from any other feature, increases the probability of a war of all against all, a catastrophe, or anyway the loss of great goods. This reason having to do with certain consequences, of course, can be advanced independently of the Contract Argument.[7] Taken just as it is, this reason for political obligation does pretty well require that we make judgements about such larger things as those just mentioned, misery and the like. This reason is therefore different from the Contract Argument in not making a false promise – that we can have an effective argument against political violence without considering larger things. Speculation about an act's illegality leading to a catastrophe or a loss of goods does inevitably bring in the opposed speculation about the act's possible gains. There is its possible contribution, still taken as an illegality, to ending or alleviating misery and the like.

There is also another clear point, related to what was said of the residue of the Contract Argument. Whatever speculations we come to about illegality and its dangers and gains, they may be at least well-matched in importance by others. In a sentence, there may be at least as much to be said against my act taken simply as a killing, in itself and for its direct consequences, as when it is taken as something with consequences as an illegality. In another sentence, it may be that there is something to be said *for* an act of mine, considered in connection with large things, escapes from distress, and that this is of greater importance than what can be said against it as something that as an illegality may have certain consequences.

There remain some other possible doctrines of political obligation, reasons for obeying the law that may deserve more attention than they have got. They are that there is fairness, or repayment of debt, or simply equality, in obeying the law if one has accepted social goods or if one has participated to some extent in a certain decision-procedure – perhaps voted in a democratic election.[8] Here too, however, there surely is no possibility of having an effective argument that avoids large questions. This will again be a matter of who has what amounts of social goods, and who has what amounts of their opposites, or a matter of the extent to which elections have in fact been fair to all voters or members of society. One wonders if the Contract Argument has been so much to the forefront, as against these other possible reasons for political obligation, because it seemed not to raise the large questions.

COMMITMENT TO MORAL NECESSITIES

Consider people of a reflective and enlightened kind, people in some degree sympathetic to the Principle of Humanity, certainly moved by its great end. Now consider proposing to them that, in the aid of progress towards the end, they shoot undefended ordinary people in the street, or give money to an organisation that does. Consider advancing to them an argument of this predictable form: that the probable and the certain consequences of inaction or of non-violent action are such that violence, with all of its probable and certain consequences, is justified. Some of the people in question would reply along certain lines, and in a certain manner, rather as follows:

It is wholly wrong to engage in attempting to weigh up what cannot be weighed up. Killing a man, killing a woman, maiming a child, destroying a family, these are atrocities that cannot be brought into a calculation of gains and losses. The things themselves are by nature inhuman or savage. It cannot be that there are common units in terms of which they are to be assigned a value. This cannot be done in terms of one category – the satisfaction of desires – or in terms of some few states of feeling or of mind. These things cannot be reduced to subtraction and addition of human experience, efficiently categorised and balanced against uncertain futures. They are outrages, and outrages are not to be measured against anything.

Precisely the large-scale horrors of recent decades have resulted from attempts to do this. It is this computational morality that issued in the grisliness of wars for which the American war in Vietnam set a pattern, and also earlier purges and massacres, and, in so far as it matters, the bestialisation of those who carried them out. One must have an overwhelming pessimism about the attempt to reason in this calculative way.

There is in fact no alternative to *a morality of necessities*: of what must be done, and what must not be done. This is not merely a matter of what ought to be done, and what ought not to be done, since moral necessities are more than merely imperatives. They have to do with the taking of life, sexual relations and relations of loyalty, the administration of justice, customs of respect and gentleness, and other things. Together they constitute the foundation of a human way of life, something needed in order to be human. We may have differences of judgement about them, but not to grant the existence of such necessities is to be other than human.

If these necessities can come into conflict in abnormal, painful and improbable situations, they are absolute none the less, and they can be so without benefit of religion or superstition. They have a truth, the truth of the human and the profoundly natural.

Chief among the necessities are those having to do with not taking life, respect for individual life, a horror of killing. The proposal, then, to shoot people or to support this killing, for purposes of generalised well-being, is unthinkable. To do so would be to be degraded in a way not to be affected at all by political success.

This response to political violence has been in a way derived from Stuart Hampshire's lecture, 'Morality and Pessimism',[9] although the lecture is wide in scope and does not mention political violence. Even if one cannot agree with its general conclusions about moral reasoning, it must be accepted as an admirable piece of work in moral philosophy. It succeeds in the rare thing of expressing a moral commitment, than which nothing is more important to morality. As for the response to political violence drawn from the lecture, surely one cannot but want to share its commitment. The force of affirmation, one may think, is not made the less by the fact that matters are not brought into clear consistency and order.

It may be, however, that there are pressing questions that are neither answered nor excluded by what is said, but in fact raised by what is said. It may be, that is, that they are questions that have a single source, in nothing other than moral passion. Can it be, perhaps, that these questions should not be asked? Can there be a proper refusal to consider questions that presuppose that atrocities may have a defence? The idea that this is so, or that something like this is so, may itself be taken to play a small part in the given response to violence.

Well, it does seem true enough that there are circumstances in which we rightly say that it is right not to consider certain questions. There is little doubt, however, that these are circumstances that can be described in a more explicit and enlightening way. They are such that we already know or believe the answers to certain questions, or already know or believe enough of the answers. They are circumstances in which it is right not to consider further. That is, we have in fact considered the questions, or done something like it. It does not seem to me that with terrorism we are always in the requisite position of knowledge or belief. My reasons will become apparent.

The sketched response to violence is of course not to be taken just as declamation that violence is terribly wrong, but rather as an argument. Moreover, its force as declamation really must be distinguished from its force as argument. What the commitment mainly comes to can be stated plainly.

There is an attempt made to reason about moral issues in a certain way, but this attempt fails, and in so doing has terrible results, such as a tolerance of terrorism, which tolerance is in fact ruled out by another way of proceeding, this being a reliance on moral necessities.

We have here another promise, a second one, of an effective means of dismissing without difficulty defences or excuses with respect to terrorism, a way of avoiding large and awful questions.

Let us begin at the end. It is allowed, as indeed it must be allowed, that moral necessities do sometimes conflict. It is allowed that they conflict, however, only in abnormal, painful, and improbable situations. What these situations are, of course, and whether they are so rare, will be determined in part by one's conception of the range or extent of the moral necessities. Hampshire's conception is such that necessities having to do with distributive justice are somehow included, and the inclusion must seem undeniably right. He mentions too the necessities of helping the poverty-stricken and the destitute.

It might be taken as intended, in such responses to violence as the one sketched, that the moral necessities having to do with not killing are the chief moral necessities, and more than that, they are such as to overwhelm all others. There is no conflict of necessities here, or only a conflict quickly ended by victory. Can we take up this simple view, that there can be no situations whatever in which killing of whatever kind is allowed? If so, we limit greatly, without further reflection, the situations in which there can be conflict between moral necessities. The simple view may be appealing, partly for its very simplicity. If we reflect for even a moment, none the less, we are unlikely to be able to take it up.[10]

Those who suppose themselves to be entertaining it are almost certain not to be entertaining precisely the view that killing is not to be done no matter what numbers of deaths ensue, no matter what wretchedness or suffering, no matter what injustice. They are in fact likely to be thinking that we must never kill outside of certain permissible situations, perhaps the extremes of self-defence, and certain wars, and when the state and society judge that execution is necessary, and circumstances when an enslaved people try to throw off tyranny.

Is it not impossible, however, to draw a confident line of this kind between the area where killing is wholly impermissible and the area where it is somehow permissible? The reason, generally speaking, is that it must be at least a possibility that the features that make killing permissible in the one given area – certain features of distress and injustice – have counterparts in the other area. To put the point in another way, there can hardly be an overwhelming moral necessity not to kill in the one area if it is inconceivable that there is such a thing in the other. There is not a sufficient factual difference between, say, certain tyrannies and all related political situations whatever not involving tyranny, or between certain 'just wars' and all related situations not involving such wars.

What we must allow is that sometimes, perhaps rarely, the conflict between moral necessities is conflict with necessities of not killing. Let us for the moment suppose no more than this, that there are some situations, perhaps few, in which such necessities conflict with others. We may have in mind a conflict between an act of killing and a course of action that will make for the persistence of some appalling injustice, the distress of a whole people. The question arises of what is to be done in such a situation.

We cannot do nothing. I do not mean that it would be wrong to do nothing, that doing nothing is not morally possible, but rather that it is not a possibility at all to avoid going against one moral necessity. It is not as if we can do A, thereby going against one moral necessity, or do B, thereby going against a different moral necessity – or do C, thereby going against no moral necessity. The position is that we can do only A or B, each one going against a moral necessity. It is only if this is the position that we in fact have a situation where there is conflict between moral necessities. To take an analogy from war, there is no conflict in the relevant sense between the need to save the civilians and the need for the army to advance if there is a way of doing both. To return to our own case, there is no conflict between the necessity not to kill and the necessity of ending the appalling distress, if in fact we can do something that respects both necessities.

If there is no possibility of an easy way, since one moral necessity or another must be denied, can we resort to something like an unre- flective leap? Can we 'act spontaneously'? In most situations, this is unthinkable. There is therefore the inevitable conclusion that in almost all situations where moral necessities conflict, we must try in a rational way to do the best thing. This is not to be avoided. No commitment can save us from it.

What hopes can we have? An answer is that we can try to *judge between alternatives*, each one including the denial of a necessity. We can try to compare the two alternatives directly, or by relating both to other circumstances of which we can conceive. Would one of the two be about as bad as a third circumstance, and the other worse? If we can or must do this, several things follow. To entertain the answer that we can try to judge between alternatives is to grant what already is sadly clear, that there is a sense of the word 'necessary' such that what we have been calling the moral necessities are *not* necessary. Simply to allow that there can be conflict between moral necessities is to move a good way in this direction. To say we can try to compare alternatives, secondly, may seem to run directly against the earlier part of the given response to violence. Is this comparing not exactly that method of moral reasoning that is said to be condemned to failure, and also to produce terrible results?

Let me try to make a bit clearer what I mean by judging between alternatives. In many forms it is not uncommon, although we overlook some instances and are not inclined to draw attention to others. Governments and also lesser offices of state weigh up possible situations such that one situation would include the taking or the loss of life, as well as a certain gain, and the other situation would involve distress or a loss, but no loss of life. This takes place in the ordinary allocation of social expenditure, notably in connection with the level of medical services. This kind of judgement has other sorts of instances. It is a part of the daily life of ordinary individuals to choose for themselves between two situations only one of which carries some risk of loss of life. Plainly, to return to governments, this judgement is part of contemplating war.

Very generally described, the procedure of judging between alternatives is one of weighing up (a) the extent to which and (b) the way in which each of two or more alternatives would probably or certainly satisfy desires or, as we are often inclined to say, needs. Would more needs or desires be satisfied in one situation? Whose needs or desires? Would the persons benefited be those who have already been more benefited than others? This is not the procedure of judging morally which of two extents and ways of satisfaction is right, but rather the procedure of assessing the extents and ways. It is almost certain to involve judgements of probability. How probable is it that certain extents and ways of satisfaction would follow from certain actions or policies? We shall look at this greatly important thing later.

This comparison is unquestionably something that in some areas and circumstances can be done well, rather than something that cannot be done at all or hardly at all. It can be done with rational confidence, very roughly speaking, when the complexity of the task is within certain bounds. It can more likely be done with such confidence, for example, when the wants or needs that would be satisfied by two possible courses of action are more or less of the same kind rather than of different kinds, or of fewer rather than more kinds. There evidently is less complication in comparing possible satisfactions of the need for food, say, than satisfactions of the needs for food on the one hand and for freedom on the other. The complexity of the task of comparison is more likely within bounds, secondly, if there are relatively simple principles as to the class or classes of people to be taken into account. It is one thing if the aim is to satisfy certain wants for as many people as possible, or indeed all persons in a society. It is another if one takes into account different classes, perhaps differentiated by the extent to which each class has already had satisfaction of wants other than those now in question. The complexity of the task of comparison increases, thirdly, to the extent that wants, needs, and satisfactions are interdependent. It is often true that the satisfaction of one want stands in the way of the satisfaction of another, and so on.

The idea that judgement between alternatives is impossible, that it cannot be done at all, seems to derive from confusing it with other things, including some things suggested by that sketched response to violence. This comparison is not a procedure whereby situations are looked at in terms of some single experienced stuff, best called the feeling of satisfaction or happiness. It is supposed, with whatever truth, that this was the recommendation of the early Utilitarians, but clearly it is true that very few of the relevant possible situations can be compared in just this way, this way alone. Indeed, many have no such ingredient. Nor can we deal in only a few such ingredients. This is not to say that situations cannot be weighed up in terms of the extent to which they satisfy desires or needs, and the way in which they do this.

It is to be granted, too, that various things that can be called calculation or computation are impossible. Again, they are not the comparison involved in judging between alternatives. It is to be granted also that there are difficulties, some of them notorious, in the way of systematising or formalising this comparison, and hence that there are no systems of a certain kind. This does not put comparison in question, or put its rationality in question.[11]

If judging between alternatives is not a method of proceeding that is always condemned to failure, it is not a method either that has an innate or general tendency to issue in terrible results. Like many other human practices, its upshots are mixed. Finally, is there any reason for thinking that comparison cannot take into account moral necessities? We have assumed that it can. There is no reason to think otherwise, since to speak of necessities is at bottom to speak of desires, no doubt great or deep desires. Not to regard them in this way would be to reduce them to mysteries.

What remains to be said, for the moment, is that it may be mistaken to think that the conflicts between moral necessities are rare or few, that the need to judge between alternatives does not arise at all often. It may be mistaken to think, more precisely, that terrorism never produces such a conflict. If that were so, it would be reasonable to say that a commitment to moral necessities offered us an effective argument against terrorism, or something close to that. On the contrary, there may be *many* circumstances where moral necessities conflict, where moral passion divides, such that a choice must be made between necessities. The deepest of moral feelings may not be able to save us from many large and dark questions. On the contrary, such feelings may *contribute to* and indeed *give rise to* such questions. Evidently the only possibility, if we cannot rely on such things as moral necessities, is the business of judging between alternatives. We shall return to it, and to the question of how confident it can be with terrorism.

We have it that neither a commitment to moral necessities nor any doctrine about political obligation will allow us to settle the question that faces us. More generally, there must be the idea that there is nothing by way of *doctrine or commitment* that enables us to settle these questions. It may be that we cannot settle our minds by way of Marx's theory of history and his propositions about terrorism and revolution, or by way of lawyer-like reflections on what is sometimes called the rule of law, or by an embracing of liberal values, or by a politician's reliance on the values of negotiation and compromise, or by any version of the idea, so refuted by the course of history, or simply by its wars, that those in authority know best.

WRETCHEDNESS AND OTHER DISTRESS

It will come as no great surprise that I think all doctrines and commitments – roughly speaking all alternatives to judging between alternatives – *are* too weak to enable us to settle the question of terrorism in an effective way. There are facts that overwhelm any arguments about political obligation, and any residue of them. There are facts that stand in the way of our thinking that violence only rarely raises conflicts between moral necessities.

It is possible to disagree, and I am aware that many people, perhaps a majority, are bound to be uncertain. There is only one way, as it seems to me, of coming to a proper view. It is by having an immediate awareness of certain facts, and by adequately reflecting on them. They can be put into different kinds, categories and orders. A first order of them has to do with average lengths of life. A second has to do with what can be called economic and social facts. A third has to do with what are underdescribed as political inequalities. Attention was given to average lifetimes near the beginning of this book,[12] and more attention is a good idea now. Let us also attend a bit to the other two orders of fact. It is only through doing so that reflection about violence comes into touch with reality.

(1) Truths about average lengths of life in Britain, the United States and so on are summed up in a certain general proposition. It is that the worst-off tenths of population in terms of income roughly speaking, in the rich societies, live about six years less long on average than the best-off tenths.[13] The proposition, of course, is a summary of various facts of death. In the worst-off tenths, there are more infant deaths, more deaths of children, more of young people and adults due to sickness, more deaths at work and because of work, and, to a small extent, more old-age but none the less premature deaths.

The average life-expectancy in the four poor societies is about 38 years, as against 77 in some of our rich societies.[14] The difference in average life-expectancy between the worst-off tenth in the poor societies and the best-off tenth in the rich societies is in the neighbourhood of 50 years, like a species-difference. Again these are summaries of various facts of death, still more grim. Again they are facts about individuals. They have precisely as much to do with individuals who have proper names as have bullets. The resulting losses of living time, to speak of them alone, are of the magnitude of many millions of years. These losses could have been prevented, and it is in fact within our power to change the future.

Shall we, as many people will want to do, give little attention to these propositions about length of life? There are particular inclinations that lead in that direction, and also several reasons, of whatever strength. I shall mention six.

There is the inclination to turn away from the subject because of the anticipation that moral or political consequences may be drawn from it. One may foresee its being argued that those who are now living shorter lives should be compensated, and that steps should be taken to change the probability that future members of the same economic classes will live shorter lives. One may foresee, too, that this argument may issue in a proposition about acts of violence directed towards compensation or change. Anticipations of this kind, while natural enough, do not give anything like a decent reason for ignoring the facts and suppositions about length of life. We need not further discuss, either, a second reluctance. It has its beginning not in the anticipation of political argument but in more unreflective feelings having to do with one's place and privilege in society, or the place and privilege of those with whom one identifies.

We must resist, thirdly, that simple disinclination to consider things that may be connected in an immediate way with what every sane person regards as the horror of violence. One reason for paying attention to the darkness of our societies is that doing so may be the only tolerable way, or even the only effective way, of moving towards an ending of violence and its horror. Nor, fourthly, are the facts and suppositions about lifetimes to be put aside because they necessarily are the beginning of an irrational appeal. By their nature they may give rise to feeling, but rationality and feeling very often come together. Indeed in certain inquiries, including our own, to inhibit feeling in certain ways is the most absurd of irrationalities.

Are the figures given in the facts and propositions to be rejected as inaccurate? The answer is that they are as accurate as a reasonable judgement requires. A careful account of them would call for many qualifications. For example, life-expectancy figures for a group at a given time are based on records of deaths in an immediately prior period. As such, they are never perfectly accurate predictions. Usually, but certainly not always, the situation will turn out to be very slightly better than predicted. Again, by way of random example, there is some degree of error in the calculation of the size of the fifth social class in England and Wales. The calculation is based on the reported occupations of individuals after their deaths and some misreportings occur. Such deficiencies in the figures, and others like them, do not begin to make our use of them improper.

Finally, are the facts and suppositions about lifetimes to be passed by because they are open to misconception? They are open to misconception, but they are none the worse for that. If we put aside everything about which mistakes can be made, we put aside everything. It would be a confusion, for example, to conceive what has been said as being about *killings* or *intended deaths*. It may be a mistake to say, even, that what we are considering are 'condoned shortenings of life'. Nor do our facts and suppositions concern *violence* being done to the people who die early. As already noted, there has been a persistent inclination in a part of the Left to describe almost any dark social or economic fact as a fact of violence. It is not one of my inclinations, and no such suggestion is meant. What we have before us are shortenings of life that are in a way natural and expected. That is not a reason for not attending to them, for not reflecting on them.

Let us do so, at least a little.

Certain people now alive will live less long on average than other people in their societies, and so they will have less of what we can call the satisfaction of life, although that thin phrase does not begin to catch the reality. There are few circumstances, even near the end of one's life, where death is preferable to life, inexistence preferable to continued existence. Whatever one may think of unnaturally prolonged life, it is evident enough that an immense majority of people in the groups in question lack something that virtually everyone desires deeply and that others do possess. The fact is independent of whether or not the individuals in question ever have a thought of the likely length of their lives. Suppose that some do not. Unequal experience does not become otherwise if those who have it are unaware of the fact.

Certainly the inequality in question is an unusual one. A man who dies, although he does not enjoy a longer life, does not miss it either. He does not feel deprived or suffer a lack. It may be that this must be regarded as of importance with respect to our response to the inequality. I shall not pursue the matter except to remark that the same question must arise in other contexts. A man who dies a death by violence is not distressed thereafter either. He too does not miss what he does not have. It is always or never important that a person whose life is shortened has a lifetime unequal to the lifetimes of others. The bare fact of inequality is always or never important.

There is also the fact that some individuals are in various ways aware that their lives will be shorter. There is then the matter of the felt distress that goes with the realisation. No doubt it is true that blacks in America and unskilled men in Britain, and the lowest economic tenth generally, are not troubled throughout most of their lives by the prospect that their lives will be shorter than those of others. (One can say the same, of course, of those who die deaths of violence.) There are times, none the less, more common in the experience of those who will die natural but earlier deaths, when there is an awareness of the prospect of a shortened life. It may be suggested, by someone resolute enough, that their feeling is unreasonable. This is so, it may be said, because they are desiring what is not possible, anguished because they will not have what in fact cannot be given to them.

Let us grant, for the purpose of argument, that it is not possible now to change their life-expectancy. While it may have been possible in the past to do something that would have issued in a different state of affairs in the present, it is not possible now. If this makes their desire 'unreasonable', it remains a truth that they have it, and suffer because of its frustrations. A man who has been incurably blinded, who wants to see, may not cease to have his 'unreasonable' desire or his anguish. He may also have a related and absolutely reasonable desire, a desire for compensation. So with the worst-off tenth. What we have before us also touches on the desire of almost every person that certain others should live longer. The fact of a shortened life is a fact for those who live on. A part, one of many, of that experience is the experience of a mother whose children die. It is an experience of death before time, and hence not relevant to us, but also of death before time.

Some may be stern enough to say that these last two considerations – about the conscious distress of some individuals because of their shorter lives, and the distress of those related to them – must be qualified in a certain way. Blacks in America do not expect to live as long as whites. Unskilled men do not expect to live as long as professional men. The families of these people do not expect them to live so long. As a consequence, whites or professional men would be more distressed if they shared the same lesser prospect of life. That is very likely a truth. Feelings and attitudes are in part the result of anticipations. Still, the truth does not very much diminish the facts we have before us. It does not begin to give us a reason for passing quickly over the facts before us.

(2) The second order of facts may need less attention. It has to do with wealth and income, but more precisely with their consequences for lives, however long or short. To glance first at rich societies, the one tenth of American families who have most wealth have in fact got 71 per cent of it. The bottom *four* tenths have 0.2 per cent. The bottom tenth has none worth speaking of.[15] The best-off tenth of American families, in terms of income or consumption, receive 30.5 per cent of the total income. The tenth of American families that receive least in fact receive 1.8 per cent of the total. The figures do not reveal that some families have quite extraordinary incomes and others have virtually no incomes at all.[16]

Will there be a great deal less inequality in the sharing of wealth 20 years from now in America? Or in Britain where the present figures are similar? Given the rate of change in the past, one can make a reasonable guess at what will be the state of affairs in a generation. It is that if there is no fundamental change in the two societies, the best-off tenths will have much the same shares and the poorest tenths will each have 1 per cent or less. In terms of income or consumption, the best-off tenth has getting on for a third of it, and the worst-off tenth something like a fiftieth. There is unlikely to be any dramatic change for the next generation. As with America and Britain, so with other rich western societies. There are similar truths about present distributions of wealth and income. We can be confident, too, to turn to the next generations, that the general picture is unlikely to be greatly different.

These facts of wealth and income are not important for themselves. They are important because they are determinants and indicators of inequalities in a great part of the things that people value and need. They are determinants and indicators, more precisely, of inequalities with respect to things people will give much or indeed almost anything to have or not to have. Some of these are health, or anyway relief from pain, some vigour rather than lassitude, shelter or a home, security in it, food, self-determination in one's own life, work, some standing and respect, hope for one's children, a life with others of one's kind, a sense of not being ignorant, religion, ways of ageing and dying.[17]

... if you're one of us, it's very bad, the water situation is. You spend a lot of your time worrying about water. That's the truth. You just don't begin a day without deciding who's going to get the water, and when, and how good it'll be when it comes back. That's why I use Coke for my children, right from the start I do. It's the best thing you can get to take away their thirst, and give them the sugar they need. They drink it all over the country, it's made for the rest of the people. If they use it, we can. We have to, though. We can't turn to much of anything else. There's the milk you have in your body to start out with, and that goes real fast I hear say because we can't get enough for ourselves. My grandma, she used to say that nothing comes free, even a mother's milk, and that you plain run dry if you can't keep yourself fed up good. The one thing you *can* do is keep plenty of water inside, and that's what Cokes do, and as I say, they give you your sugar. And when the babies get on their own, they drink those Cokes and you can see them perk up, perk right up. They'll be lying around, tired-like, and waiting on me to figure out what I can find for them, and then I'll get the bottle opener and they know what's coming. My grandma, she said we'd be all dried up and dead and gone from starvation if God didn't send us Cokes.[18]

The differences between classes within the rich societies are but one part of the present subject, the smaller part. There are also the yet more terrible differences between the rich and the poor societies.

In the United States, the gross national product per person has recently been an average of $29,240. In four African countries, it has been about $220 per person.[19] These figures, of course, do not give one any direct grasp of actual incomes within the two groups of countries. They would do so if each gross national product issued in an equal income for each member of society. The bottom tenth of population in the poor societies has an average income some thousands of times smaller than the income of the top tenth of population in rich societies. This comparison does not pertain only to small groups of people, but to several hundred million.

It has been a generally accepted fact that since 1965, and indeed before then, economic inequalities between these two parts of the world have been increasing rather than decreasing. Comparatively speaking, the poor countries have been getting poorer and the rich countries richer. Their rates of growth are such that the gap has been widening. The only thing that could reverse the trend is what amounts to an absolute transformation in the economic relations of the poor and rich countries. If it does not occur, economic inequalities between the two groups of countries, and between classes within them, will be much greater in 20 years.

It is again the consequences of these economic facts that are important. These consequences, other than those having to do with lengths of lifetimes, constitute those ways of existence that come to the attention of most of us by way of the newspaper advertisements of such charities as War on Want and the Save the Children Fund. These are such consequences as the awfulnesses and horrors of hunger over a lifetime, the experience of starvation, disease and other distress, disdain, being without help, ignorance, degradation. I have maintained that we must know more of these things. Still, it seems that to say so little of them as could be said here in a page or two would go against decency. For that reason or some other one, I shall not offer a brisk list of the facts of trachoma, leprosy or Aids. Nor shall I attempt to quicken anyone's appreciation of being a life almost without hope. Each of us has a clear obligation to inform himself or herself, and to come to have the feelings required not by this or that moral or political or economic outlook, but by what can be called humanity.

(3) The history of men and women, looked at in one direct way, has been a struggle for freedom, most importantly the freedom of those groups best described as peoples and nations. That is, it has been a struggle in which groups have sought to achieve some approximation to the freedom and power of other groups. This autonomy of a people consists, roughly, in the independent governance of a homeland. It is governance by the group as distinct from some minority of it, and it is also governance free from external oppression or constraint.

It is remarkably easy, if one has always been a member of a group that attained freedom and power long ago, to think that groups who have not, and who struggle for autonomy, are in fact pursuing something not worth the shedding of blood. It is also remarkably easy, if one has always been a member of an autonomous group, to count the worth of autonomy for little as against the worth of something else – say, some level of material well-being, or peace, or 'participation' in the governance of a homeland.

There is a clear unreality about this. How can it be that an ideal of community or of generous humanity should lead to the idea that it is the groups having less or no autonomy that should be the first to give up what they have, or the hope of some? As for the worth of autonomy, there is a kind of absurdity in attempting to devalue it. Something for which sane and admirable men have always been willing to risk and to accept death, torture, punishment, and also self-accusation and the experience of guilt is something worth having if anything is. There is no alternative to this conclusion.

To say these things, inevitably, is again to raise problems. What groups count? What is a 'homeland'? I am inclined to the proposition that the most relevant answers, those to be heard first, are those given by those people who are the weaker and who define themselves as a group, an autonomy-demanding group. Their definition of themselves is most relevant, and their claim that something is their homeland is to be heard first. There is a proper presumption that they are right. No doubt it has happened that definitions and claims of this kind have sometimes been mistaken, in a large sense of the word. Perhaps this has been rare.

Certainly there are clear and indubitable cases. The rape of Palestine by Zionist Israel is one of these. There is no need for an inquiry into passages of political and other history over half a century, accounts of agreements broken or offers refused, or even of atrocities committed. There is no need, even, for records of the murdering of children by soldiers in tanks or airmen with missiles, and the crimes against humanity of those who subsequently became prime ministers. The changing population figures for the region, Jewish and Arab, overcome all of that. A people's homeland has been taken and violated by settlement.[20] A people has been violated. Nothing conceals it, certainly not any refrain about democracy against terrorism.

FOUR CONCLUSIONS

The first of four main conclusions of this essay is that large and dark facts ensure that no doctrine or commitment can give us an effective condemnation of all terrorism for humanity. No doctrine or commitment enables us to settle the question. Large and dark facts stand in the way of any progress by way of the Contract Agreement for political obligation, and any progress by way of the doctrine of moral necessities. It is impossible to believe that there can be only very few relevant conflicts between moral necessities, conflicts involving the given violence. On the contrary, there can be many. In these conflicts, as in the case of reflection on the Contract Argument, we are led to judgement between alternatives. Let us return to that inevitable subject, about which the essential thing remains to be said. We can begin by recalling particular ends of terrorism for humanity, and the terrorism itself, and by considering the relation between the two things.

Terrorism can be directed to undeniably good ends, first of all democracy, perhaps a better democracy than ours. Indeed, that terrorism can be directed to undeniably good ends is an understatement. It can be directed to the changing of circumstances such that there will be a general agreement in the future that they were circumstances of moral barbarity. Terrorism can be directed, to speak differently, to ends that make for progress towards well-being for those who are deprived of it. As already remarked, what I have to say mainly concerns terrorism for humanity. It is a certainty that in order to consider it one must also take account of responses of state-terrorism and terrorism of the Right, but neither of these latter things raises large moral difficulty. There is a want of seriousness in a refusal to distinguish, say, between violence with the aim of securing a distribution of food that would allow children to live, and terrorism with the aim of defending the aggression of a people or race or class.

It hardly needs adding that not all of the interim goals of terrorism for humanity are on a level. That is, some advances are of greater value, either for themselves or as means. No doubt it is generally true that the alleviation of the situation of the very worst off is the first priority. Those who are slowly starving to death have needs even greater than those who are seeking autonomy, or defending only their liberties.

Sometimes, as with a struggle for freedom, the end of a campaign of terrorism is specific enough. There was a clear end in the case of black terrorists in South Africa – to end apartheid and a pretence of democracy. There has been a clear-enough end in the case of the Irish Republican Army and its successors in Northern Ireland. Certainly there is a clear end in the case of the Palestinian terrorists seeking to free their people and to end the violation of their homeland. It is now not a mistake or a self-deception, but merely a tactic, to confuse it with the destruction of the nuclear power Israel.[21]

In other cases the end in view has been less specific, or indeed not specific. To the extent that a specific end is insufficiently defined in a public way, or to the extent that in fact there is no specific end but only a general one, there is likely to be less chance of achieving the specific end or something of an intended sort, perhaps something within an intended range. Terrorism is an attempt to coerce peoples and governments in a certain way; that is to say that it attempts to bring them to have certain attitudes and to make certain decisions. It is distinct from an exercise of force that leaves no place for decision.[22] It follows that governments and peoples must have more or less unavoidable knowledge of what is being demanded of them, less room for pretence of ignorance. One way in which a campaign of violence may fail, then, is through insufficient definition. This would be true, perhaps, of any campaign that had as its announced end anything so general as what I have given as the goal of terrorism for humanity.

So much for ends. The second matter is terrorism itself. It is a mistake to avoid its true description, a description that keeps its true nature in mind. Terrorism consists, in part, in atrocity and carnage.

Its reality for us at this time is more or less immediate. That it is immediate, while the related facts of wretchedness and other distress are in several senses distant, is reason enough for not dwelling further on terrorism. This is not one-sidedness.[23]

Third, and most importantly, there is the resulting large matter of the relation of the means of terrorism for humanity to its ends, of the relation of any campaign of violence to its specific or general purpose. This has to do with probabilities, and with the required sort of judgement between alternatives. Let us approach it by noticing five possible upshots of terrorism. Perhaps these are not quite all the relevant possibilities, and it will be apparent that they could be replaced by somewhat different classifications. This will not affect my argument.

Individuals decide on a campaign of terrorism directed to a specific and well-defined end, the changing or ending of an appalling circumstance, one whose persistence will cause suffering to many victims. These victims of this circumstance will live badly, and mostly briefly, if the circumstance is not changed. This decision in favour of terrorism is of course the result, in part, of a conviction that non-violent means, including civil disobedience, will not succeed in ending or alleviating the circumstance of injustice.

The campaign is taken forward, and it is resisted by the relevant state or government, for whatever reason. It is resisted, to speak more plainly, by individuals in power, perhaps democratically elected individuals. Their resistance is successful, and so there persists the appalling circumstance to which the terrorism was directed. The upshot of the violence, then, is useless distress and death. This is the first of our five possible upshots of terrorism.

Whether the campaign of terrorism that would fail was right or wrong, clearly, was a matter of judgement between alternatives. In one essential part, this was the question of how probable it was in the beginning and later, to a reasonable judgement, that the outcome would be what it was. Also, if a knowing judge would have found it difficult to estimate the probability of the outcome, necessarily there was uncertainty as to whether the right course of action, whatever it was, would in fact turn out for the best.

I take it that kinds and degrees of ignorance or uncertainty about the results of possible actions do not make it impossible to tell which of two is right. Almost always there is a discoverable right action, an answer to the question of what ought to be done.[24] The answer is determined in part by the available knowledge, however small that knowledge. Of course, whether the right action will turn out for the best is another question. One may be less than confident about that. I shall return to this fundamental matter, and also, incidentally, to the question of the morality of the state resistance to the terrorism in question.

To turn now to a second possibility, the terrorism in question is like the first in terms of the circumstance to which it is directed and the conviction that alternative non-violent means would not change that circumstance. The total result of this terrorism is worse. The appalling circumstance of suffering is not changed, and, because of state-terrorism, a 'war on terror', terrorism of the Right, war itself and perhaps a military take-over or open oligarchy, there is yet more distress and death than would have been required by the state simply to defeat the campaign of violence. The upshot, then, is useless distress and death, more than in the first case.

A third kind of violence is such that the end is achieved, but by means that cannot be justified by that end. That is, the total result is worse than it might have been, perhaps for the reason that the given end would have been achieved by non-violent means, which in fact were operating, or for the reason that the given end would have been achieved by non-violent means that would have been operating if there had been no violence. Again the upshot includes useless suffering. The fact is not of importance, but I think there has been relatively little violence of this sort, where a circumstance of injustice or misery is in fact ended, but the means of violence were unnecessary or excessive.

A fourth possibility is that terrorism achieves its end, the end being worth it. A circumstance of viciousness is ended within a given time, and the terrible cost was none the less not too great. Non-violence would not have worked. Many of the revolutions and struggles of the past that now are celebrated as beginnings of national histories are taken to be in this category. Again, of course, the question of the rightness of the actions in question is to be settled, in an essential part, by what the probability was of achieving the given end.

A fifth possible situation is one where the violence does not achieve its specific end, but does issue in a related state of affairs, or where violence has a general rather than a specific end, and does achieve something of the envisaged general kind. Non-violence would not have worked. The total result is better than the alternative. Certainly there has been violence of this fifth kind. I doubt that there is any serious outlook, short of an absolute passivism, which in this twenty-first century can perhaps no longer be serious, that does not have the consequence that there have been many cases of the fifth kind, and also the fourth.

The essential and principal issue, of course, is whether anyone can say, with rational confidence, at or near the beginning, that some envisaged terrorism will have one of the five possible upshots rather than others. What is needed is an answer to that question; or rather to a question, or indeed many questions in a campaign over the course of time, of this general form:

> Which is right, non-violent action with no immediate harm to anyone, and with a certain probability of ending or altering a circumstance of suffering and injustice within a certain time, or terrorism at a certain immediate cost of death and destruction, with a certain probability of ending or altering a circumstance of suffering and injustice within a certain time?

To answer a question of this form is of course to do what was called judging between alternatives.

Suppose for a moment that in a given circumstance we can know that the immediate harm of non-violence will come to nothing, or not much at all. Suppose too, although this will certainly be harder, that we can say with some assurance what the immediate effect of the contemplated violence will be. Finally, suppose we have a grasp of the suffering and injustice to be affected by the non-violence, and the suffering and injustice that may be affected by the terrorism – which two things may or may not be the same. A crucial matter remains. Can there be confidence in judging the two probabilities of success? Can we say with confidence what probability there is of the non-violence being successful, and what probability there is of the violence being successful?

Given knowledge of each of the other matters it may be taken that if the non-violence probability is below a certain level, and if the violence probability is above a certain level, then an answer to the question can be had with confidence. That is, if the probability of non-violence being successful is below a certain critical level, and the probability of terrorism being successful is above a certain critical level, then an answer that terrorism is the right course can be made with confidence. On the other hand, if the non-violence probability is above the critical level, or if the violence probability is below the other critical level, then another answer can be had with confidence.

That is, if the likelihood of non-violence being a success is above the critical level, and the likelihood of violence being a success is below the other critical level, then the answer that violence is wrong can be made with confidence.

In the nature of things, however, both probabilities will usually be near their critical levels. This guarantees difficulty, at least. In the nature of things, to speak differently, it will be unlikely that a state and society are such as to make it relatively highly probable (well above a critical level) that they will give in to non-violence, while it is of relatively low probability (well below the critical level) that they will give in to violence. The general reason for this is a certain rationality.

To express this simply, if the opponents of a state or government have a 75 per cent chance of winning by resort to violence, then it will be reasonable for the state to bargain or compromise. There will be, that is, a decent probability of the opponents of the state achieving their goal non-violently. It is unlikely to happen that the opponents of the state have a 75 per cent chance of winning by violence while there is a relatively low probability of their winning by non-violence. It is unlikely, indeed, that the opponents have a 50 per cent chance of winning by violence while there is a relatively low probability of their winning by non-violence. On the other hand, if the opponents have only a 5 per cent chance of winning by violence, then there will be less incentive for the government to bargain. There will be little probability of the opponents getting their way by non-violence. It will be a rare case where the opponents have so small a chance of getting their way by violence and a relatively large probability of getting it non-violently.

In general, then, the probabilities will be close to their critical levels. There is the consequence, a large consequence, that a rational confidence will require fairly precise judgements of probability. Ordinarily, rough and hence more secure judgements will not be sufficient. A rough and secure judgement of probability will leave one with no decision whatever on the critical issue. There is no use in the judgement that there is a 60 per cent or 70 per cent chance of success, if the question of whether or not to go ahead depends on whether the chance is over or under 65 per cent.

I am inclined to the unhappy view that for the most part we cannot judge the relevant probabilities with the precision needed for rational confidence. Certainly judgement between alternatives is necessary, and almost certainly there is a right judgement. That it can be made with rational confidence is unlikely.

There is an argument of another kind for this conclusion. Essentially it is that there has been a general failure to estimate such probabilities precisely in the past, and that the reasons for this are likely to persist into the future. There has not been anything like confirmation of claims to the effect that a certain proportion of campaigns of terrorism of a given sort will result in situations of a certain kind. No one has found identifying marks by which to decide that a conceived campaign is to a certain extent probable to have one of the first three upshots rather than the fourth or fifth. Indeed there has not been much success in even the formulating of such claims. This essential prior activity, which might also be called the devising of hypotheses, has itself turned out to be pretty well impossible. It has been impossible to produce testable claims which have some possibility of being useful.

The formulating and confirming of such claims would have been the result, of course, of study of the past. In fact, this endeavour of formulating and confirming claims could hardly have been distinct from another one, the giving of explanations of past sequences of events, past successes and failures. There is very little available by way of such explanations. If anything remotely like 'laws of history' have been discovered, they have not been such as to enable historians to offer persuasive explanations of successes and failures in past political struggles. Certainly there should now be universal agreement that speculative philosophy of history, the pursuit of 'laws of history', has been a dismal failure. If we can be confident that some past event was a necessary condition of a subsequent one, we cannot be anything like confident about what set of events was a sufficient condition for the subsequent one.

This failure to explain the outcomes of past struggles, and hence to arrive at claims for use in the present and future, has several explanations, and they are truisms. One is that so many different factors enter into the producing of successes and failures. The range of relevant factors for a violent political struggle is exceedingly wide. The outcome of a violent struggle depends on: (a) the opposition to the state or government, which may be taken to vary as a function of at least its size, social base of support, principles, ideology, aims and strategy, leadership, finances, organisational competence, and weapons; (b) the state's strength, which has to do with at least the government's form, popularity, competence, resources and stability; and (c) the international environment, which includes the influence and support of other governments, movements and groups, the changing relationships between them, and also the influence and pressure of international opinion.[25]

A second explanation of failure in explaining and predicting violent political struggles is that there is relatively little data to go on. This will only seem surprising or paradoxical to those who forget that we cannot for purposes of experiment increase the number or kind of such struggles. In most of science, by contrast, we can so act as to produce more and more data. A third and large explanation is the nature of history: there is not enough repetition in it to enable us to learn enough from it. Changes in technology are part of this story. Changes in ideology are as important, as are changing conceptions of what is within the realm of the possible. History is the product of human invention of several kinds, and endless invention gives rise to endless change.

These explanations of past failure to explain and predict political struggles evidently suggest that the failure will persist. Particularly the third explanation, the nature of history, makes it unlikely that we shall come to do better.

For the most part, then, we cannot make adequate assessments of the probability that political action or inaction will have a certain result, that an envisaged campaign of violence will be of one of the five kinds. We cannot make assessments adequate for a rational confidence. For the most part, for we cannot be at all confident that our judgements that a campaign of terrorism is wrong or right will turn out well. We cannot have the reassurance that doing the right thing, as we see it, will have the best upshot. For the most part we are subject to uncertainty.

This does leave it open that there are cases where we can judge probabilities with confidence, and so come to decently based verdicts. These will include some in which terrorism is judged right and some in which it is judged wrong. It is my view that some democratic terrorism, and in particular such terrorism as also has the aim of liberating a people from invasion and occupation, can be defended as right. This is so with respect to Palestinian terrorism now against the Israeli state. I have no doubt that the Palestinians have a moral right to their terrorism against the Israelis. They have at this time a moral right to their only possibility of redress against the resolution of the Zionist state of Israel and its state-terrorism. Never has terrorism had a better claim also to the good names of self-defence, resistance, response to state-terrorism and so on.[26]

My second general conclusion, however, is that we are subject to an extensive uncertainty about terrorism, an uncertainty with relatively few exceptions. Some will be inclined to agree that an extensive uncertainty is indeed unavoidable, and then pass on to this proposition: even when it is judged to be right, the judgement will quite possibly turn out badly, and so there is the general conclusion that violence must not be used. We cannot have the reassurance of such a proposition. There is as much reason to move from the given uncertainty to the proposition that even when violence is judged to be wrong the judgement will quite possibly turn out to involve a mistake, and so we can conclude that violence *may* be used. There is, of course a long tradition that derives kinds of reassuring conservatism from claims about our ignorance. We must not do this or that, leaving the well-tried path, because we do not know what dangers lie to one side. Whatever is to be said of all that, my claim about our uncertainty is such that it has neither a reassuring nor an unreassuring upshot. If we are uncertain in the given way, any inference to conservatism is worthless. The well-tried path is no more known to be correct than any other path.[27]

Despite all of what has been said, this general conclusion about uncertainty would have about it a certain strangeness if it were, so to speak, the whole truth. This strangeness, looked at one way, would be the strangeness of finding very little of a substantial kind in the long historical endeavour of so many people, including moral and political philosophers and theorists. To speak differently, the strangeness would derive from a conviction that while our position with respect to much violence may be one of uncertainty, it is not only that. Surely we do also have certainty of certain kinds, or anyway decently grounded belief. There is then something else to be said in connection with the general moral question of terrorism for humanity. It is my third conclusion. It pertains, incidentally, to other general moral questions, not only to violence.

We have been concerned so far, essentially, with an overriding question. However, we can attempt to have other moral views of an action or campaign or practice than just an overriding one. This seems always overlooked in such contexts as our present one. It is not that we can attempt only two possible views, expressed indifferently by such pairs of terms as 'right' and 'wrong', 'justified' and 'unjustified', 'correct' and 'mistaken', 'ought' and 'ought not', 'morally necessary' and 'not morally necessary'. Or rather, it is not that we can take up only one of several overriding moral views, since, to mention one other, there is also the overriding view that the fundamental question is one whose answer must be uncertain. It is also true, to come to the point, that actions can have features and effects about which we are certain, perhaps many. An act can then stand in comparison to many other acts.

Let us say that both of two acts of bombing were wrong. It remains of obvious importance that one had a definition having to do with a struggle against suffering and injustice, while the other did not. It is probable that each act made for some progress or movement in the direction supported by the respective agents. This is then a way in which the first act, although it will not achieve a given end, and hence was wrong, has something to be said for it that the second does not. This sort of argument has a fairly wide application. Consider again the first act of bombing, and also the state-terrorism in response. We may suppose that there is no killing or wounding in the latter activity, except in self-defence. We may suppose that, but for the opposition of the state, the suffering and injustice in question would be ended or affected. It is possible, then, while taking both the violent act and the replying activity of the state to be wrong, to see a respect in which the act has a recommendation not had by the activity. There is also the clear respect, having to do with death and injury, in which the state's activity is superior.

It seems to follow from this view of terrorism, as being open to more judgements than just two or three, that a certain policy with respect to certain movements should be adopted, a policy that comprehends realities. It is unlikely that it will be, except in so far as the interests of national states conflict. It is, roughly, that the treatment accorded to terrorist movements, some of them, should be different. By way of one illustration, it seems to be an indubitable moral necessity that the Palestinians should have the possibility of stating their claims to Americans, whose role in the crime against them is plain. They should have the possibility of having their case heard regularly on American television and in American newspapers, the violation of their lives and homes made clear. My third conclusion, then, is that if we cannot with confidence make overriding judgements about violence we can make lesser judgements, and they are of some value as guides to action.

The last of my conclusions also has to do with comparisons, two comparisons between campaigns of terrorism on the one hand and, on the other, the policies and practices of the individuals who are the reality of sovereign states. We can proceed here in terms of overriding views.

Of the mentioned categories of campaigns of terrorism, the first three worsen situations rather than improve them, and the others do the opposite. For the most part, it is impossible to have a rational confidence at the outset that a judgement for or against will turn out well. There are, of course, also some other situations where it is possible to have a rational confidence, or perhaps to be rationally certain. Let us have one of these in mind in connection with the first comparison. Let us suppose that there is rational certainty that an ongoing campaign of terrorism is in fact of the first kind. That is, it is directed to the ending of circumstance of misery, but it will not succeed because of resistance by the individuals who constitute the executive of the relevant state.

If the perpetuation of the campaign of violence is wrong, there can be an argument to the conclusion that resistance by the individuals of the state, who also bear proper names, is as wrong as the campaign of terrorism. Without their resistance the circumstance of misery would be ended. There is also another comparison. The campaign of violence is mistaken only because of the resistance of the state. That is, without the resistance the campaign would not be mistaken. On the other hand, it is not true that the governmental resistance is wrong because of the campaign of violence.

Many will want to resist something here. One inapposite line of resistance has to do with making a moral assessment of the two groups of persons or agents involved. Such an assessment is not the main thing. There are individuals who engage in violence out of non-moral motivation, and there are individuals who oppose them out of equally non-moral motivation, having been corrupted by power, or having become representatives of no more than the self-interest of a group, perhaps vicious self-interest. There are individuals who engage in terrorism and by so doing show themselves to be of moral motivation, whether or not their judgements as to their actions are correct, and the same is true of some of those in power who oppose them.

The main thing is not in this way about agents, but about actions. It is about questions of this form: Taking an action in itself and for its consequences, ought it to be performed? Of course, as we know, the question can be couched in terms of conceivable agents. Characterising the act in terms of possible motives and beliefs, we may ask if it is an act that would be performed by a certain knowledgeable judge. I do not have in mind what might be called an Ideal

Agent, one who has greater sympathy or knowledge than can humanly be had, but something in the line of an actual person, although one with some attributes and not others.

The kind of violence-situation described is one in which violence would be wrong, but where the state's response of violence would also be wrong. Without that response – or rather, with a different response that is a possibility – there would be a changing or ending of the relevant unjust circumstance, perhaps one of misery. Can this be resisted appositely? Can it be shown that there are no such cases? It seems likely that many attempts will involve recourse to a doctrine of political obligation, about which we know, or perhaps to some sort of commitment to moral necessities, of which we know something, or to some other essentially indecisive consideration. What would be decisive would be the proposition that if national states were to end a circumstance of injustice, that would in fact always result in a greater one. It seems to me that this cannot be shown.

There is also the second comparison, my main one. Suppose that the situation is the more common one where it is not possible to have confidence about one's judgement that the campaign of violence is right or wrong. What is also true of the situation is that the circumstance of misery might be changed or ended by govern-mental action. Individuals in government have a considerable opportunity to secure this end, without violence. I speak of politi-cians, very many politicians.

They have considerable opportunity to end misery without thereby causing suffering. That they do not do this, at any rate try to do it, is wrong. This judgement is not like the other in being so open to the possibility of going wrong. Here we have a small asymmetry, but one that throws into sharp definition the historic and continuing practices of sovereign states, or rather the individuals at their heads. It is a settled fact, about which there can be hardly any doubt, that their obligations are great. An increasing perception of this great obligation, and of great failure in it, will be a recommendation of much terrorism. This is my fourth conclusion.

Certain propositions about political obligations, like others about moral necessities, do not enable us to settle the general moral question of terrorism for humanity. Nor does any other doctrine or commitment. This is so because of certain grim facts of distress in its several forms. All that we can do is attempt to judge between alter-natives. This, for the most part, cannot be anything like confident.

Relatively few cases are like the Palestinian one. For the most part we cannot escape uncertainty about the overriding question. It is an uncertainty, however, in which certain limited perceptions and responses are possible. The most important of these may be the perception of the wrongfulness of the historic and continuing practices of states, or, more to the point, of the individuals who are the reality of those sovereign states.

It was said at the beginning of this essay that I wished to say some things in advocacy of a certain response to the question of terrorism for humanity. In finishing, it is worth saying that I do take decent political philosophy not only to have the nature of all decent philosophy, but also to consist in advocacy. It is a kind of analogue to the adversarial system in some systems of law, including the British. Political philosophers are inevitably more like barristers, as distinct from judges – or anyway impartial judges – than is allowed by certain high conceptions of their subject, and it is best to admit it. No doubt they are advocates more or less convinced of the rightness of their cases, but they are advocates none the less.

Acknowledgements

I am grateful for comments on essays in this book, at one stage or another of their histories, to Brian Barry, George Brennan, Malcolm Budd, Myles Burnyeat, Ingrid Honderich, Jerry Cohen, James Griffin, David Hamlyn, Alastair Hannay, John Honderich, Kiaran Honderich, David Lloyd-Thomas, Mihailo Markovic, Helen Marshall, Janet Radcliffe Richards, Adam Schaff, Amartya Sen, Timothy Sprigge, Allen Wood, undergraduate and graduate students at University College London, and critics in many university audiences.

The histories of the essays, under different titles, are as follows.

Earlier versions of the first, second and fifth were published as *Three Essays on Political Violence* (Blackwell, 1977) and *Political Violence* (Cornell University Press, 1976).

Earlier versions of all but the third were in the first edition of *Violence for Equality: Inquiries in Political Philosophy* (Penguin, 1980).

Versions of all the essays were in *Violence for Equality: Inquiries in Political Philosophy* (Routledge, 1989).

The original version of the first one was first published in *Nature and Conduct: Royal Institute of Philosophy Lectures* (Macmillan, London, 1975), edited by Richard Peters.

Much of the second comes from 'Appraisals of Political Violence', in *Issues in Law and Morality, Proceedings of the 1971 Oberlin Colloquium in Philosophy* (Press of Case Western Reserve University, 1973), edited by Norman S. Care and Thomas Trelogan. The essay also comes from 'The Use of the Basic Proposition of a Theory of Justice', *Mind*, 1975.

The third essay is an enlargement of 'The Problem of Well-Being and the Principle of Equality', *Mind*, 1981.

The fourth comes originally from 'Clean Hands', a lecture to the Workshop on Justice at the University of Calgary in 1977.

A version of the fifth appears in *Violence and Aggression, Proceedings of the Third International Conference of the International Society for the History of Ideas* (Rutgers University Press, 1974), edited by Philip P. Weiner and John Fisher. A version also appeared in the journal *Philosophy and Public Affairs*, 1973.

The sixth essay comes from a speech to a UNESCO conference on 'The Rights and Duties Deriving, for States and Groups, from the Establishment of a New International Economic and Cultural Order', Paris, 1978.

I am grateful to the various publishers for permissions.

Notes

INTRODUCTION

1. Other books of political philosophy on terrorism are J. Angelo Corlett, *Terrorism: A Philosophical Analysis* (Kluwer, 2003); Trudy Govier, *A Delicate Balance: What Philosophy Can Tell Us About Terrorism* (Westview, 2002); Richard Norman, *Ethics, Killing and War* (Cambridge University Press, 1995); Paul Gilbert, *Terrorism, Security and Nationality: An Introductory Study in Applied Political Philosophy* (Routledge, 2003). With respect to both political philosophy and sceptical examinations of our politics, economics and international relations, the outstanding works are those of Noam Chomsky, the great moral judge of our age: *9–11* (Seven Stories Press, 2001); *Pirates and Emperors, Old and New: International Terrorism in the Real World* (Pluto, 2002); *Necessary Illusions* (Pluto, 1989), etc. For religious morality, see Rowan Williams, the Archbishop of Canterbury, *Writing in the Dust* (Hodder & Stoughton, 2002).
2. The piece in question seems to have been published first on a University of California website (as http://ist-socrates.berkeley.edu/~jsearle/pdf/terrorism.pdf) and then elsewhere on the web (e.g. http://www.dianahsieh.com/). It was recommended in collections of readings on terrorism (e.g. http://ontology.buffalo.edu/war/).
3. See below, pp. 15, 153–5.
4. *After the Terror* (Edinburgh University Press, 2002), pp. 25–9, 150–1; 'After the Terror: A Book and Further Thoughts', *The Journal of Ethics*, 7, 2003, pp. 161–81.
5. A larger bundle consists in this book with *After the Terror* and the collection of papers *On Political Means and Social Ends* (Edinburgh University Press, 2003), and also *Conservatism* (Pluto Press, Revised edition, 2004).

ESSAY 1

1. *National Vital Statistics Report* (2001), vol. 48, no. 18, 7 Feb., p. 33. National Center for Health Statistics.
2. In 1970 the gap between blacks and whites was 7.5 years and in 1980 it was 6.3 years. *Statistical Abstract of the United States: 1988* (Washington, 1988), Table 105, p. 70.
3. 'Trends in Life Expectancy by Social Class, 1972–1999' (2000), Table 1. Office for National Statistics.
4. One indication of this is the fact about the men of the fifth social class in England and Wales just reported.
5. *The World Guide 2001–2002* (New Internationalist Publications). The figures were derived by this reference work from the World Bank, UNICEF,

the World Health Organization, and so on. There is little change in *The World Guide 2003–2004*.

6. Source: *Statistical Abstract of the United States*, 1974, Table 80, p. 58.
7. Cf. pp. 99–100.
8. Robert Coles, *Still Hungry in America* (Cleveland, 1969), pp. 27–8.
9. For more on the definition, and on a good deal else in this book, see *After The Terror* (Edinburgh University Press, 2002) and *On Political Means and Social Ends* (Edinburgh University Press, 2003).
10. See Essay 2 and Essay 5.
11. For the other, see Essay 6.
12. Cf. *After the Terror*, Ch. 2, *On Political Means and Social Ends*, Essay 6.
13. If they may be concealed from some of us by attitude, so to speak, it is easy enough to find certain related but different agents of distress. These are those men in uniform engaged in state terrorism, as in Palestine against the Palestinians, under the cover of talk of war. They are not our concern.
14. See below, Essay 6.
15. *Herr Eugen Duhring's Revolution in Science (Anti-Duhring)*, trans. E. Burns (New York, 1966), p. 109. The view is shared with Marx and others in their tradition, of course.
16. *J. S. Mill On Liberty In Focus* (Routledge, 1991), ed. John Gray and G.W. Smith, p. 27.
17. For a kind of introduction to Burke, see my *Conservatism* (Penguin 1991 and forthcoming in a revised edition, Pluto Press).
18. J.J.C. Smart and Bernard Williams, *Utilitarianism: For and Against* (Cambridge University Press, 1973), pp. 97–8.
19. *Ibid.*, pp. 116–17, 103–4.
20. *Ibid.*, p. 94.
21. *Ibid.*, pp. 102–3.
22. *Ibid.*, p. 103. For further relevant reflections, see my *A Theory of Determinism: The Mind, Neuroscience, and Life-Hopes* (Oxford University Press, 1988), pp. 420ff.
23. *Ibid.*, pp. 88–9.
24. Williams considers this sort of suggestion, that consequentialist attitudes may be seen as supporting the chemist's decision. His remarks, I think, do not really undercut the suggestion.
25. Essay 6.
26. *Conjectures and Refutations: The Growth of Scientific Knowledge* (Routledge, 1963), p. 355.
27. *Ibid.*, p. 363.
28. *Ibid.*, p. 358.
29. *Ibid.*, p. 357.
30. Stuart Hampshire discusses and defends Bertrand Russell's relevant condemnation of governments in 'Russell, Radicalism, and Reason', in *Philosophy and Political Action* (Oxford University Press, 1972), ed. Virginia Held, Kai Nielsen, and Charles Parsons.
31. Essay 6.
32. For more general remarks on egalitarian items, see pp. 90–1, 100–8. For more on Rawls, see pp. 58–82, 91–2.

33. Consider, in this connection, *The Ideal of Equality* (St. Martin's Press, 2000), ed. Matthew Clayton and Andrew Williams.

ESSAY 2

1. Robert Paul Wolff, 'On Violence', *Journal of Philosophy*, 1969; *In Defence of Anarchism* (Harper, 1970).
2. John Rawls, *A Theory of Justice* (Harvard and Oxford University Presses, 1972); 'Distributive Justice', in *Philosophy, Politics and Society*, 3rd series, ed. Peter Laslett and W. G. Runciman (Blackwell, 1969); 'The Justification of Civil Disobedience', in *Civil Disobedience: Theory and Practice*, ed. Hugo Adam Bedau (Pegasus, 1969).
3. I mean to cast no aspersion on either Wolff or Rawls. The first has demonstrated a high moral concern inside and outside philosophy. Rawls evidently had the sense of responsibility of a liberal. But philosophers can get caught up in things, maybe captivated by the logic that is their line of life.
4. Can this concession be expressed even covertly as the concession that the distinctive political concept of violence is empty and that talk that uses it is incoherent? Is there no sense in talk of a use of force prohibited by a government that has a right to unreflective obedience? Well, we can conceive of a government that is in fact accorded a right it ought not to have. We can conceive, further, that it puts the usual prohibitions on certain uses of force. There are more problems here. The substantial conclusion of the argument is preserved in the overt form given above, however, so let us stick to that. I mean the proposition that the violent cannot be condemned for failing in a certain obligation, for going against a certain authority.
5. We are told that 'claims to authority', the authority related to unreflective obedience, 'have been defended on a variety of grounds, most prominent among which are the appeal to God, to tradition, to expertise, to the laws of history, and to the consent of those commanded' ('On Violence', p. 603). Later (p. 612) it seems to be assumed that the argument of the essay has shown 'the classical theory of political authority' to be mistaken.
6. *A Theory of Justice*, p. 302.
7. *Ibid.*, pp. 17, 21, 42, 167 and 577–87. The basic proposition is also thought to have two other uses, which I do not consider here. See my article 'The Use of the Basic Proposition of a Theory of Justice', *Mind*, 1975. It is revised and reprinted as 'The Contract Argument in a Theory of Justice' in my *On Political Means and Social Ends* (Edinburgh University Press, 2003).
8. *Ibid.*, pp. 12, 120; cf. pp. 15, 18, 120, 121 and 521.
9. Rawls has in mind different things in different places. In 'The Justification of Civil Disobedience', he appears to be dealing with actual societies.
10. For a relevant discussion by Rawls, but not one which materially affected the point, see *A Theory of Justice*, pp. 577–87.
11. *Ibid.*, pp. 14–21, 587.

12. I have left out, incidentally, some formal conditions on principles that might be taken to be part of the first premise of the Contract Argument, and also some practical considerations. Both can evidently also go into the Ordinary Argument. *Ibid.*, pp. 146, 175.

13. *Ibid.*, p. 13.

14. Rawls, in passing and perhaps implicitly, grants the point. *Ibid.* p. 139.

15. A second objection to my fundamental criticism would have to do with a view of the Contract Argument as other than a plain matter of premises and conclusion. See *A Theory of Justice*, pp. 21, 48–9, 579. One can, however, take the same view of the Ordinary Argument.

16. Do by all means consult Rawls's subsequent work, *Political Liberalism* (Columbia University Press, 1993), which has not been studied by me.

17. 'Distributive Justice', pp. 73–5.

18. For a view of our capitalism, see *After the Terror*, pp. 129–40.

19. Essay 6.

ESSAY 3

1. Systematic accounts of human goods, basic values and things which it is rational to desire for their own sake have not been popular and have been attempted by few philosophers, for whatever reason, perhaps because they are unlikely to issue in a universality that does not suit conventional moralities. See W.K. Frankena, *Ethics* (Englewood Cliffs, 1973), p. 71f.; Morris Ginsberg, *On the Diversity of Morals* (London, 1956), Chs 7 & 8; John Finnis, *Natural Law and Natural Rights* (Oxford, 1980), Chs 3 & 4. There is a further statement of my six goods at the beginning of Essay 8. See also my *After the Terror* (Edinburgh University Press, 2002), Chs 1 & 2.

2. Rawls, *A Theory of Justice*, p. 440f., gives a satisfactory account, and defines self-respect as the most important primary good.

3. There is an excellent discussion of forms of the assumption in Amartya Sen, *Collective Choice and Social Welfare* (San Francisco, 1970), Ch. 7.

4. Robert Nozick, *Anarchy, State and Utopia* (Oxford, 1974), esp. Ch. 7, section 1.

5. D.A. Lloyd-Thomas in 'The Ones in Darkness', *Philosophy* (1979), rightly notices a mistaken line of mine in favour of this, the Principle of Any Equality, and a correct one against in *Three Essays on Political Violence* (Blackwells, 1976), p. 41 and p. 10, respectively. His main contention, that in so far as there is a connection at all between serious need and equality, it holds doubtfully between need and the Principle of Formal Equality, noticed below, seems to me mistaken. Need, as explained in this essay, is bound up with the Principle of Humanity.

6. *A Theory of Justice*.

7. *Ibid.*, p. 61. More light is shed in Rawls's later book *Political Liberalism* (Columbia University Press, 1993), on which I have found it hard to get a hold.

8. Cf. *After the Terror*, and also 'John Stuart Mill's *On Liberty*, and a Question About Liberalism' and 'The Contract Argument in a Theory of Justice' in *On Political Means and Social Ends* (Edinburgh University Press, 2003).

9. Moralities of relationship are examined and criticised in *After the Terror*, Ch. 3.
10. See also p. 13 above.
11. There is another argument, more basic, to the effect that it is the human nature of each of us to put our personal demands for satisfaction of our great desires ahead of the demands of others for the satisfaction of their secondary rather than great desires, and that consistency then commits us to the Principle of Humanity. See *After the Terror*, Ch. 2. There is also the argument for the principle that consists in the strength of its kind of thing, and the weakness or worse of other kinds of thing. See, in *On Political Means and Social Ends*, 'Consequentialisms, Moralities of Concern, and Selfishness'.
12. See my *Punishment, The Supposed Justifications* (Polity, 1989; forthcoming in a revised edition from Pluto Press) and also *A Theory of Determinism: The Mind, Neuroscience and Life-Hopes* (Oxford University Press, 1988), Ch. 10.
13. For a full discussion see my 'Determinism and Politics', *Midwest Studies in Philosophy*, 1982, to be reprinted in *On Freedom* (Edinburgh University Press, 2004).
14. See Essay 6 below, and also 'After the Terror: A Book and Further Thoughts' in *On Political Means and Social Ends*.

ESSAY 4

1. See, for beginnings of such recent reflection, the admirable book by Jonathan Glover, *Causing Death and Saving Lives* (Penguin Books, 1977) particularly Ch. 7, and an alarming short article, 'The Survival Lottery' (*Philosophy*, 1975) by John Harris.
2. Of which you heard a good deal in Essay 1.
3. See my *A Theory of Determinism*, pp. 420ff.
4. A good deal more is said, and different is said, of the natural fact and practice of morality in *After the Terror*, Ch. 2. For more on acts and omissions, see Ch. 3 of that book. For an examination of consequentialist moralities, and one kind in particular, see 'Consequentialisms, Moralities of Concern, and Selfishness' in *On Political Means and Social Ends*.
5. In ordinary morality there is a distinction between what we are obliged to do and what is done by those who are or used to be called saints and heroes. They are those individuals, such as Albert Schweitzer, who are said to be moved by an ideal, and so to do more than their duty. It is said that they do things of moral excellence, but they would not do wrong if they did not do them. They do some of the things that we omit to do.

ESSAY 5

1. Jean-Paul Sartre, preface to Frantz Fanon, *The Wretched of the Earth*, trans. Constance Farrington (Penguin, 1970). A similar idea is at the centre of George Sorel's *Reflections on Violence* (Cambridge University Press, 1999).

For an enlightening account of Sorel's thought, see Isaiah Berlin, 'George Sorel', in his *Against the Current* (Oxford University Press, 1979).

2. Herbert Marcuse, 'Ethics and Revolution', in *Revolution and the Rule of Law*, ed. Edward Kent (Prentice Hall, 1971).
3. Essay 1.
4. Essay 2.
5. Compare, for example, Robert Dahl's classic work, *A Preface to Democratic Theory* (University of Chicago Press, 1956), p. 84.
6. I now take the characterisation of democracy having to do with equality in these paragraphs to be an idealisation, whether innocent or self-serving, a characterisation not in sight of being true of our actual democratic systems. See my 'Hierarchic Democracy and the Necessity of Mass Civil Disobedience', reprinted in *On Political Means and Social Ends*. There is a reason or anyway a good excuse for not changing the rosy picture here by intruding some reality into it. That democracy *rosily conceived* allows for the idea of democratic terrorism says even more about that terrorism than could be said by way of a properly realistic picture of our democracy.
7. Essay 1.
8. See, for example, the essays by Robert Audi, Robert L. Holmes and Ronald S. Miller, in *Violence*, ed. Jerome A. Schaffer (New York, 1971).
9. Marcuse, in an article in the *New York Times Magazine*, October 27, 1968, associates himself with this view. See also John Harris, 'The Marxist Conception of Violence', *Philosophy and Public Affairs*, 1974.
10. See above, Essay 2.
11. p. 15.
12. Dahl, *A Preface to Democratic Theory*, p. 72.
13. Here and elsewhere, as indicated in note 6, I now think differently. It is reasonable to argue that economic power destroys the rule having to do with equality. See 'Hierarchic Democracy and the Necessity of Mass Civil Disobedience'.
14. As, of course, does Rawls.
15. All or most of them are given by Henry B. Mayo, *An Introduction to Democratic Theory* (Oxford University Press, 1960).
16. Rawls (*A Theory of Justice*, p. 366 and elsewhere) suggests that violence cannot be a 'mode of address', a form of notice given to a society that injustice exists. If it is true that violence cannot be described as a 'mode of address', it is also true that typically it does not consist in the coercion of force. My argument depends in part on this latter point rather than any doubtful suggestion about a close connection between violence and more formal or venerable proceedings. In my view, as may be anticipated, violence may on occasion be described as 'an appeal to the sense of justice of the majority', which Rawls appears to deny.

ESSAY 6

1. Essay 2.
2. *Leviathan* (various editions), Chs 26 & 30.
3. John Locke, *Second Treatise of Government* (various editions), Chs 16–19.

4. J.-J. Rousseau, *A Discourse on Political Economy* (various editions).
5. Essay 4.
6. See Peter Singer, *Democracy and Disobedience* (Oxford University Press, 1973).
7. See R.M. Hare, 'Political Obligation', in Ted Honderich (ed.), *Social Ends and Political Means* (Routledge, 1976).
8. See Singer, *Democracy and Disobedience*. See also above, Essay 2.
9. Stuart Hampshire, *Morality and Pessimism*, the Leslie Stephen Lecture, 1972 (Cambridge University Press, 1972). Hampshire has not written substantially about political violence, but a transcript of a television talk by him came to my attention after this essay was written (*The New Review*, March 1967). He says, in part:

> I ... suggest the beginnings of a rough criterion for justified killing in very extreme situations in peacetime. Four conditions are necessary: first, that it is a response to a great injustice and oppression, as of a resistance movement against a foreign power ruling by force and terror so that the victim is the reverse of innocent; secondly, that it is certain that no lawful and non-violent means of remedying the injustice and oppression will be given; thirdly, that the political killing will certainly cause far less suffering, and less widespread suffering than the present injustice and cruelty are causing; lastly, that it really is very probable that the killing will end the oppression, and that it will not provoke more violence and more horror; this last condition is very rarely satisfied, but sometimes it may have been. These principles give the outline of a possible morality of political violence, though of course a highly disputable one.

10. Views and problems of this kind are admirably discussed by Jonathan Glover in *Causing Death and Saving Lives* (Penguin Books, 1977).
11. See James Griffin's excellent inquiry, 'Are There Incommensurable Values?', *Philosophy and Public Affairs* (1977).
12. See Essay 1.
13. See Essay 1.
14. See Essay 1.
15. Edward N. Wolff, 'Recent Trends in Wealth Ownership, 1983–1998' (Jerome Levy Economics Institute, 2000), working paper no. 300, Table 2.
16. *The World Guide 2001–2002* (New Internationalist Publications), pp. 24–5, 602–9.
17. Cf. Essay 3.
18. Robert Coles, *Still Hungry in America* (Cleveland, 1969), pp. 40–1.
19. *The World Guide 2001–2002*, pp. 24–5, 602–9.
20. *After the Terror*, pp. 24–9.
21. See p. 3, above.
22. See Essay 5.
23. See Essay 1.
24. Essay 4 includes more on these matters, of course.
25. See Paul Wilkinson, *Terrorism and the Liberal State* (London, 1977), pp. 82–3.

26. See *After the Terror*, pp. 24–9, 94, 150–1; 'After the Terror: A Book and Further Thoughts', *The Journal of Ethics*, no. 7, 2003, pp. 161–81.
27. For thoughts on the subject, see my *Conservatism*, forthcoming from Pluto in 2004 in a revised edition, and 'Conservatism, Its Distinctions and Its Rationale' in *On Political Means and Social Ends* (Edinburgh University Press, 2003).

Index